Contents

Introduction

The Office of the Comptroller of the Currency's (OCC) *Comptroller's Handbook* booklet, "Residential Real Estate Lending," is prepared for use by OCC examiners in connection with their examination and supervision of national banks and federal savings associations (collectively, banks). Each bank is different and may present specific issues. Accordingly, examiners should apply the information in this booklet consistent with each bank's individual circumstances. When it is necessary to distinguish between them, national banks and federal savings associations (FSA) are referred to separately.

For the purposes of this booklet, residential real estate (RRE) lending comprises loans for purchasing RRE (properties designed to house one-to-four families), refinancing loans used to purchase RRE, and extending closed-end loans or open-end lines of credit secured by the borrower's equity in RRE. RRE loans and lines of credit are generally protected by liens against the residential properties.

This booklet addresses the risks inherent in RRE lending generally as well as risks unique to specific lending activities and products. It also discusses the OCC's supervisory expectations and regulatory requirements for prudent risk management. For information related to originating mortgages for sale, refer to the "Mortgage Banking" booklet of the *Comptroller's Handbook*.

This booklet includes supplemental procedures to facilitate the supervision and examination of RRE lending activities. The procedures include an internal control questionnaire and verification procedures to support the examination process. Further, this booklet uses three distinct categories of lending operations: (1) a portfolio lender, such as a community bank or FSA with limited product offerings; (2) a departmental or divisional lender, such as a larger community bank or FSA with wider product offerings and more robust staffing; and (3) a large lender, such as a regional bank or FSA with a large menu of products and a dedicated staff of lending personnel. The size, scope, and complexity of each activity affect associated risks and the required risk management systems. Appendix C contains a table that details the basic characteristics of each category relative to RRE lending activities. The goal is to help the reader determine if the quality of the bank's risk management practices is commensurate with the quantity of risk being assumed by offering RRE loan products.

Overview

Banks have long been subject to laws and regulations that govern the making of loans secured by RRE. The laws and regulations exist because of the extended maturity of such loans and the fundamental requirement of banks to meet the credit needs of the communities they serve. With the passage of the Dodd–Frank Wall Street Reform and Consumer Protection Act of 2010 and implementation of its requirements governing FSAs in July 2011, national banks and FSAs are both subject to the OCC's supervision. For national banks, the authority for RRE lending is set forth in 12 USC 371, "Real Estate Loans"; the authority for FSAs is set forth in 12 USC 1464, in the Home Owners' Loan Act (HOLA). Both national banks and FSAs are subject to a uniform rule on real estate lending, which incorporates the "Interagency Guidelines for Real Estate Lending Policies." This rule can be found in 12 CFR 34, subpart D, for national banks, and in 12 CFR 160.101, for FSAs, both titled "Real Estate Lending Standards."

Depository institutions in the United States traditionally have engaged in lending secured by liens on one- to four-family residential properties. RRE lending has long been regarded as a primary retail or consumer lending activity for banks. An RRE loan is made primarily to purchase RRE or to refinance a loan used to purchase RRE. The Tax Reform Act of 1986 changed the income tax laws so that interest on loans secured by the borrowers' residences became the only deductible interest on debt. This change led to increases in both direct loans and lines of credit secured by first or second liens on RRE. The change also led to increased refinancing of purchase-money loans that included the extension of new money or credit. The proceeds of these loans and lines of credit were used for many purposes, including home renovations, repairs, education, debt consolidation, and other general needs.

In the most traditional sense, RRE lending follows a specific chain of events. First, the lender accepts a written application from the borrower that is processed and underwritten against predefined standards for creditworthiness and collateral valuation. The lender often funds these loans through the deposit-taking activities of the bank or through borrowings from long-term lenders, such as the Federal Home Loan Banks (FHLB). The lender then disburses the funds to the approved borrower and records all appropriate mortgages or deeds of trust to perfect the lender's secured position in the collateral. Next, the lender services the loan by collecting payments, including interest, principal, and any escrows required for insurance and taxes, until the loan is paid in full. If the borrower defaults, the lender bears the consequent expenses and losses associated with collection and foreclosure proceedings against the borrower. If title to the real estate securing the loan transfers to the bank as the result of these foreclosure proceedings, the bank is responsible for abiding by the laws and regulations governing ownership of real estate assets. For more information, refer to the "Other Real Estate Owned" booklet of the *Comptroller's Handbook*.

RRE lending may include submarkets of real estate lending that require special knowledge, skills, and controls (e.g., Federal Housing Administration [FHA], U.S. Department of Veterans Affairs [VA], and jumbo loans[1]). As with other specialized lending markets, the lack of such skills and controls, including inadequate staffing with appropriate experience, can increase operational risk. Specialized RRE lending may require increased controls, such as close monitoring and higher servicing requirements throughout the life of the loan.

Mortgage banking generally involves an expansion of RRE lending activity that goes beyond the bank's abilities to fund and hold loans until their maturity. Mortgage banking typically involves large-scale mortgage origination processes that may include the purchase of third-party-originated loans from affiliated and nonaffiliated correspondent lenders and brokers. Mortgage banking involves the sale of originated and purchased mortgages into the

---

[1] Jumbo loans are mortgage loans that exceed the maximum purchase amount accepted by Fannie Mae and Freddie Mac.

secondary market to government-sponsored enterprises (GSE) or other third-party independent investors. The servicing of the loans sold, including collection activities, may be maintained by the originating bank ("servicing retained") or sold with the loan to other entities ("servicing released"). For more information, refer to the "Mortgage Banking" booklet of the *Comptroller's Handbook.*

This "Residential Real Estate Lending" booklet provides information and examination procedures for RRE lending activities, in which the majority of the loans are retained by the bank ("held for investment"). This booklet also discusses the different scales and nature of RRE lending activities and the risk management practices deemed appropriate for each level of operations. Expanded residential lending operations may include some mortgage banking operations that warrant reference to and use of the procedures in the "Mortgage Banking" booklet. This RRE booklet primarily provides information and examination procedures for first-lien mortgage loans, home equity loans, and home equity lines of credit (HELOC). When appropriate, guidance detailing elevated risk management expectations that has been issued on an interagency basis by the bank regulatory agencies (i.e., the OCC, the Federal Deposit Insurance Corporation [FDIC], and the Board of Governors of the Federal Reserve System [FRB]) is incorporated into this booklet.

Dodd–Frank made some significant changes to consumer protection laws and created the Consumer Financial Protection Bureau (CFPB). To implement Dodd–Frank, the CFPB has undertaken various rulemakings, including ability-to-repay (ATR) requirements, known as the ATR rule,[2] applicable to virtually all closed-end residential mortgage loans. The changes also include the development of a category of mortgages called qualified mortgages (QM). Additionally, there are new rules for high-cost and higher-priced mortgages (2013 Home Ownership and Equity Protection Act [HOEPA] Rule, Truth in Lending Act [TILA] Higher-Priced Mortgage Loans [HPML] Appraisal Rule, and TILA HPML Escrow Rule); on integrated disclosures for mortgage loans (Integrated Mortgage Disclosures Under the Real Estate Settlement Procedures Act and the Truth In Lending Act); the servicing of mortgages (mortgage servicing rules); the availability of appraisals and other valuations (Equal Credit Opportunity Act [ECOA] Valuations Rule); and the compensation of mortgage loan originators (Loan Originator Rule).

The CFPB's rulemaking efforts are ongoing. To the extent that any of the guidance described in this booklet conflicts with the CFPB's rules, the guidance is superseded by the CFPB's rules. Examiners should contact the OCC's Credit Risk Division and Compliance Policy Division to obtain information on recent developments that may not be in this booklet.

Mortgage Products

Traditionally, there are two kinds of residential mortgage loans: government mortgage loans and conventional mortgage loans. Government loans are insured by the FHA, guaranteed by the VA, or subsidized by the U.S. Department of Housing and Urban Development (HUD),

---

[2] 12 CFR 1026.43.

the U.S. Department of Agriculture (USDA), or a state or local program. These loans have limits on the maximum amount that may be borrowed, have specific underwriting standards, and are subsidized using federal or local funds or bond financing to reduce the interest rate, monthly payments, or down-payment requirements for the borrower.

Conventional mortgage loans are not directly insured, guaranteed, or subsidized by the U.S. government or a state or local government. Conventional mortgage loans often are categorized as conforming or nonconforming mortgage loans. Conforming mortgage loans typically must meet the secondary-market purchasing agency's (Fannie Mae and Freddie Mac) loan size limitations, amortization periods, and underwriting guidelines.

Nonconforming mortgage loans do not meet the standards for eligibility and purchase established by Fannie Mae or Freddie Mac. Nonconforming loans may include jumbo mortgages, Alt-A mortgages, A-minus mortgages, individual taxpayer identification number (ITIN)[3] mortgage loans, and subprime mortgage loans. Alt-A mortgage loans may have limited or reduced income and asset documentation, or may be secured by alternate property types such as an investment property for rental or a second home.

Lending to ITIN borrowers should be effectively managed because it may be difficult to conduct a traditional credit review for ITIN loan applicants due to a number of factors, including the borrower's immigration status. When evaluating ITIN loan applications, institutions may have to rely on a variety of sources to verify credit history, employment status, and income.[4] Risk management programs for ITIN lending may include (1) a comprehensive credit review function to mitigate risk when unable to conduct traditional credit assessment; (2) a determination of the true identity of the borrower; (3) an assessment of the borrower's job stability; and (4) consideration of the risk posed by the borrower's immigration status and ties to the community.[5]

Other examples of nonconforming mortgages include

- a graduated payment mortgage (a loan in which the payments increase over the years).
- a zero down-payment mortgage (a loan that requires no down payment).
- an energy-efficient mortgage (a loan that gives underwriting leeway for energy efficiencies).

---

[3] The Internal Revenue Service issues ITINs to help individuals comply with U.S. tax laws and to provide a means to process and account for tax returns and payments from those not eligible for social security numbers. ITINs are issued regardless of immigration status because both resident and nonresident aliens may have U.S. federal tax filing and payment responsibilities under the Internal Revenue Code. Refer to IRS Publication 1915 (Rev. 6-2013), p. 6.

[4] Lenders must consider the extent to which Regulation Z, including the ATR rule, applies to such lending. Refer to 12 CFR 1026, Supp. I, Comment 1(c)-1. Lenders must also consider fair lending risks when lending to ITIN borrowers to ensure they do not discriminate on a prohibited basis under applicable fair lending laws such as such as ECOA and the Fair Housing Act.

[5] Refer to 12 CFR 1002.6.

- a reverse mortgage (a loan to a borrower who is at least 62 years of age and resides in the property, in which repayment occurs when the borrower dies, sells the house, or moves out of the house for more than 12 consecutive months).

Conventional mortgage loans (both conforming and nonconforming) can be further broken down into traditional mortgage loans and nontraditional mortgage loans. Traditional mortgage loans commonly include amortizing fixed-rate mortgages, adjustable rate mortgages (ARM), hybrid ARMs, and balloon mortgages that give the borrower the option to extend the amortization period. These products typically offer terms that require the orderly payment of interest and reasonable amortization of principal.

Nontraditional mortgages, on the other hand, allow the borrower to defer the payment of principal and sometimes interest. Examples include interest-only (IO) mortgage loans, payment option ARMs, and balloon mortgages that do not give the borrower the option to extend the amortization period. Risks associated with and regulatory restrictions regarding nontraditional mortgages are discussed throughout this booklet.

This booklet is not intended to set forth all the potentially applicable requirements. As new regulations concerning mortgage lending are issued in final form, examiners should consult the topic-specific *Comptroller's Handbook* booklets. For example, refer to the "Real Estate Settlement Procedures" booklet for Regulation X and the "Truth in Lending Act" booklet for Regulation Z. To the extent that regulations concerning mortgage lending impose requirements that are inconsistent with previously issued guidance, the regulations supersede the guidance.

Home Equity Loan and Line of Credit Products

Home equity loan and line of credit products, while secured by RRE properties, are different from permanent residential mortgage loans in many ways. First, home equity loans and lines of credit are typically acquired from existing customers through the bank's branch locations or consumer lending activities. Some larger banks offer preapproved or invitation-to-apply solicitations to their customer bases or within their operating areas to obtain applications. Second, home equity loans and lines may have shorter maturities than mortgage loans and often require a bank to perfect its interest in the collateral by placing a second (i.e., junior) lien on the real estate property. Loan origination activities may be conducted by the same personnel who handle mortgage loans, but the home equity loan and line underwriting and processing functions may also be handled by personnel trained in consumer credit functions and use a consumer loan platform.

Home equity loans are closed-end loans with either a fixed or variable rate of interest and a structured repayment schedule. A lien is recorded on the borrower's residence pledged as collateral. In a home equity loan, all of the loan proceeds are normally disbursed at origination to either the customer's account or another designated payee such as a contractor for home improvements,[6] or to other creditors for debt consolidation.

As opposed to home equity loans, HELOCs are primarily open-end credit facilities secured by a lien against the equity in residential property. Numerous combinations of rates, terms, and repayment plans exist. The HELOC typically has a draw period of five or 10 years. The draw period usually has a variable interest rate, and repayment of at least the interest accrued each month is required. Some lenders require that a percentage of the payment amount cover interest accrued and achieve some amount of principal reduction. Advances on a HELOC are initiated by the customer by telephone, e-mail, or in-person request; draw checks tied to the line; or credit or debit cards tied to the line.

At the end of the draw period, the line typically converts to an amortization period of five to 25 years with interest and principal payments required that fully amortize the balance. As part of the underwriting of a HELOC, the lender should evaluate the borrower's ability to repay the loan according to its fluctuating terms, including a fully drawn status. Accordingly, the lender should evaluate the borrower's ability to amortize the fully drawn line over the loan term and to absorb potential increases in interest rates during the variable rate draw period. Additionally, the lender should evaluate whether the borrower will be able to repay the line when it moves from the draw period terms, which may require repayment only of the interest accrued, to the full repayment amortization terms. For example, if a HELOC requires full repayment at the conclusion of the five-year draw period, the borrower's repayment capacity should be evaluated based on a fully drawn amount, using the highest possible interest rate and principal payments designed to achieve full amortization over the five-year term of the balloon payment contract.[7] Banks should also consider the new ATR rule in Regulation Z for open-end high-cost mortgages under 12 CFR 1026.34.

Each bank should have specific policy guidelines to address HELOCs that are approaching the end of their draw period, especially in cases in which it is unlikely that the borrower will move seamlessly into any required amortization terms or meet the full repayment requirement in a balloon maturity. Such guidelines should address the criteria necessary to proactively evaluate the borrower's capability and collateral position for renewal of the draw period, placing the loan into amortization status on market terms, or restructuring the loan into amortization on below-market terms due to deterioration of the borrower's financial condition, the collateral value, or both. The modification of repayment terms may result in a troubled debt restructuring (TDR) status and possible classification of the loan relationship. OCC Bulletin 2014-29, "Risk Management of Home Equity Lines of Credit Approaching the End-of-Draw Periods: Interagency Guidance," identifies HELOC end-of-draw (EOD) risks and provides additional guidance.

---

[6] If the loan at issue qualifies as a high-cost mortgage, the creditor may pay a contractor from the loan's proceeds only if the disbursements are made (1) by an instrument made payable to the consumer, or made payable jointly to the contractor and consumer, or (2) if the consumer agrees, to a third-party escrow agent (12 CFR 1026.34).

[7] Refer to OCC Bulletin 2005-22, "Home Equity Lending: Credit Risk Management Guidance."

Home equity loans and lines of credit are offered with either fixed or variable rates that are based on market conditions as well as credit risk factors determined by the applicant's credit score or credit history, the term of the loan, the lien position, and the loan to value (LTV or combined LTV [CLTV] when the loan is in a second-lien position) ratio. HELOCs are normally offered with variable rates during the draw period. These may continue into the repayment period, or the rate may become fixed at that time. The variable rate of interest is tied to a prime rate published in a newspaper or a Treasury rate. For variable rate loans, the bank must disclose the frequency of adjustment (monthly, quarterly, etc.).[8]

Additionally, HELOCs generally do not have interest rate caps that limit periodic rate increases (under Regulation Z, however, the lender must state in the consumer credit contract the maximum interest rate that may be imposed during the term of the obligation). Rising interest rates could subject a borrower to significant payment increases, particularly if the line originated during a period of low interest rates. Therefore, the underwriting standards should effectively require that the borrower's repayment requirements be analyzed in a stressed environment as part of the approval process.

Subprime Mortgage

The term "subprime" refers to the credit characteristics of the individual borrower. Subprime borrowers display a range of credit risk characteristics that may include one or more of the following:

- Two or more 30-day delinquencies in the last 12 months, or one or more 60-day delinquencies in the last 24 months.
- Judgment, foreclosure, repossession, or charge-off in the previous 24 months.
- Bankruptcy in the last five years.
- Relatively high default probability as evidenced by, for example, a credit bureau score (FICO) of 660 or below (depending on the product or collateral), or other bureau or proprietary scores with an equivalent default probability likelihood.
- Debt service-to-income ratio of 50 percent or greater, or otherwise limited ability to cover recurring living expenses after deducting total monthly debt-service requirements from monthly income.[9]

Loans provided to subprime borrowers (subprime loans) often have a higher interest rate than the prime rate offered on traditional loans. Because lenders charge a premium for the added risk of default, subprime loans can be more profitable than standard risk loans if the lender has accurately estimated default and loss rates and has adequately priced the loans.

Elevated levels of credit and other risks arising from subprime lending activities require more intensive risk management and additional regulatory capital. Generally, OCC and

---

[8] Refer to 12 CFR 1026.40(d)(12).

[9] Refer to OCC Bulletin 2001-6 ("Expanded Guidance for Subprime Lending Programs," as adopted by the OCC, FRB, FDIC, and Office of Thrift Supervision [OTS]).

interagency rules, guidance, and statements detail the risks involved in subprime lending, including credit risk, and discuss supervisory expectations.[10] These issuances highlight the importance of comprehensive policies and risk management infrastructure to effectively manage the risks associated with subprime lending, and note the need to comply with ECOA and consumer protection statutes and regulations.

A bank that is or plans to become engaged in subprime mortgage lending (or subprime mortgage purchase or servicing) should consider the additional risks inherent in this activity. A bank should determine if these risks are acceptable and can be controlled, given its staff, financial condition, size, and level of capital support. If management and the board decide to enter the subprime RRE lending or servicing business, they should establish board-approved policies and procedures as well as internal controls to identify, measure, monitor, and control the additional risks. Failure to implement the appropriate risk management infrastructure before engaging in subprime RRE lending or servicing activities may be an unsafe or unsound banking practice that could be criticized in supervisory letters and reports of examination (ROE) and requires corrective actions.

Guidance sets forth general supervisory expectations for all real estate lending, including (1) the establishment of prudent underwriting standards and loan portfolio management (LPM) processes, and (2) consideration of the borrower's ATR and other underwriting factors.[11] OCC and interagency guidance specifically requires examiners to carefully assess management's ability to administer the higher risk in subprime portfolios.[12] In particular, examiners should judge management's willingness to accept increased risk exposure, the quality of the risk management and control processes in place, and, just as importantly, the extent to which management is adhering to those processes. When examiners determine that risk management practices are deficient, either because the processes as crafted are deficient or because management is not following procedures that otherwise are acceptable, the examiners should criticize management and initiate corrective action. Such examiner actions may include formal or informal enforcement actions or other actions requiring the bank to prepare a plan to achieve adequate capitalization.

The OCC also has issued "Expanded Guidance for Subprime Lending Programs,"[13] which applies specifically to banks that have subprime lending programs with an aggregate credit

---

[10] OCC Bulletin 2007-26 ("Statement on Subprime Mortgage Lending," as adopted by the OCC, FRB, FDIC, OTS, and National Credit Union Administration [NCUA]); OCC Bulletin 2001-6 ("Expanded Guidance for Subprime Lending Programs," as adopted by the OCC, FRB, FDIC, and OTS); OCC Bulletin 1999-10 ("Subprime Lending Activities," as adopted by the OCC, FRB, FDIC, and OTS); OCC Bulletin 1999-15 ("Subprime Lending: Risks and Rewards"); and 12 CFR 34, part D, "Real Estate Lending Standards," which includes appendix A, "Interagency Guidelines for Real Estate Lending," as adopted by the OCC, FRB, FDIC, and OTS in 1992 and revised in 1993.

[11] Refer to 12 CFR 34, appendix A.

[12] Refer to OCC Bulletins 1999-10, "Subprime Lending Activities," and 1999-15, "Subprime Lending: Risks and Rewards."

[13] OCC Bulletin 2001-6, "Expanded Guidance for Subprime Lending Programs."

exposure equal to or greater than 25 percent of tier 1 capital. (Aggregate exposure includes principal outstanding and committed, accrued and unpaid interest, and any retained residual assets relating to securitized subprime loans.) This guidance is meant to intensify examination scrutiny of banks that systematically target the subprime market through programs that employ tailored marketing, underwriting standards, and risk selection. Such lending should be conducted in a segregated program, portfolio, or portfolio segment. The average credit risk profile of such programs or portfolios likely displays significantly higher delinquency and loss rates than prime portfolios. The expanded guidance discusses supervisory expectations for allowance for loan and lease losses (ALLL), regulatory capital, examination review of subprime activities, classification of risk, and documentation for re-aging, renewing, or extending delinquent accounts. The expanded guidance also discusses regulatory expectations for the review and treatment of certain potentially abusive lending practices.

The OCC may also apply this expanded guidance to certain smaller subprime portfolios, such as those experiencing rapid growth or adverse performance trends, those administered by inexperienced management, and those with inadequate or weak controls.

More recent interagency guidance set forth expectations for sound lending practices and clear communications with borrowers, including supervisory expectations that the bank should consider the borrower's ATR; document the borrower's income, assets, and liabilities; limit prepayment penalties; and communicate with borrowers.[14] The guidance indicates that consumers need to be informed of potential payment increases, prepayment penalties, balloon payments, and the requirement to pay taxes and insurance. The guidance also confirms that institutions should develop strong control systems to address safety and soundness concerns and monitor whether actual practices are consistent with their policies and procedures.

Many of the risk management measures and supervisory expectations discussed in the OCC and interagency guidance were incorporated, clarified, or expanded on in the mortgage rules adopted by the CFPB and effective beginning in January 2014 (the 2014 mortgage rules).[15] All OCC-supervised institutions must comply with these rules. For example, the 2014 mortgage rules require consideration and verification of borrower information (income, assets, employment, and liabilities) and consideration of a borrower's ability to repay loans based on at least the fully indexed interest rate, fully amortizing principal payments, and mortgage-related obligations (such as taxes and insurance).[16] The 2014 mortgage rules also

---

[14] Refer to OCC Bulletin 2007-26, "Statement on Subprime Mortgage Lending".

[15] The 2014 mortgage rules comprise amendments to Regulation Z, 12 CFR 1026, implementing TILA, 15 USC 1601 et seq; Regulation X, 12 CFR 1024, implementing the Real Estate Settlement Procedures Act (RESPA), 12 USC 2601 et seq; and Regulation B, 12 CFR 1002 et seq, implementing ECOA, 15. USC 1691 et seq.

[16] Refer to 12 CFR 1026.43.

restrict prepayment penalties.[17] Further, when a loan is higher-priced, additional restrictions and prohibitions apply.[18] In addition, the 2014 mortgage rules require disclosures that show how monthly payments can change.[19] Finally, the 2014 mortgage rules may require policies and procedures for loss mitigation, and certain other requirements may apply to loss mitigation programs.[20]

Examiners should continue to assess management's ability to administer higher-risk subprime portfolios as described in interagency guidance and supplemental OCC-specific guidelines, and to ensure compliance with applicable provisions of the 2014 mortgage rules. In particular, examiners should focus on the applicable provisions of OCC guidance with respect to considerations of risk management, capital, ALLL, and capital considerations. When considering ATR and the potential for payment shock, examiners should refer to the 2014 mortgage rules.

Reverse Mortgage Loans

Reverse mortgage loans are a form of credit extension secured by first mortgages on single-family residences and are available to borrowers 62 years of age and older. Banks provide two basic types of reverse mortgage products: the lenders' own proprietary reverse mortgage products and reverse mortgages offered under the home equity conversion mortgage (HECM) program insured by the FHA. Both HECMs and proprietary products are subject to various laws governing mortgage lending, including TILA, the Real Estate Settlement Procedures Act (RESPA), the Federal Trade Commission (FTC) Act, and the fair lending laws. The remainder of this discussion generally reflects HECM rules, because HECM products are predominantly used.

As the term implies, reverse mortgage loans are the reverse of traditional mortgage loans. Instead of borrowing a lump sum and repaying it over time, borrowers receive loan proceeds (typically about 30 percent to 40 percent of the property's value) in the form of a lump sum or line of credit or in regular monthly advances. The advances may either be for a specified number of months (term loans) or be paid as long as the borrower lives in the home (tenure loans). Regardless of the advance feature of the loan (term, tenure, or line of credit), reverse mortgage loans do not have fixed maturity dates. If there is only one borrower and one mortgagor, a reverse mortgage loan matures when the borrower either dies or moves. If there

---

[17] Refer to 12 CFR 1026.43(g) and 1026.32.

[18] Refer to 12 CFR 1026.32 and 1026.35.

[19] Refer to 12 CFR 1026.18(s), 1026.19(e),(f), 1026.37, and 1026.38.

[20] Refer to 12 CFR 1024.38 and 1024.41.

are two borrowers, the loan matures when the survivor dies or moves.[21] At that time, lenders are repaid out of the proceeds from the sale of the home, and the lender's recovery from the borrower or the estate is limited to the proceeds from the sale of the home. While borrowers do not repay the loan through the traditional monthly principal and interest (P&I) payment, they still are responsible for paying taxes and insurance. As with conventional mortgage loans, the lender accrues interest on the outstanding balance until the loan is repaid.

The amount of the monthly payments or advances the borrower receives for either term or tenure reverse mortgage loans depends on the estimated borrower life expectancy, the interest rate, and the value of the home. Lenders may use mortality and relocation tables to estimate the loan maturity. For tenure loans, the number of months to maturity equates to the number of payments the lender has to make to the borrower. Other factors that affect monthly payments are the expected appreciation or depreciation of the home, and whether the borrower draws down the full or partial amount of the loan in lieu of monthly payments.

Reverse mortgage loans are attractive from a consumer standpoint because they enable eligible borrowers to remain in their homes while accessing their home equity to meet emergency needs, supplement their incomes, or, in some cases, purchase a new home—without subjecting the borrowers to ongoing repayment obligations during the life of the loan. As long as borrowers perform according to the loan terms, they may remain in their homes even if there is no remaining equity in the property. Further, the lender has recourse against the property but not against the borrowers personally and not against the borrowers' heirs.

The OCC encourages banks to engage in lending programs that meet identified community credit needs, provided the bank conducts them in a safe and sound manner, complies with all applicable laws, and treats customers fairly. While reverse mortgage loans may be responsive to a particular community's credit needs, they can be highly complex loan products, involve the application of prescriptive HUD rules (for HECMs), and may present substantial reputation risk because the loans become due and payable upon the death of the borrower. Therefore, it is important for the bank to provide customers with clear and balanced product information and other consumer protections.

To ensure that regulated banks appropriately manage the compliance and reputation risks associated with reverse mortgages, the bank regulatory agencies issued specific guidance in 2010. The interagency guidance is available in OCC Bulletin 2010-30, "Reverse Mortgages: Interagency Guidance."

Consequently, it is incumbent on management and the board to carefully assess all risks associated with any proposed HECM or proprietary reverse mortgage lending program and to determine to what degree the risks are within the bank's articulated risk appetite. Further,

---

[21] On April 25, 2014, HUD issued Mortgagee Letter 2014-07, which stated that the FHA's HECM documents must contain a provision deferring due and payable status until the death of the last surviving non-borrower spouse or another covered event. Consult HUD's Web site for current guidance relating to the treatment of non-borrower spouses and other HECM-related issues.

banks should have appropriate performance and monitoring systems in place to allow them to assess whether their new reverse mortgage products are meeting operational and strategic expectations. Because reverse mortgages are RRE-secured loans, they are subject to the interagency guidelines for real estate lending activities.[22]

Investor-Owned RRE

Banks are also authorized to make loans to investors for the purpose of purchasing or refinancing one- to four-family RRE properties for rental to others. In many banks, investor-owned residential real estate (IORR) financing is managed like owner-occupied one- to four-family residential loans. The credit risk presented by IORR lending, however, is more similar to that associated with loans for income-producing commercial real estate. Because of this similarity, the OCC expects banks to use the same types of credit risk management practices for IORR that are used for commercial real estate lending. This expectation does not change the regulatory capital, regulatory reporting, or HOLA requirements for IORR.

Banks should report IORR loans that meet the call report definition of one- to four-family residential lending in that category. IORR loans continue to qualify as RRE property loans under HOLA. IORR loans qualify for the 50 percent risk-based capital category if certain regulatory requirements are met. IORR loans that do not meet the criteria fall into a higher risk-based capital category. Refer to the call report instructions and the OCC's capital regulations (12 CFR 3) for further detail on these topics. For more information, refer to the "Commercial Real Estate Lending" booklet of the *Comptroller's Handbook*.

Manufactured Housing

"Manufactured housing" describes homes built to HUD building code (24 CFR 3280) pursuant to the National Manufactured Housing Construction and Safety Standards Act of 1974 (42 USC 5401 et seq). The HUD code preempts local building codes and is intended to ensure that the design, safety, and quality of new manufactured homes are superior to those of manufactured homes constructed in the past. States, however, may still regulate the support systems and foundations for the manufactured home (42 USC 5403(d)). Today's manufactured homes have a permanent chassis. Modular, panelized, kit, and other homes without a permanent chassis are not considered manufactured homes. Modern manufactured homes have evolved from their distant origins as travel trailers or mobile homes and are almost never moved from their original sites. Today, the majority of new unit sales are multi-section homes, and most are permanently placed on the buyer's land.

There are a number of similarities between manufactured housing loans and other indirect lending. The transaction originates with a dealer, who then submits the application to various institutions. The financing is typically completed using a retail sales contract. In most states, manufactured homes are originally titled as personal property or chattel. To be considered real estate, the home's wheels, axles, and hitch must be removed and the home must be

---

[22] Refer to 12 CFR 34, subpart D, appendix A, and the appendix to 12 CFR 160.101.

permanently attached to the land. In such cases, the personal property title is surrendered and the home is converted to real property in accordance with state and local requirements.

Banks may invest in manufactured housing loans. Pursuant to HOLA, an FSA may specifically invest in interests therein without limitation as to percentage of assets (12 USC 1464(c)(1)(J)).

Additionally, banks may invest in manufactured home loans secured by a combination of the manufactured home and real estate. If a manufactured home is permanently affixed to a foundation, banks can usually treat a loan that is secured by a combination of the manufactured home and the lot on which it sits as a "home loan" for regulatory reporting purposes. Such loans are subject to the LTV and other requirements of the interagency guidelines for real estate-secured lending activities.[23]

Banks engaged in manufactured housing finance should carefully manage the risk of collateral depreciation. Lenders should establish prudent underwriting standards, including appropriate LTV limits and amortization terms. Appraisals and evaluations should be conducted by personnel with specific expertise in valuing manufactured homes. Any manufactured housing loans originated for sale to the secondary market should adhere to specific investor requirements. In some cases, mortgage insurance may be available from private mortgage insurers and the FHA for loans secured by manufactured homes.

Affordable Housing

The OCC has long encouraged banks to extend prudent credit to promote community development. By taking the initiative in community development, banks may establish new markets, reinforce their identity as community institutions, and enhance their performance.[24] Community development loans often are made in conjunction with state or local housing programs, reinvestment corporations, or as part of community development projects and corporations.

Banks can hold affordable housing mortgage loans in portfolio or originate such loans for sale into the secondary market according to specific investor requirements. Servicing for such loans can be retained or transferred at the time of a sale. Additionally, banks may participate in affordable housing mortgage loan programs established by city, county, and state governments. These loans may have specialized servicing requirements, and banks should ensure that their servicing processes sufficiently address these requirements.

A bank's RRE lending policies and procedures for its affordable housing mortgage programs should contain prudent underwriting standards, portfolio monitoring expectations, and

---

[23] Refer to 12 CFR 34, subpart D, appendix A, and the appendix to 12 CFR 160.101.

[24] These activities potentially may receive consideration when the bank's performance under the Community Reinvestment Act (CRA) is evaluated.

appropriate appraisal and evaluation requirements, with associated LTV limits. Successful affordable housing mortgage portfolio risk management practices include

- providing comprehensive home buyer education as well as pre- and post-mortgage credit counseling.
- using available subsidies, grants, abatements, and guarantees, as these enhancements can reduce the funds needed for down payments, closing costs, or monthly payments.
- limiting the use of risk-layering practices such as approvals with both high debt-to-income ratios and minimal borrower reserves for unexpected expenses and repairs.[25]
- ensuring that management information systems (MIS) for affordable mortgage portfolios can effectively evaluate loan volumes, delinquency rates, losses and profitability consistent with management's comprehensive community development strategies, goals, and key underwriting factors.
- using enhanced reporting and monitoring for affordable mortgages that have an adjustable rate to ensure that rising rates do not unduly increase credit risk by increasing debt service requirements to unsustainable levels.
- ensuring that affordable mortgage early delinquency intervention efforts provide a structured, systematic, and rapid response, including contact immediately after the grace period or missed payment.
- providing incentives for affordable mortgage borrowers to set up an automatic payment plan, either through automatic debit of an existing deposit account or by payroll deduction.
- considering a requirement for private mortgage insurance (PMI), limits on the volume of non-PMI loans, or the use of master mortgage insurance on future affordable mortgage loans.
- establishing a dedicated enhanced servicing unit with personnel trained in collection techniques or enhancing the bank's contracted servicing arrangements to work more closely with the entities that provide counseling to the bank's customers.
- contracting with a community development-related firm that has experience in managing affordable mortgage portfolios and a good track record of delinquency reduction and prevention.

A bank that extends credit for development of affordable housing projects should consider the financial assistance that frequently accompanies these projects, such as low-income housing tax credits, subsidies, and grants. Such financial assistance creates an incentive for developers and investors to undertake such projects. Accordingly, the benefits of such financial assistance should be appropriately reflected in a project's appraisal such that the estimated cash flow of the project is not negatively affected, resulting in a lower market value. (Refer to OCC Bulletin 1995-16, "Appraisals: Affordable Housing Loans and Market Value.") The guidance states that when a bank obtains an appraisal for an affordable housing project, the appraisal should contain a market value estimate that reflects the real estate collateral and interest in the real estate on a cash or cash-equivalent basis. The agencies'

---

[25] Lenders also should consider the extent to which Regulation Z, including the ATR rule, applies to such lending.

appraisal regulations permit the appraiser to include in the market value estimate any significant financial assistance that would survive sale or foreclosure, such as the value of low-income housing tax credits, subsidies, and grants.

A bank should ensure that an appraiser engaged to appraise an affordable housing project is competent to perform such an appraisal. Specifically, appraisers should be knowledgeable about the various types of financial assistance and programs that are associated with an affordable housing project. In addition, while certain types of financial assistance do not necessarily transfer to new ownership upon sale or foreclosure, the lender should ensure that the appraiser appropriately considers the effect of these items in the cash flow analysis, when applicable.

RRE Activities and Functions

RRE lending activities for both mortgages and home equity loans and lines involve three primary activities—production, servicing, and collection—that are further broken down into specific functions. Production functions include origination, processing (including collateral valuation), underwriting, and closing. Servicing functions include portfolio supervision and assessment, escrow account administration, account management for open-end lines of credit, and loan modifications. Collection functions include early stage delinquency assessment, renewals, extensions, deferrals and re-aging,[26] TDRs, and foreclosure assessment and execution.

RRE Loan Production Functions

Mortgage Loan Origination

There are two primary channels for obtaining mortgage loan applications. One is the retail channel, consisting primarily of the bank's retail offices and branches located within the geographic boundaries served. The other is the wholesale channel, which includes loans generated by other third parties, such as correspondents and brokers who may or may not operate within the bank's geographic boundaries. Additionally, mortgage loan applications may be available through the Internet. This channel may be limited to prospective applicants within the bank's geographic boundaries or open to outside applicants.

Mortgage originators and bank lending officers take applications from prospective borrowers. These originators may use face-to-face customer contact, telemarketing, and direct mail to solicit applications. While some smaller banks may still use traditional written application forms, most originators are now taking applications electronically with a mortgage application software program. The program initiates the application process by requesting credit bureau data and scores as well as initial information about property value

---

[26] Examiners can refer to SM 2009-07, "Guidance for the Treatment of Residential Real Estate Loan Modifications" (December 7, 2009); also refer to CNBE 2010-01, "Policy Interpretation—Supervisory Memorandum 2009-7" (February 23, 2010).

and lien status. Electronic applications also are acquired directly from prospective applicants using their home computers and an Internet application site. Banks may also use third parties such as mortgage brokers or correspondents to originate mortgage loans (and home equity loans and lines). When doing so, prudent lending practices dictate that a bank should have strong control systems to ensure the quality of originations and compliance with all applicable laws and regulations, and to help prevent fraud.

Brokers are firms or individuals, acting on behalf of either the bank or the borrower, who match the borrower's needs with the bank's mortgage or home equity origination programs. Brokers take applications from customers. Although they sometimes process the application and underwrite the loan to qualify the application for a particular lender, they generally do not use their own funds to close loans. Whether brokers are allowed to process and perform any underwriting depends on the relationship between the bank and the broker. For control purposes, the bank should retain appropriate oversight of all critical loan processing activities, such as verification of income and employment and independence in the appraisal and evaluation function.

Correspondents are financial companies that close and fund loans in their own names and subsequently sell them to a lender. Banks commonly obtain loans through correspondents and, in some cases, delegate the underwriting function to the correspondent. In delegated underwriting relationships, a bank grants approval to a correspondent financial company to process, underwrite, and close loans according to the delegating bank's processing and underwriting requirements and commits to purchase those loans. The delegating bank should have systems and controls to provide assurance that the correspondent is appropriately managed, is financially sound, and provides mortgages that meet the bank's prescribed underwriting guidelines and comply with applicable consumer protection laws and regulations. A quality control (QC) unit or function in the delegating bank should closely monitor the quality of loans that the correspondent underwrites. Prudent lending practices include post-purchase underwriting reviews and ongoing monitoring of portfolio performance management activities.

Both brokers and correspondents are typically compensated based on mortgage (or home equity loan or line of credit) origination volume and, accordingly, have an incentive to produce and close as many loans as possible. Therefore, banks should perform comprehensive due diligence on third-party originators before entering a relationship. In addition, once a relationship is established, the bank should have adequate audit procedures and controls to verify that third parties are not being paid to generate incomplete or fraudulent mortgage applications and are not otherwise receiving referral or unearned income or fees contrary to RESPA prohibitions or loan originator compensation in contravention to Regulation Z.[27]

By monitoring the quality of loans by origination source, and uncovering such problems as early payment defaults and incomplete packages, bank management learns if third-party originators are producing quality loans. If ongoing credit or documentation problems are discovered, the bank should take appropriate action, which could include terminating its relationship with the third party.

Some larger banks have developed internal credit scoring tools for electronic evaluation of loan applicants. Other banks that want to sell their mortgages in the secondary market use application software programs and scoring models developed by Fannie Mae (Desktop Underwriter, or DU) or Freddie Mac (Loan Prospector, or LP). These credit scoring tools are used for efficiency, to reduce costs and time for application decisions, and to promote consistency in underwriting. Moreover, these tools have proven effective in evaluating residential applications within short time frames. The components of any scoring system, however, should be reviewed to ensure the factors contribute to creditworthiness, and that the system is periodically monitored and revalidated. (Refer to OCC Bulletin 2011-12, "Sound Practices for Model Risk Management.") One drawback of rigorous scoring models is that they may not be able to recognize applicants who would make satisfactory borrowers but fail to meet the scorecard cutoff criteria. If management uses automated scoring systems and also chooses to allow "overrides" of a model's decisions on extension of credit, then management should have specific criteria and documentation requirements for justifying such override determinations. In smaller judgmental credit operations, management should also implement and adhere to specific criteria and documentation requirements for justifying a decision to override a loan policy requirement.

Bank personnel must also be aware of the federal and state laws and regulations, especially the regulations that implement consumer protection laws, including ECOA, the Fair Housing Act, the Fair Credit Reporting Act, the Home Mortgage Disclosure Act, RESPA, HOEPA, TILA, and the Bank Secrecy Act. Management's lending processes and origination platforms should be designed to ensure that the bank complies with all applicable laws and regulations and provides timely and accurate disclosures to mortgage applicants. Mortgage loan originators and bank staff must be diligent in safeguarding applicants' and borrowers' confidential information.

Mortgage loan originators and loan officers should provide sufficient information to customers so they fully understand material terms, costs, and risks of the loan products offered. Communication with customers, including advertisements, oral statements, and

---

[27] In addition, a bank that purchases loans subject to TILA's rules for home equity loans with high rates or high closing costs (loans covered by HOEPA) can incur assignee liability for all claims and defenses with respect to that mortgage that the consumer could assert against the creditor unless the institution can reasonably show that it could not determine the transaction was a loan covered by HOEPA. Also, the nature of the bank's relationship with brokers and correspondents may have implications for liability under ECOA and for reporting responsibilities under the Home Mortgage Disclosure Act.

promotional materials, should provide clear and balanced information about the relative benefits and risks of mortgage products.

SAFE Act Registration for Mortgage Originators

The Secure and Fair Enforcement for Mortgage Licensing Act of 2008 (SAFE Act) was passed as part of the Housing and Economic Recovery Act of 2008. This law created federal licensing and registration requirements for mortgage loan originators. Since January 2011, all employees of banks that serve as mortgage loan originators are required to register with the Nationwide Mortgage Licensing System and Registry. The employees must obtain a unique identifier from the registry and maintain their registration. Detailed examples of what does and does not constitute mortgage origination activities may be found in 12 CFR 1007, appendix A.

Mortgage Loan Originator Compensation

On January 10, 2014, amendments to Regulation Z implemented requirements and restrictions imposed by Dodd–Frank concerning loan originator compensation. These changes include the definition of and qualifications for a loan originator.[28] They also include requirements for the registration and licensing of loan originators as well as requirements for training, screening, and compensation practices, including written policies. Compensation prohibitions generally include basing the originator's compensation on the terms of a transaction or a proxy for a transaction term.[29] Regulation Z also prohibits loan originators in a transaction from being compensated by both a consumer and another person, such as a creditor. The rule establishes tests for when loan originators can be compensated through certain profits-based compensation arrangements. Finally, the rule contains requirements for specific loan originator identification information to be included on loan documents as well as other record-keeping requirements. Refer to the "Truth in Lending Act" booklet of the *Comptroller's Handbook* for Regulation Z.

Mortgage Loan Processing

Mortgage loan processing consists of information or data gathering and verification. The loan processor (loan officer, administrative staff, or dedicated personnel) should ensure that the loan files contain all of the documents necessary to support the credit analysis and decision, such as the applicant's income and employment verification, the collateral valuation (appraisal or evaluation) and lien status, and the funds necessary for any down payment and

---

[28] For employers whose employees are not required to be licensed, including depository institutions and bona fide nonprofits, Regulation Z requires them to (1) ensure that their loan originator employees meet character, fitness, and criminal background standards similar to existing SAFE Act licensing standards; and (2) provide training to their loan originator employees that is appropriate and consistent with those employees' origination activities. The rule also contains special provisions with respect to criminal background checks and the circumstances in which a criminal conviction is disqualifying, and with respect to situations in which a credit check on a loan originator is required. Refer to 12 CFR 1026.36(f).

[29] Refer to the CFPB's "2013 Loan Originator Rule: Small Entity Compliance Guide."

---

closing. For most mortgages, the information that the bank relies on in determining a customer's repayment ability must be verified using reasonably reliable third-party records. The loan processor should ensure that all the necessary steps are performed in accordance with internal requirements. This process should also include steps that ensure that all property taxes are paid current and that appropriate hazard and flood insurance, as applicable, is in effect with accurate loss payee instructions. In addition, home owners association (HOA) dues or fees must be considered when determining the borrower's ATR.[30] FHA, VA, and USDA loans contain unique requirements that may require specific training for loan processors handling these government-insured or government-guaranteed loans.

When the processing environment is less automated, the processor's responsibilities also include preparing the final loan application forms, obtaining support documents, and verifying the information on the loan application. Once a loan package is complete, the processor submits the information to the underwriting department manually or electronically. In banks that use the automated underwriting systems of Fannie Mae or Freddie Mac, loan applications are assigned a processing status and preliminary grade. Any additional documentation requirements that must be satisfied for underwriting and closing are identified. In other cases when documentation requirements vary because of specific situations, such as streamlined investor products, the processors should use product-specific checklists or automated checks to ensure all required steps have been completed properly.

The processing of an RRE loan application requires a valuation of the real estate collateral. (Refer to 12 CFR 34, subpart C, "Appraisals.") Depending on the level of automation involved, the real estate appraisal or evaluation may be automatically ordered from a specific appraiser or through an appraisal management company (AMC). In less automated environments, the loan processor may order the appraisal or evaluation based on internal policies and procedures. Once the completed appraisal or evaluation is obtained, the processor includes it in the loan file to be reviewed by the underwriter.[31] In some cases, the processor may complete a checklist designed to help evaluate the integrity of the appraisal or evaluation as well as compliance with regulatory requirements.

Mortgage Loan Underwriting

The function of the mortgage loan underwriter is to approve or deny the loan application in accordance with the bank's lending policy, including any secondary-market investor requirements. Underwriters are responsible for determining if a prospective borrower qualifies for the requested mortgage product and if repayment capacity, collateral protection, and other appropriate requirements have been met. Underwriters must also take into account the need to comply with Regulation Z's requirement that the creditor make a reasonable and

---

[30] Refer to 12 CFR 1026.43(c); for open-end high-cost mortgages, refer to 12 CFR 1026.34(a)(4).

[31] Regulation B at 12 CFR 1002.14 requires lenders also to provide a copy of the appraisal or valuation to the applicant.

good faith determination at or before consummation that the consumer will have a reasonable ability to repay the loan according to its terms for most closed-end consumer mortgages.[32]

Common underwriter review procedures include

- evaluation of the borrower's repayment capacity by looking at income information, employment status and consistency of employment, current debt obligations, alimony, and child support; credit score; credit history using a conventional credit bureau report or other alternative credit documentation; and financial resources (deposit accounts and other liquid investments) consistent with the underwriting considerations and verification requirements of the ATR rule, as applicable.[33]
- determination of the borrower's ability to close on the loan from sufficient funds or resources.
- determination that all calculations such as DTI ratios, disposable funds, LTV ratios, and required disclosures are accurate.
- identification of any special loan requirements or closing conditions, such as flood insurance or mortgage insurance.
- determination that real estate appraisals or evaluations are complete, have integrity, and are appropriately accurate to support the loan. (**Note:** OCC Bulletin 2010-42, "Sound Practices for Appraisals and Evaluations," requires that a bank's appraisal review function be independent of the lending function to the highest degree possible.)
- determination that the title search has not identified any circumstances that could impede the security of the mortgage.

Depending on the size and nature of the bank's RRE lending activities, a quality assurance (QA) or QC process that reviews mortgage loan underwriting may be necessary. A QA process reviews a sampling of underwriter-approved loans, typically before funding, to ensure consistency with lending standards. Smaller banks may have 100 percent reviews while larger departmental lenders may randomly sample a group of approvals. Some banks only review exception approvals (loans approved outside of normal policies and standards) to ensure the underwriter's decision was justified by effective mitigation of the risks.

For the largest mortgage lenders that are active in selling to the secondary markets, agencies and investors typically require a review of an independent and statistically sound sampling of loans each month by a QC function, generally post-funding. The QC function may be completed internally by designated personnel or through an external vendor. If performed internally, the QC manager and function should be independent of the loan production function. The QC process usually occurs after a loan has been closed and funded. It is designed to effectively alert management to any deficiencies that may have existed in recently completed loan originations. The QC function should also be designed to detect

---

[32] Refer to 12 CFR 1026.43(c).

[33] If covered by the ATR rule, third-party record verification is generally required (except that, in certain instances, oral confirmation of employment is permitted).

fraudulent transactions so management can effectively address the causes and report perpetrators to the proper authorities.

Well-designed QC processes effectively categorize the nature of deficiencies found (noncritical, critical, etc.) and result in timely feedback to the responsible loan processor(s) and underwriter(s). Additionally, monthly QC reporting should be designed to reflect not only the results of the most recent review but also trends in the monthly review results. Such reports more effectively alert management, the audit committee, or the board to the true nature of QC findings and whether trends are improving or deteriorating.

The underwriting area may also implement a second review process. Many banks implement a second review process to assure themselves and the loan applicants that every effort has been made to qualify an applicant for a mortgage loan. Second review procedures examine loan applications that were not approved to determine alternative ways for approval. A variety of internal review panels or external review procedures can be created. Banks should establish strict criteria for second review eligibility.

Mortgage Loan Closing

After a mortgage loan application is approved by the loan officer or underwriting unit, a loan closer or closing unit ensures that the loan is properly closed, funded, and settled. This process includes execution of the documents required to create a valid obligation to repay the loan and those necessary to perfect the bank's security interest in the RRE collateral. The closing person or unit also ensures that the bank has all appropriate documentation in the file after closing. This process may entail the use of a trailing documents function that collects documents after appropriate courthouse filings are completed. In addition to an internal closing person or unit, escrow agents, title companies, and attorneys commonly perform closings for a bank. Whoever performs the closing should obtain all appropriate documents and signatures before disbursing the loan proceeds. To the extent this service is provided by a third party, a bank should ensure proper management of its third-party vendors. Some banks use a "pre-funding" review process and checklist that reviews each file to determine its integrity before providing the file to the closing employee or agent.

The closing person or unit should obtain the executed note, final title insurance, mortgage assignments, insurance and guaranty certificate, etc. If a loan is being sold to the secondary market, the closing person or unit should protect the closing package and ensure delivery to the agency or investor within the time frames required.

A post-closing review of each loan file should be performed, normally within 10 days of closing. This review should be designed to ensure that the bank or its agent closed each loan according to the underwriter's instructions and that all documents were properly executed. Missing or inaccurate documents should be identified, tracked, and obtained by personnel responsible for trailing documents. Weekly or monthly aging reports should tell management what documents still need to be obtained, executed, or corrected and for how many days they have been unresolved. Management and the board should set thresholds for effective resolution and actively address any situations that extend beyond the tolerances.

When the bank anticipates selling loans to secondary-market investors, the bank's closing function must disclose to an applicant whether the servicing of the loan may be assigned, sold, or transferred within three days after application for a first-lien mortgage.[34] For these situations, many banks use the Mortgage Electronic Registration Systems registry known as MERS Residential. MERS Residential, a national, central database of mortgage loan information, was created as a utility for the mortgage finance industry to track the sale of ownership and servicing rights of loans. For more information, refer to the "Mortgage Banking" booklet of the *Comptroller's Handbook*.

Home Equity Lending Originations

Depending on the size and nature of the bank's RRE lending activities, home equity lending functions may either be coordinated with the mortgage lending functions or occur as part of a separate and distinct consumer lending function. In many smaller banks, home equity origination activities are performed by the same lending officers and administrative staff that have RRE lending expertise. In larger community banks, the home equity origination activities are often part of a larger consumer lending operation. In the largest community and regional banks, home equity lending is done by specialists within the consumer lending division or by a mortgage banking department or division.

In most community banks, applications for home equity loans and lines of credit come from existing customers or customers who reside in the bank's operational geographies. Most applications come through the retail locations and branches. Applications may also be sourced through the bank's Internet site, through telephone or mail solicitations, or from brokers and correspondent banks. As noted previously for mortgage loans, whenever a bank uses third parties such as brokers and correspondents in the origination process, the bank should have strong control systems to ensure the quality of originations and compliance with all applicable laws and regulations, and to help prevent fraud. Additionally, the quality of third-party-sourced originations should be monitored closely to uncover such problems as early payments defaults and incomplete packages. If the bank discovers ongoing credit quality or documentation integrity problems, it should take appropriate action against the third party, which could include terminating its relationship.

The home equity application process may still be paper-based and manual in the smallest banks. In most banks, however, the application process is usually completed using an automated platform that captures the applicant's data (through applicant or employee input). The information is then evaluated against predefined lending standards for the products offered by the bank. Standards typically include a credit bureau score or an application score, the quality of the customer's employment and credit history, the expected lien position of the loan or line (first or second), LTV or CLTV ratio if a prior first mortgage balance exists, and the condition and value of the real estate to be used as collateral. If the loan or line is in a second-lien position, the lender should consider repayment capacity based on whether the

---

[34] Refer to 12 CFR 1024.5(b)(7). A bona fide transfer of a loan obligation in the secondary market is not covered by RESPA and 12 CFR 1024, except with respect to section 6 of RESPA (12 USC 2605) and subpart C of Regulation X, 12 CFR 1024.30–1024.41. The servicing disclosure requirement is in 12 CFR 1024.33.

first lien is a fixed-rate, ARM, IO, or pay-option ARM and in accordance with the ATR rule, as applicable.[35] To the degree that the bank uses automated scoring models for credit decisions and loan pricing, these models should be periodically monitored and revalidated. (Refer to OCC Bulletin 2011-12, "Sound Practices for Model Risk Management.")

Home Equity Lending Processing

Personnel who process home equity loan and line applications follow steps similar to those used by personnel who process mortgage loan applications. First, the processor should ensure that the loan file (or automated application platform) contains all of the documentation necessary to support the credit analysis, decision, and pricing, such as the applicant's income, employment, and debt obligations. If a second-lien position on the equity in the RRE is contemplated, the processor verifies the amount of the first mortgage position as well as the existence of any other outstanding encumbrances, such as liens for unpaid taxes, mechanic's liens, or recorded judgments against the applicant.

In most cases, the processor or the automated platform orders the appropriate collateral valuation and condition documentation, such as the appraisal or evaluation. Smaller banks may use lending personnel to perform real estate evaluations of applications assigned to others. Larger community and regional banks may use an internally generated list of approved appraisers, staff appraisers, or an external vendor like a real estate AMC to obtain an appropriate collateral valuation or condition report. Whenever an evaluation is used to document the real estate collateral's condition and value, management should ensure that the evaluation meets all of the standards in OCC Bulletin 2010-42, "Sound Practices for Appraisals and Evaluations."[36]

Competition, cost pressures, and advancements in technology have prompted banks to streamline their appraisal and evaluation processes. These changes, coupled with banks underwriting to higher LTV ratios, have heightened the importance of strong collateral valuation management policies, procedures, and processes, especially for second-lien home equity loans and lines. A bank's collateral valuation process should establish criteria for determining the appropriate valuation method for a particular transaction based on the risk in the transaction. For example, higher-risk transactions (lower credit quality, higher LTV) or

---

[35] Refer to 12 CFR 1026.43. Repayment capacity for high-cost HELOCs is addressed in 12 CFR 1026.34(a)(4). Further, 12 CFR 34.3(b) requires that national banks not make consumer real estate loans based predominantly on the bank's realization of the foreclosure or liquidation value of the collateral, without regard to a borrower's ability to repay the loan according to its terms.

[36] Under 12 CFR 1026.35, additional appraisal requirements apply to loans classified as HPMLs. Under this regulation, an HPML is a closed-end loan secured by the consumer's principal dwelling with an annual percentage rate (APR) that exceeds the average prime offer rate for a comparable transaction, as of the date of rate set, by (1) 1.5 or more percentage points for loans secured by a first lien if the loan's principal amount at the time of consummation does not exceed the maximum principal obligation eligible for purchase by Fannie Mae or Freddie Mac (conforming loans, generally $417,000; exempt locations, $625,000); (2) 2.5 or more percentage points for loans secured by a first lien if the principal at the time of consummation exceeds the maximum principal obligation eligible for purchase by Fannie Mae or Freddie Mac (i.e., jumbo loans); or (3) 3.5 or more percentage points for loans secured by a subordinate lien on a dwelling.

---

non-homogenous residential property such as custom homes should be supported by more thorough evaluations. Additionally, the bank's collateral valuation processes should effectively preclude "value shopping" when more than one valuation method is available. The bank should require the use of the most reliable collateral valuation method for the transaction versus using one that returns the highest value.

Home Equity Lending Underwriting

Once the information in the loan file or automated application platform is complete, a loan officer or underwriter reviews the information and makes a final decision to approve or deny the loan or line. In a process with limited automation, the officer or underwriter's input could be substantial and involves file checklists and worksheets to justify the credit decision. In a more automated environment, the officer or underwriter may interact with the system, review information and preliminary decisions on screen, and then input his or her approval or disapproval. When there are any deviations from predefined standards, the officer or underwriter should enter comments that reflect his or her justification for the final decision and any mitigating factors noted relative to compromised tolerances.

Depending on the scale and nature of the home equity lending activities, QA or QC processes similar to mortgage loan underwriting may be necessary. In larger home equity lending operations, management may have procedures to review loan documentation before final loan funding and settlement.

Home Equity Lending Closing

The closing of home equity loans and lines is less formal than a mortgage loan closing. Home equity loans and lines are usually closed and funded at a bank location or branch. Proceeds may be provided directly to the customer by check or a deposit to his or her account. In some cases, depending on the expected purpose of the loan or line, the proceeds may be provided directly to a third-party lender (loan consolidations) or vendor (home remodel or repairs).[37] When a line of credit is closed and not immediately drawn upon, the customer has the ability to initiate a draw during the contractual draw period through specific methods identified by the bank.

In some areas, as required by state laws or situations involving first-lien positions on previously unencumbered RRE collateral, a bank may use a title company or attorney as the bank's agent to close a home equity loan or line. A bank should have effective post-closing review functions to determine that all final recorded documentation supports its lien position.

---

[37] As noted previously, when a loan is a high-cost mortgage, the creditor cannot make payments from the loan's proceeds exclusively to a contractor. Instead, the loan proceeds need to be disbursed through either the consumer or an escrow agent (12 CFR 1026.34).

RRE Loan Servicing Functions

Mortgage Loan Servicing

Once a mortgage loan has been closed, funded, and settled, its information is placed in a loan servicing system to facilitate future supervision of the loan, including the collection and recording of the customer's payments. In smaller banks that retain most of their mortgage loans, the servicing system may be their standard loan platform. Alternatively, banks can use a specialized mortgage loan platform that ensures they can effectively address any unique loan characteristics such as variable interest rate calculations or conversions from fixed interest terms to variable interest terms.

Depending on the scale and nature of the bank's mortgage loan activities, it may sell closed loans to the secondary market with servicing retained. This means that the bank continues to receive and record the customer's loan payments even though the loan is actually held in another entity's portfolio. In some situations, the bank may service the loan for a short period and then transfer both ownership and the rights to service to an investor. Regardless of a loan's disposition, the bank's loan servicing system should differentiate between loans that the bank owns and services and loans that the bank services for other investors.

Mortgage Servicing Rules

Dodd–Frank made several amendments to RESPA and TILA regarding the servicing of certain residential mortgage loans. In January 2013, the CFPB issued amendments to TILA's Regulation Z and RESPA's Regulation X to implement the new requirements. These changes are known as the Mortgage Servicing Rules, and they generally became effective January 10, 2014. The changes to Regulation X specifically address requirements for

- error resolution and information requests.
- force-placed insurance.
- general servicing policies, procedures, and requirements.
- early intervention with delinquent consumers.
- continuity of contact with delinquent consumers.
- loss mitigation, including requirements when servicing is transferred (12 CFR 1024, subpart C).

The rules address a servicer's obligation to establish reasonable policies and procedures to achieve many of the delineated objectives. The changes to Regulation Z specifically address requirements for

- interest rate adjustment notices and timing for ARMs (12 CFR 1026.20(c)-(d)).
- prompt crediting of mortgage payments and responses to requests for payoff amounts (12 CFR 1026.36(c)).
- periodic statements for mortgage loans (12 CFR 1026.41).

These rules also exempt certain small servicers from parts of the Mortgage Servicing Rules.[38]

Mortgage Loan Escrow Account Administration

In addition to the collection of mortgage loan payments for P&I, the bank may also be responsible for the collection and payment of periodic real estate property taxes and hazard and flood insurance premiums, as applicable. In addition, HOA fees may be escrowed because some jurisdictions may grant a super-lien status (priority over the bank's loan) to unpaid HOA fees. These payments are collected from the customer and held in an escrow deposit account until the payments are required by the taxing authority, insurance vendor, or the HOA. Flood insurance must be escrowed if other insurance and taxes are escrowed.[39] Under the Homeowner Flood Insurance Affordability Act of 2014, regardless of whether taxes or hazard insurance are escrowed, an institution or its servicer must escrow flood insurance premiums and fees for loans made, increased, extended, renewed, or refinanced on or after January 1, 2016, unless an exception applies. Under RESPA, the bank is required to analyze the timing and amount of payments made from the escrow account, to revise them if necessary to avoid an account deficit, and to disclose the results to the consumer. Depending on the amount of the deficit, the consumer may resolve the deficiency with a lump sum extra payment or an increase in his or her monthly payment that resolves the deficit over the next 12 months.

In smaller banks, escrow deposit account activity is usually limited, and borrowers are expected to directly pay their hazard insurance premiums and property tax payments. Nevertheless, the bank should have monitoring that ensures that timely payments are being made by the borrower, that the bank's RRE collateral remains adequately covered by hazard insurance with the bank as loss payee, and that the bank's lien is not compromised by any liens from unpaid property taxes.

When the bank extends additional credit to a borrower for an unanticipated payment of insurance premiums or property taxes, the extensions should be based on specific guidance in the loan policy. In this situation, management should also evaluate the relationship for possible classification if the circumstances indicate deterioration in the borrower's financial condition.

Servicers must comply with applicable law regarding their management of escrow accounts, including collecting, holding, and escrowing funds on behalf of each borrower in accordance with RESPA (12 USC 2609) and Regulation X (12 CFR 1024.17 and 1024.34). When the escrow account is first created, the amount allowed is the "amount sufficient to pay the charges respecting the mortgaged property, such as taxes and insurance, which are attributable to the period from the date such payment(s) were last paid until the initial payment date" plus a two-month cushion (12 CFR 1024.17(c)(1)(i)). RESPA allows servicers to hold up to the amount required to make expected payments over the next 12 months plus

---

[38] Small servicers are defined at 12 CFR 1026.41(e)(4).

[39] Refer to 12 CFR 22.5 and 172.5.

an additional one-sixth of that amount. This limit applies to funds collected at closing as well as those collected throughout the life of the loan. RESPA also requires the servicer to provide various disclosures, including the initial and annual escrow statements. Effective in January 2014, the requirement for timely escrow disbursements generally includes the payment of hazard insurance premiums when the borrower is more than 30 days overdue on his or her mortgage, unless the servicer is unable to disburse funds from the borrower's account.[40] Insufficient funds in a borrower's escrow account do not mean that the servicer is unable to disburse the funds.

TILA Escrow Rule for Higher-Priced Mortgages

Before passage of Dodd–Frank, creditors were required to set up and administer escrow accounts for HPMLs for a minimum of one year for property taxes. Effective June 1, 2013, the TILA Escrow Rule (12 CFR 1026.35(b)) generally lengthened the time creditors must collect and manage escrows for HPMLs to five years.

For an HPML secured by a first lien on a principal dwelling, the TILA Escrow Rule requires the escrow account to be maintained until (1) the underlying debt obligation is terminated, or (2) after the five-year period, the consumer requests that the escrow account be cancelled.[41] For the consumer to cancel the account, however, the loan's unpaid balance must be less than 80 percent of the original value of the property securing the loan, and the consumer must not be delinquent or in default on the debt obligation. The TILA Escrow Rule does not require a creditor to escrow insurance premiums in common interest communities (e.g., condominiums) when the homeowners must participate in governing associations that purchase master insurance policies. Furthermore, the rule defines limited exceptions from the requirements for smaller creditors that operate in predominantly rural or underserved areas.

Mortgage Loan Portfolio Management

Prudent lending practices dictate that a bank effectively monitors the quality of the loans it originates. Effective monitoring is crucial for loans held for investment that have the most direct impact on the bank's earnings and regulatory capital. Loan reporting and tracking systems should allow management to isolate key products, channels of origination, borrower characteristics, loan features, and layers of additional risks. Portfolio volume and performance reporting should be tracked against management's expectations of performance given the approved internal lending standards and policies. Deviations from expected performance metrics should allow management to identify and isolate the causes of deterioration in performance. The impact of changing markets and market conditions should also be assessed when evaluating performance deviations. Banks should perform stress tests

---

[40] A servicer is unable to disburse funds from the borrower's account only if the servicer has a reasonable basis to believe that either the borrower's property is vacant or the borrower's hazard insurance has terminated for reasons other than nonpayment.

[41] Refer to 12 CFR 1026.35.

on key portfolio segments to help identify and quantify events that can increase risk within a segment of the overall portfolio.

Examples of key financial information, credit statistics, and statistical analyses that should be monitored over time include original and updated credit bureau scores, LTV ratios, DTI ratios, housing and debt coverage ratios, owner occupancy and concentrations in product types, and terms and channels of origination. These analyses can be used to develop trends in performance and provide insights into delinquency, losses, prepayment activities, and foreclosures.

Banks originating and investing in nontraditional mortgage loans should adopt more robust risk management practices and portfolio reporting, which are capable of managing such exposures in a thoughtful and systematic manner. Such practices include the establishment of portfolio concentration limits measured as a percentage of total capital for key segments such as loan types, third-party originations, geographic area, and property occupancy status, and active reporting of volumes against those limits. Concentrations should also be monitored by key portfolio characteristics like loans with high CLTV ratios, loans with high DTI ratios, loans with potential for negative amortization, loans to borrowers with credit scores below established tolerances, loans with risk-layering features, and non-owner-occupied investor loans. Reporting should include proactive reviews of portfolio condition through refreshed credit scores, refreshed collateral valuations, and the possible use of other credit bureau statistics that may indicate potential issues, such as missed payments with another primary creditor. The existence of any nontraditional portfolio concentrations that are not effectively managed through appropriately elevated MIS may become the subject of supervisory letter or examination report comments and may be criticized as unsafe and unsound practices that require corrective action.

Home Equity Lending Payment Administration

The payment processing for closed-end home equity loans is very similar to that for mortgage loans. The bank receives the payments and applies them to P&I based on the daily or monthly accrual of interest and the amount of time since the last payment was received. Because home equity loans are typically second liens, the payments generally include only P&I. In some cases, a home equity loan may be a first-lien loan and the payments may consist of principal, interest, taxes, and insurance, and have an associated escrow deposit account.

HELOCs are open-end credit arrangements and have several different potential payment arrangements. During the draw period for a line of credit, payment requirements are typically IO with principal payments made at the option of the borrower. When a payment is received, the proceeds are typically applied to the interest that has accrued since the last payment date. If the payment contains an amount above the interest accrual amount, these proceeds are applied to the principal balance to lower the outstanding balance and increase the amount of credit available under the line. Some banks require payments during the draw period that consist of both interest accrued and some amount of principal repayment. These payments are based on some percentage of the outstanding balance. For example, the regular monthly payment may be the interest accrued during the month plus 1 percent of the outstanding principal amount.

While the interest rate on a HELOC is usually a variable rate during the draw period, it may remain variable during the repayment period or become a fixed rate. Other structures for HELOCs include a balloon maturity at the end of the draw period rather than a conversion to a repayment period. In such structures, the entire balance outstanding at the maturity of the agreement is due and payable. Depending on the sophistication of the bank's HELOC offerings, varying levels of technological infrastructure are needed to handle changes in repayment requirements.

When conversion from the draw period payment to a full amortization period payment involves a substantial increase in the customer's monthly payment, the bank should monitor the customer's ability to fulfill the new payment requirements. When a customer cannot meet the full amortization payment requirement, the bank's policy and procedures for credit risk management should have predefined criteria for acceptable actions. These actions may include prudent restructures of the loan balances to achieve an acceptable repayment within a reasonable amount of time. In addition, management should assess whether there is a need to classify the relationship, earn interest income on the relationship, and potentially account for and report the relationship as a TDR. Renewing a relationship on IO market terms if the borrower's creditworthiness does not justify such terms is an unsafe or unsound lending practice.

Home Equity Lending Account Management

For home equity loans, account management activities primarily involve monitoring a borrower's financial condition by periodically obtaining updated credit scores when practical, such as part of a portfolio score refresh activity. Collateral values and LTV information also should be monitored and updated through portfolio valuation activities. This information should be used to target accounts for specific collection activities if the borrower becomes delinquent in making payments.

Because HELOCs often have long-term, IO payment features, banks should have risk management techniques that identify higher-risk accounts and adverse changes in account risk profiles. Such techniques enable management to implement timely preventative action (for example, freezing or reducing available lines). Further, a bank should have risk management procedures to evaluate and approve additional credit on an existing line or extend the IO period. Account management practices should be appropriate for the size of the portfolio and the risks associated with the types of home equity lending.

Effective account management practices for larger portfolios or portfolios with high-risk characteristics include

- periodically refreshing credit risk scores on all customers.
- using behavior scoring and analysis of individual borrower characteristics to identify potential problem accounts.

- periodically assessing account utilization rates.
- periodically assessing payment patterns, including borrowers who make only minimum payments over a period of time or those who rely on the line to keep payments current.
- monitoring of home values by geographic area.
- obtaining updated information on the collateral's value when significant market factors indicate a potential decline in home values, or when a borrower's payment performance deteriorates and greater reliance is placed on the collateral.

The frequency of these actions should be commensurate with the size and risk in the RRE portfolio as determined by borrower and market conditions. Bank policies should require management to conduct annual credit reviews of HELOC accounts to determine whether the line should be continued based on the borrower's current financial condition.[42]

When appropriate, banks should refuse to extend additional credit or should reduce the credit limit of a HELOC, bearing in mind that Regulation Z provides important protections for consumers when a HELOC account is terminated, suspended, or reduced.[43] For example, a bank can freeze or reduce a credit line under a limited set of circumstances, including when (1) the value of the collateral declines significantly below the appraised value for the purposes of the home equity line; (2) the consumer is in default of a material obligation under the loan agreement; or (3) the bank reasonably believes the consumer will be unable to fulfill the repayment obligations under the plan because of a material deterioration in the borrower's financial circumstances.

Additionally, under ECOA and its implementing regulation, 12 CFR 1002 (Regulation B), the Fair Housing Act, and other fair lending guidance, banks may not discriminate on a prohibited basis when making credit decisions. When taking action to terminate, reduce, suspend, or reinstate HELOC accounts, banks should follow policies that are consistent with prudent risk management principles and should carry them out without regard to prohibited factors. As with all actions related to RRE lending, banks must not violate section 5 of the FTC Act, which prohibits unfair or deceptive acts or practices, or the prohibition against unfair, deceptive, or abusive acts or practices found in Dodd–Frank.[44]

Account management practices for HELOCs should also include risk management controls and criteria for the approval of advances or draws against the approved line. These controls may be implemented manually in a smaller bank (for example, a teller or other representative

---

[42] Under the capital rule (effective January 1, 2014, for advanced approaches banks, and January 1, 2015, for all other banks), like the prior general risk-based capital guidelines, an unused HELOC commitment with an original maturity of one year or more may be allocated a 0 percent conversion factor if the bank conducts at least an annual credit review and is able to unconditionally cancel the commitment, at its option (i.e., prohibit additional extensions of credit, reduce the credit line, and terminate the line with or without cause), to the full extent permitted by relevant federal law. Refer to 12 CFR 3.

[43] Refer to 12 CFR 1026.40(f).

[44] For federal savings associations, also refer to OTS CEO Memo #276, "HELOC Account Management Guidance" (August 28, 2008).

---

may review specific account information to ensure the customer's good standing before authorizing the draw). In larger community and regional banks, the process for draw approval typically is automated and likely includes a review of the customer's payment status and most recent credit score information. Any authorizations that would allow the home equity line to go over its approved limit should be restricted and subject to specific policies, procedures, and approval authorities. Draw authorization approval processes that do not adequately control authorizations may be criticized. Furthermore, bank practices should require any over-limit borrowers to repay the over-limit amount in a timely manner. The existence of over-limit HELOCs may significantly increase a portfolio's credit risk. Therefore, MIS should be sufficient to enable management to identify, measure, monitor, and control the unique risks associated with over-limit accounts.

Home Equity Lending Portfolio Management

Banks should implement an effective portfolio credit risk management process for their home equity portfolios that is commensurate with their size, operational nature, and risk profile. Such processes should include compliance with regulatory real estate lending standards requiring lending policies that are consistent with safe and sound banking practices and are approved by the board of directors annually. Before implementing any changes to policies or underwriting standards, management should assess the potential effects on the bank's overall risk profile, including concentrations, profitability, and credit performance such as delinquency and loss rates. The accuracy of these assessments should be tested by comparisons to subsequent actual experience.

Effective portfolio management should clearly communicate portfolio objectives, such as growth targets, utilization rates, expected rate of return hurdles, default expectations, and losses. For banks with significant concentrations of home equity loans and lines, capital and portfolio limits measured as a percentage of total capital should be established and monitored for key portfolio segments, such as geographic area, loan type, and higher-risk products. When appropriate, consideration should be given to the use of risk mitigation tools such as PMI, pool insurance, or securitization. As the portfolio approaches concentration limits, the portfolio managers should analyze the situation sufficiently to enable the bank's board of directors and senior management to make a well-informed decision to either raise concentration limits or pursue a different course of action.

Effective portfolio management also requires an understanding of the risk characteristics of the home equity portfolio. Management should analyze the portfolio by segment using criteria such as product type, credit risk score, DTI ratios, LTV ratios, property type, geographic area, collateral valuation method, lien position, size of credit relative to prior liens, and documentation type (such as full, low doc, or no doc).

RRE Loan Collections and Foreclosure Functions

Mortgage Loan and Delinquent Loan Collections

An effective collection process is vital to controlling and minimizing credit losses. The process should be guided by well-established policies and procedures and should be managed effectively at each stage for optimal and legal collection of P&I to occur. For smaller banks that are primarily servicing and collecting loans from their portfolios, collections may be conducted by the same loan officer who originated the loan. The process likely involves phone calls, letters, and consultations with a foreclosure attorney if the loan becomes excessively past due.

For larger community banks, the collection process may be conducted by dedicated collection staff whose primary responsibilities are the collections of the bank's consumer loans, including those secured by RRE. Because of the nature of real estate-secured collection activities, there may be designated specialists within the collection staff who handle residential loans (mortgages and home equity). For larger regional banks that service and collect mortgage loans held in their portfolios as well as loans held by other investors, a specialized mortgage loan collection staff likely exists to ensure that collections and foreclosures are handled properly.

When a bank services and collects mortgage loans for third-party investors, it must ensure that it follows all applicable state and federal laws (including the Fair Debt Collection Practices Act) and other legal obligations in connection with the timing and manner of collection activities. In addition, banks must comply with the procedures set forth in the Mortgage Servicing Rules in Regulation X, subpart C.

For loans in the early stages of delinquency, the collection staff contacts borrowers by telephone and letters. Except for small servicers, Regulation X requires banks that service covered mortgage loans to make good faith efforts to establish live contact with delinquent borrowers by the 36th day of delinquency and to assign personnel to the borrower by the time it provides required written notice, but no later than 45 days from delinquency. Early intervention efforts apprise borrowers of their status, provide information about possible loss mitigation options, and give the bank the opportunity to obtain a payment or promise to pay from the customer that can either make up the loan arrearage or keep the loan from becoming more past due. A secondary goal is to obtain current financial information from the borrower in order to make more informed collection decisions going forward about the borrower's ability and willingness to perform.

Once an account becomes more than 90 days delinquent, it is subject to possible classification under the interagency "Uniform Retail Credit Classification and Account Management Policy" issued in June 2000 (refer to OCC Bulletin 2000-20, "Uniform Retail Credit Classification and Account Management Policy"). At that point, prudent lending policies for portfolio loans typically require the bank to evaluate the overall situation and determine the appropriateness of continued income recognition and the desirability of pursuing more intense collection activities, loan modification, or foreclosure.[45] This activity includes review of as much credit information as possible (credit scores, credit reports, or financial information provided by the borrower) as well as some type of update on the current value of the collateral through an automated valuation model (AVM), a broker price opinion (BPO), an evaluation, or an appraisal.

Once the RRE-secured loan reaches 180 days past due, the interagency classification guidance requires the bank to have a current assessment of the value of the collateral securing the loan and to charge off any exposure above the collateral's value less expected cost to sell the property. When the bank transfers the RRE securing the loan to other real estate owned (OREO) in accordance with generally accepted accounting principles (GAAP), the value of the collateral must be supported by a regulatory conforming appraisal or evaluation.[46]

Mortgage Loan Renewals, Assumptions, Deferrals, Modifications, and TDRs

For banks that are servicing and collecting mortgage loans held in their portfolios, prudent RRE lending policies should have predefined standards for working with delinquent borrowers. These standards should include parameters for when it is acceptable to renew the loan at current market terms or to execute a deferral of a loan's payment(s). The standards may also include circumstances when it would be acceptable for the loan to be assumed by another willing and capable obligor. Finally, the standards should include parameters for negotiating a modification of the loan's repayment requirements. These parameters should be comprehensive and attempt to achieve a permanent result that facilitates the borrower's ability to reasonably perform and minimizes the bank's potential for future loss. Depending on the nature of the borrower's financial distress and the degree of modification of the loan's terms, the modification may be reported within the bank's call reports as a TDR and consistent with GAAP. TDR accounting occurs when the bank's modifications or concessions to standard market terms are prompted by deterioration in the borrower's financial condition.

During periods of market deterioration (e.g., declining housing prices and tightening credit standards), loan modifications should be presumed to be TDRs, unless that presumption can be overcome by a preponderance of evidence to the contrary. Banks should document the analysis performed for each loan modification to support whether the modification is or is not a TDR. In order to support that a loan modification is not a TDR, the borrower's file should include new underwriting documentation (updated property value, credit report, and income analysis) as evidence that the modification reflects market rates and terms for a new loan with comparable risk.

---

[45] The bank should also consider whether the loan modification procedures in 12 CFR 1026.41 are applicable.

[46] 12 CFR 34.85 and 160.172 require national banks and FSAs, respectively, to obtain an appraisal or evaluation, as appropriate, to substantiate the market value of each parcel upon transfer to OREO.

Regulatory guidance consistently encourages lenders to work constructively with distressed RRE borrowers to the greatest extent possible within prudent banking practices to avoid unnecessary foreclosures. The bank should not, however, use workout strategies to defer identifiable losses. The lender, while working with a borrower, should always follow regulatory guidance for classification of, and loss recognition on, problem loans. Lenders also should follow appropriate income recognition or use of nonaccrual status, if appropriate, and accurate accounting of the loan's condition based on the circumstances consistent with call report instructions and GAAP. Working with distressed borrowers does not result in regulatory forbearance from long-standing and proven regulatory asset classification and loss recognition standards.

Mortgage Loan Foreclosures

When a borrower defaults, the lender follows the specific requirements under state law to obtain its interest in the property and gain title through a foreclosure process. Each state has laws and regulations on perfecting a security interest in the collateral and for obtaining title to the property through the secured interest if a borrower defaults on a loan. Depending on the state, security interest perfection occurs through the recording of a security deed of trust or a mortgage in the appropriate jurisdiction, usually the county where the property is located. The foreclosure process (whether judicial or nonjudicial) takes place between the perfection and obtaining title. Once title has been obtained, the lender then works to sell the property to recoup the losses suffered from the borrower's default on the loan. In some states, if the lender's sale of the property does not sufficiently cover the bank's losses and associated expenses of collection, the bank may pursue a deficiency judgment against the borrower for the amount remaining. Borrowers have certain rights under state law, including a right of redemption in some states. (A right of redemption gives property owners who pay off the taxes or liens on their property the ability to prevent foreclosure, sometimes even after the auction or sale has occurred.)

During periods of financial stress, the banking and mortgage industry may suffer a high level of financial and reputational harm because many lenders, or their contracted servicers of loans, are unable to manage the large volume of defaulted RRE loans and fail to diligently follow state foreclosure requirements. The "Interagency Review of Foreclosure Policies and Practices," published by bank regulatory agencies in April 2011, identifies deficiencies in the administration of delinquent mortgage loans, loss mitigation practices, and foreclosure processing requirements, including

- inadequate oversight, controls, policies and procedures, and audits of mortgage collection functions.
- insufficient resources to ensure proper administration of loss mitigation and foreclosure processes.
- failure to properly oversee outside counsel and other third-party providers of foreclosure-related services.
- submission of affidavits that improperly asserted personal knowledge of facts contained within foreclosure case files.
- lack of or improper notarization of documents.

- failure to ensure proper endorsement of promissory notes or mortgage documents.

Because of such banking industry deficiencies, new laws and regulations were enacted at both the federal and state level to improve consumer safeguards. In addition, certain borrowers may be entitled to additional protections in the foreclosure process because they (1) are covered by the Servicemembers Civil Relief Act of 2003; (2) filed for bankruptcy shortly before the foreclosure action; or (3) qualified for or were paying in accordance with a trial modification.

New safeguards were adopted to prevent harm to borrowers that may result from inappropriate servicing practices. For instance, as of January 2014, under Regulation X, a servicer may not make the first notice or filing for any judicial or nonjudicial foreclosure process until the borrower is more than 120 days delinquent. If a borrower submits a complete loss mitigation application before the bank has begun the foreclosure process, the bank may not begin the foreclosure process until one of the following occurs:

- The bank sends the borrower a notice that the borrower is not eligible for any loss mitigation option, and the consumer has exhausted the appeal process.
- The borrower rejects all loss mitigation options the bank offers.
- The borrower fails to perform under an agreement on a loss mitigation option.[47]

In addition to any new legal obligations, the OCC specifically expects banks that service residential mortgages to act responsibly in their administration of delinquent mortgages and cases involving borrowers at imminent risk of foreclosure. Banks must comply with safe and sound banking practices; applicable federal, state, and local laws; third-party investor requirements; and the Home Affordable Modification Program requirements, if applicable, as well as other existing contractual and programmatic commitments.

Prudent business practices in servicing residential mortgage loans include ensuring, before proceeding to a foreclosure sale, that

- the loan is in default under terms of the note.
- any borrower complaints, appeals, or escalations have been considered and addressed.
- the borrower is not subject to specific legal protections such as those afforded under the Servicemembers Civil Relief Act and bankruptcy law.
- the bank has appropriate legal authority to foreclose.
- all appropriate notices have been provided to the borrower.
- appropriate outreach and other loss mitigation efforts have been made.
- the loan is not currently in an active loss mitigation program.
- the borrower is not currently qualified or being considered for a loss mitigation action.
- the bank is in compliance with all applicable federal, state, and local legal requirements, contractual requirements, and other legal and regulatory requirements.

---

[47] Refer to 12 CFR 1024.41.

Appendix E of the "Mortgage Banking" booklet of the *Comptroller's Handbook* contains the OCC's guidelines that establish minimum standards for the handling and prioritization of borrower files that are subject to an imminently scheduled (within 60 days) foreclosure sale.[48] These minimum review criteria are intended to ensure a level of consistency across servicers and should be used to determine whether a scheduled foreclosure sale should be postponed, suspended, or cancelled because of critical foreclosure defects in the borrower's file. The purpose of these guidelines is to ensure that borrowers do not lose their homes without their files first receiving pre-foreclosure sale reviews conducted according to the standards listed in the guidelines. These standards are applicable to all OCC-supervised banks. As part of examinations of RRE lending activities, examiners determine if these standards have been effectively implemented. Failure to effectively implement and adhere to standards such as those provided in the guidelines may be criticized in supervisory letters and ROEs.

For banks that service and collect loans held in their portfolios, the decision to foreclose on the property often comes after extensive negotiations with the borrower. While the bank is pursuing a foreclosure action, there are some additional measures to mitigate loss that may be pursued to avoid a protracted foreclosure period. These actions include pre-foreclosure or short sale, in which the lender agrees to accept the proceeds of the sale in satisfaction of the loan even though the proceeds may be less than the amount owed on the mortgage. Another potential option would be a deed in lieu of foreclosure, in which the borrower voluntarily conveys the property to the lender to avoid a lengthy process with additional accruals of interest and legal expenses and in many cases satisfying any remaining debt.[49] Some banks provide cash payments to encourage borrowers to agree to a deed in lieu of foreclosure, and banks have found that this can be more cost-effective than proceeding through foreclosure and also can limit the negative impact on neighboring home values. These loss mitigation efforts may be used in addition to other attempts to sell the property before foreclosure.[50]

The state laws governing foreclosure vary, and the services of an attorney specializing in foreclosure law may be necessary and, in some states, required. State laws govern the time period that a lender must wait before initiating foreclosure proceedings, govern whether there is a right to redemption, and prescribe a judicial proceeding necessary for a deficiency judgment. In some states, foreclosing requires a judicial proceeding, while in other states, no judicial proceeding is required.

For banks that service loans for third-party investors, banks must follow the investors' standards as well as applicable laws pertaining to collection, loss mitigation, and foreclosure

---

[48] Refer also to 12 CFR 1024.41 (loss mitigation procedures under Regulation X/RESPA). Small servicers are not subject to most of 12 CFR 1024.41 but are subject to the 120-day ban on foreclosures.

[49] Examiners should consider consulting with district accountants or Accounting Policy regarding applicability of FASB Accounting Standards Update No. 2014-04, "Reclassification of Residential Real Estate Collateralized Consumer Mortgage Loans Upon Foreclosure."

[50] Refer to the "Managing Foreclosed Properties" section in the "Other Real Estate Owned" booklet of the *Comptroller's Handbook.*

actions. If a mortgage loan is part of a government loan guaranty program, such as the VA's or the FHA's program, the servicer must follow additional regulations and guidelines in the collections process. (For more information, refer to the "Mortgage Banking" booklet of the *Comptroller's Handbook*.)

Home Equity Lending Delinquent Loan Collections

The collection process for home equity loans and lines is operationally similar to that for mortgage loans. Depending on the size and nature of the bank's home equity lending activities, collections are handled by loan officers, a consumer loan collection staff, or specialists within a consumer loan collection staff. The primary distinctions between collections on mortgage loans and home equity loans and lines depend on the lien position of the bank. If the bank's home equity loan or line has a first-lien position, then collection activities closely resemble those for first-mortgage loans. If, however, the bank's home equity loan or line is subordinate or has a second-lien position, then collection activities have some additional areas of focus.

When a HELOC becomes delinquent, management should first act according to its predefined processes or standards to determine if the customer's access to the line should be, and legally can be, suspended. While many banks automatically terminate line access at a certain number of days past due (15, 30, 45, or 60), proactive managers of credit risk seek to terminate access sooner rather than later, such as through an evaluation of the customer's credit situation through a credit score or credit report. Proactive managers would also likely include some type of update of current collateral value. Based on evaluation of this information against the standards, management may act to terminate line access in compliance with Regulation Z requirements.

In the early stages of delinquency (less than 90 days), the loan officer or collections staff uses phone calls and letters to contact the borrower and attempt to obtain a loan payment and current financial information. Staff should also ascertain and document the borrower's willingness and ability to return the loan or line to a current status. Finally, the lender should obtain an updated estimate of the collateral's current value as well as the amount of the first lien and its repayment status. This information is used to determine the potential need to classify the loan or line, recognize any loss, discontinue income recognition, and decide the next steps in the collection process.

Under the interagency "Uniform Retail Credit Classification and Account Management Policy," the loans and lines are subject to classification when they become 90 days or more past due. The loans and lines are subject to loss recognition when identified or generally no later than when the loan becomes 180 days or more past due. Loss recognition involves charging the loan or line down to available value of the collateral less the cost to sell the property, if repossession of collateral is assured and in process. In cases when there is no available equity in the collateral, the bank's loss is 100 percent of the loan or line amount. Management may maintain the lien on the property to negotiate some amount of recovery in response to releasing the lien.

During times of economic downturn, banks may experience situations in which financially distressed borrowers make specific choices about paying on a home equity loan or line with a subordinate lien. In some cases, given the protracted nature of the foreclosure process, borrowers may have chosen to continue paying on a subordinate lien while ceasing to pay on the first lien. These payments effectively give the subordinate lien lender little incentive to proceed with collection or foreclosure activities even though an evaluation of the situation indicates that these activities would otherwise be warranted. In other cases, a borrower may choose not to pay on the subordinate lien while continuing to pay on the first lien. In situations when the combined liens exceed the total current value of the property, this action usually results in a loss for the subordinate lender and a decision to not pursue foreclosure due to a lack of viable equity.

Finally, some borrowers file for bankruptcy protection under federal law. The filing usually stops mortgage lenders from instituting collection and foreclosure activities. In some cases, the borrowers continue to make payments on their subordinate lien home equity loan during the bankruptcy process. The borrowers may not, however, reaffirm their contractual obligation to pay during the bankruptcy proceedings. The effect of these actions, in states where they are allowed, is known as a "ride through" the bankruptcy process. The ride-through effectively allows a borrower to stay in his or her home as long as payments continue to be made according to the loan's terms, but it eliminates the contractual obligation to do so.

From the bank's point of view, appropriate credit risk management dictates that a bankruptcy ride-through be subject to the asset classification process. In this case, the bank's only source of repayment is its right to proceed with redemption of its secured interest in the collateral. While such an asset has value, it also exhibits the characteristics of a substandard asset because it is no longer protected by the paying capacity or net worth of the obligor. Furthermore, the defaulted loan contract is dependent on the value and sale of the collateral for repayment if the customer chooses to stop payments. In those situations when the bank is unable to evaluate the borrower's repayment capacity and determines that loss classification is appropriate, the bank should write down the loan to the estimated collateral value less cost to sell, based on the most appropriate evaluation method or recent appraisal. Management should evaluate the appropriate application of each subsequent payment received, applying payments to further reduce the principal balance of the loan, cash basis recognition of income, or a combination of the above methods, consistent with the condition of the loan.

Home Equity Lending Renewals, Deferrals, Re-Ages, Modifications, and TDRs

In some cases, management may choose to pursue a renewal, deferral, re-age, or modification to a home equity loan or line based on predefined standards in the RRE loan policy. These standards should include criteria for evaluating the borrower's willingness and ability to perform on the loan or line going forward as well as the bank's potential equity position in the collateral property. Simply renewing a home equity line on draw-period IO terms because the borrower cannot meet amortizing repayment terms typically is criticized as an imprudent lending practice. Re-aging a HELOC to current status or deferring payments to the end of a home equity loan without a documented review of the borrower's renewed willingness and capacity to repay also generally is criticized. Finally, if the terms of the home equity loan or line are substantially modified, the bank should evaluate the loan or line for TDR status for financial reporting purposes.[51]

Home Equity Lending Foreclosures

The decision to foreclose on a home equity loan or line when the bank has a subordinate lien position involves a comprehensive assessment of all relevant circumstances and factors. Because foreclosure likely involves paying off the first-lien position to gain title to the property, management should ensure that the collateral's estimated value justifies this expense. Management should also evaluate the amount of time and other estimated expenses that may be incurred to effectively accomplish foreclosure and marketing of the property. If, after evaluating the facts, management decides not to pursue foreclosure, the entire amount of the loan or line should be charged off no later than 180 days or more past due.

Risks Associated With RRE Lending

From a supervisory perspective, risk is the potential that events, expected or unexpected, will have an adverse effect on a bank's earnings, capital, or franchise or enterprise value. The OCC has defined eight categories of risk for bank supervision purposes: credit, interest rate, liquidity, price, operational, compliance, strategic, and reputation. These categories are not mutually exclusive. Any product or service may expose a bank to multiple risks. Risks also may be interdependent and may be positively or negatively correlated. Examiners should be aware of this interdependence and assess the effect in a consistent and inclusive manner. Refer to the "Bank Supervision Process" booklet of the *Comptroller's Handbook* for an expanded discussion of banking risks and their definitions.

The risks associated with RRE lending are credit, interest rate, liquidity, operational, compliance, strategic, and reputation.

Credit Risk

The primary credit risk associated with RRE lending is that borrowers will be unable to repay their loans. Another credit risk concern is that a combination of all real estate loans against a single property to a single borrower will exceed the realizable market value of the residential property. For borrowers who cannot or do not repay their debt, the bank may need to initiate collection activities, consider loan modifications, or begin foreclosure proceedings.[52] Therefore, underwriting standards should emphasize the borrower's ability and willingness to service the loan from cash flow or net income rather than the sale of collateral. A bank is precluded from making an RRE loan based predominantly on the bank's realization of the

---

[51] A creditor's ability to change the terms of a HELOC is limited by 12 CFR 1026.40; if the borrower is in default, however, the lender can prohibit any further extensions of credit or reduce the credit line.

[52] Banks should ensure that loss mitigation and foreclosure activities conform with the requirements set forth in 12 CFR 1024.41.

foreclosure or liquidation value of the borrower's collateral, without regard to the borrower's ability to repay the loan according to its terms.

Both traditional and nontraditional mortgage loans and home equity loans and lines of credit can be subject to risk-layering practices. Risk layering results in a cumulative effect of risk factors that increases the overall level of a transaction's credit risk. Examples of risk layering include

- the combination of payment deferral (liberal repayment requirement) and other risk factors, such as a simultaneous second lien or higher LTV ratios (less overall borrower equity).
- reduced documentation (less verified borrower information).
- non-owner-occupied investor property (potential volatility in a borrower's ability to pay).

If risks are layered, the loan terms should reflect the increased risk by including strong risk mitigation factors that support an underwriting decision and the borrower's overall repayment capacity. Such mitigating factors could include a lower overall LTV ratio, a lower DTI ratio, higher disposable income or cash reserves, other credit enhancements, or mortgage insurance.

A bank's use of risk-layering practices should be well articulated in its RRE loan policies and lending standards. Mortgage loans and home equity loans and lines of credit that are subjected to risk-layering practices should be identified within a bank's MIS reports to ensure appropriate measurement and monitoring. Management and the board should effectively limit the volume of loans and lines of credit subjected to risk-layering practices and avoid undue concentrations of layered risk in relation to regulatory capital and earnings.

Acceptable collateral valuation practices, including prudent LTV standards, should be established. Additionally, prudent ATR standards should be established, such as acceptable DTI ratios.[53] Proper credit and collateral documentation, including appropriate applications, credit reports, appraisals, and evidence of lien priority status and amounts, should be required.

Special lending programs often are used to provide financing to low- and moderate-income borrowers. Management undertakes these programs to prudently serve the credit needs of the bank's communities, with the additional benefit of potential consideration in the assessment of the bank's performance under the Community Reinvestment Act (CRA). Management should set prudent policy limits for commitments to these programs before implementation. First-time home-buyer programs with limited or no down-payment requirements may permit borrowers to become overextended more easily than conventional programs. Overextension is more likely if the program simultaneously permits a layering of credit risk through increased LTV ratios, higher DTI ratios, or reduced savings on hand. Any of these methods of layering risk can result in a borrower quickly becoming overextended due to an

---

[53] For virtually all closed-end residential mortgage loans, the ATR standards are prescribed by 12 CFR 1026.43.

unexpected financial crisis. These methods need responsive, and possibly enhanced, loss mitigation efforts, such as working with the borrower to minimize delinquencies and foreclosures.

Another issue affecting credit risk is continued lien priority. A bank should ensure that its lien has priority over the liens of other creditors. For example, some state laws dictate whether subsequent advances under a HELOC continue to hold lien priority status. To ensure continued collateral adequacy, lenders should be aware of what laws apply.

The greater the volume and types of RRE lending programs offered, the higher the potential credit risk exposure. The amount of credit risk taken should drive the level of sophistication in the bank's systems and controls. The risk management infrastructure and controls should be commensurate with the articulated appetite for risk. When nontraditional RRE products are used or credit risk is layered in a transaction, risk management processes should include periodic review of the borrower's repayment history, as such a review would help identify potential repayment problems before a crisis occurs.

When a borrower lacks sufficient equity to meet down-payment requirements, lenders normally require some type of enhancement, such as PMI. Borrowers purchase PMI either through private companies or by participating in the FHA and VA loan programs, which are government guaranteed. Banks may also consider whether the borrower qualifies for other government-guaranteed loan programs as a way to reduce credit risk.

HELOCs can cause unique credit risk issues because borrowers potentially can use the undrawn portions of their lines to make their monthly payments. A bank that provides draw checks as part of its home equity program can determine if this situation is occurring by reviewing the payee information on the check. If so, a prompt review of the account and the borrower's financial capacity to repay is recommended. Curtailing additional extensions under the home equity line should be considered, if allowed by contract terms and in compliance with Regulation Z requirements.

Interest Rate Risk

RRE loans and lines of credit expose a bank to interest rate risk because they can be written on a fixed-rate basis, a variable-rate basis, or a combination of the two, in which either the rate is fixed for a period and then becomes variable or the rate is variable and then becomes fixed. All of these scenarios should be adequately identified and addressed in the bank's primary processes and tools for managing interest rate risk. In times of rising interest rates, interest income on loans made on a fixed-rate basis may fall below the bank's cost of funds. With variable rates, when different indexes are used for loans than for the cost of funds, exposure to interest rate risk may increase.

Periods of increasing interest rates can reduce home buyers' willingness or ability to finance a real estate loan and therefore can adversely affect a bank that needs a minimum level of loan originations to remain profitable. Decreasing interest rates, by contrast, normally result in faster loan prepayments, which can reduce a bank's projected interest income from the mortgage loan portfolio.

Liquidity Risk

Liquidity risk includes the inability to access funding sources or manage fluctuations in funding levels. The degree of liquidity risk is affected by a variety of factors, including whether portfolio production is underwritten to secondary-market standards and the need to fund commitments to borrowers. Portfolio lenders make RRE loans with the intention of maintaining these loans in their portfolio; liquidity needs, however, may require a bank to sell some of the RRE loans in the secondary market. If the mortgages considered for sale are not underwritten in compliance with investor guidelines, like those of Fannie Mae, Freddie Mac, or private investors, the bank may be unable to sell them at an acceptable price.

Operational Risk

Operational capabilities should fully incorporate RRE lending activities. Management should have expertise in appropriate mortgage and home equity lending processes. Staffing levels and experience of personnel should be commensurate with the volume and nature of risks being assumed. Strategic and ongoing tactical plans should ensure that support systems, controls, and personnel are in place to accommodate the volume of planned loan origination, servicing, and collection activities inherent in residential mortgage and home equity portfolios.

Other operational risks in RRE lending that should be controlled include documentation or record-keeping management, escrow account administration, payments processing, and the management of collection or foreclosure activities. Any functions of a successful mortgage operation may be performed internally or contracted out to a third party. If a bank uses third-party vendors, the bank should ensure that these relationships are effectively managed.[54] During times of financial crisis, banks may suffer significant operational problems or losses when high volumes of delinquent mortgage loans overwhelm mortgage servicing systems or when third-party contractors fail to meet their contractual obligations.

Compliance Risk

Numerous consumer protection and fair lending laws and regulations, listed in the "References" section of this booklet, affect RRE lending. Refer to the relevant *Consumer Compliance* booklet for each of these laws and regulations for updated information and complete examination procedures. In addition, examiners should address non-consumer compliance risks, such as appraisal and lending limit regulations.

Extensive changes to governing regulations such as Regulation Z, which implements TILA, and Regulation X, which implements RESPA, have occurred since the financial crisis of

---

[54] Refer to OCC Bulletin 2013-29, "Third-Party Relationships: Risk Management Guidance."

2008. Additionally, the CFPB was created by Dodd–Frank and given the responsibility to regulate the offering and provision of consumer financial products or services under the federal consumer financial laws enumerated in that statute (for example, RESPA and TILA).[55] In connection with the federal consumer financial laws, Dodd–Frank conferred authority on the CFPB to issue rules (for example, amendments to Regulations X and Z) interpreting those laws. With regard to banks with assets more than $10 billion, Dodd–Frank also assigned to the CFPB exclusive examination authority, and primary enforcement authority, to ensure compliance by banks with the federal consumer financial laws.

RRE lending activities also expose banks to fair lending requirements, such as the requirements under ECOA and the Fair Housing Act. Management must be aware of these standards and implement effective procedures and controls to help it identify practices that could result in discrimination against any class of borrowers. For example, discretionary pricing that is not properly controlled may increase fair lending risk, and potentially lead to violations of ECOA and the Fair Housing Act. For more information, refer to the "Fair Lending" booklet of the *Comptroller's Handbook*.

Strategic Risk

Strategic risk from RRE lending may be increased if a bank has a substantial number of loans concentrated in one geographic area, market, or property type, or if a large number of borrowers share the same employer or industry income source. When evaluating a bank's RRE strategic risk, consider, among other things, economic dynamics and market conditions, new products and services, growth from new channels, concentrations of loans, and borrower income sources. The structure and managerial talent of the organization must support its strategies and levels of sophistication and innovation.

Reputation Risk

Reputation risk arises from negative public opinion, which can result from sources such as interactions with individual customers, an operational breakdown, publication of a formal enforcement action, and litigation. An operational breakdown or general weakness in any part of a bank's RRE lending activities can harm the bank's reputation if it causes customers and the general public to become dissatisfied. Reputation risks can include the perception that a bank (or a contracted third-party vendor) is engaged in discriminatory, predatory, unfair, deceptive, or abusive practices, or has otherwise failed to comply with applicable consumer laws and regulations. Additionally, high levels of past-dues, foreclosures, and losses can affect the bank's reputation because these statistics are tracked by bank analysts and communicated to investors, depositors, and others.

For example, if a bank decides to eliminate its affordable-housing loan program because the program is not performing well, the bank's reputation may suffer. To reduce the impact on a

---

[55] Refer to 12 USC 5481(14) for the definition of federal consumer financial law.

bank's reputation, adequate policies, commitments, and expertise should be in place to meet affordable housing market needs.

During periods of financial stress, the banking industry may suffer from reputation risk caused by negative public perception of the RRE lending activities. Questionable activities may involve over-lending to borrowers with high-risk credit profiles or limited down payments. Furthermore, a high volume of RRE loan delinquencies may overwhelm the operational abilities of many banks and servicers to effectively administer collection and foreclosure activities in strict adherence to federal and state legal requirements. In addition, the volume of loan repurchase requests from investors may increase substantially, which can negatively affect both a bank's reputation and its liquidity positions.

Risk Management

Each bank should identify, measure, monitor, and control risk by implementing an effective risk management system appropriate for the size and complexity of its operations. When examiners assess the effectiveness of a bank's risk management system, they consider the bank's policies, processes, personnel, and control systems. For more information, refer to the "Bank Supervision Process" booklet of the *Comptroller's Handbook*.

In organizations with more complex and sophisticated RRE lending products and activities, a strong credit risk management function is especially important to the success and profitability of residential lending operations. The risk management function, whether embedded in the line of business, performed corporately, or both, should be responsible for evaluating ongoing credit standards, monitoring the quality of the portfolio(s), and making changes to the underwriting standards as necessary to maintain the desired level of risk in the portfolio(s). The risk management function should promote early and accurate identification of existing and potential problems as well as identification of policy revision needs. Risk management also should provide bank management with the information it needs to identify and respond promptly to changes in the lending environment. This information includes monitoring trends in portfolio delinquency, in aggregate losses and account-level loss severity, and in forward-looking risk profile as determined by periodic refreshes of account-level credit scores or behavior scores. The risk management function also should help manage and maintain all credit scoring systems used for RRE lending activities.

As part of examining RRE lending activities, examiners assess the level and frequency of audit and loan review coverage to determine if it is commensurate with the size and nature of the bank's residential lending strategy and operations. To the degree a bank has larger, more complex RRE lending activities, examiners assess the existence, adequacy, and independence of a dedicated QC function. In the largest banks, examiners assess the existence and adequacy of the credit risk management function.

If an examination reveals deficiencies in audit and loan review coverage in relation to the size and nature of RRE lending activities, the bank could be subject to supervisory criticism and needs to take appropriate corrective action. If an examination reveals that a QC function or a credit risk management function is necessary to properly supervise the bank's RRE lending activities, the lack of such functions commensurate with the size and nature of the lending strategy and operations is communicated as a deficiency that requires corrective action.

Risk management systems typically include the internal and external audit functions and the loan review functions in all banks. Depending on the size and nature of a bank's RRE lending operations, these risk management systems also may include specific consumer compliance management or audit functions and QC functions. In the largest, most complex banks, these systems typically involve a risk officer and staff within each line of business or within the corporate governing entity, or both.

Management and Oversight

RRE lending traditionally has been a primary focus of FSAs and has become more prevalent in national banks since the 1970s. The lending process has also become more automated and sophisticated, and the nature of the products offered has become widely varied. Given these trends, a bank's RRE lending operations must have the management and organizational structure, expertise, staffing levels, information systems, training programs, internal controls, and loan review processes to operate effectively in this environment.

A bank's RRE strategy should include pro forma depictions of the expected portfolio mix by product or credit score and the expected performance by delinquency and losses. Internal reports should monitor portfolio performance according to the expectations set forth in the strategy and the pro forma expectations. Any significant deviations from expectations should be highlighted and discussed by appropriate management or the board. Examiners should assess the adequacy of the strategy and the strategic planning process in relation to management's ability to achieve the desired outcomes.

Regardless of a bank's size and the scope and nature of RRE lending activities, the strategy for this activity should clearly identify and articulate the level of risk the bank wants to accept and generate within its book of business (held for investment or held for sale). The strategy should reflect realistic objectives based on reasonable data and assumptions. The objectives should include the type of programs and products offered for both residential mortgage lending and home equity lending. For each major program and product, management should fully understand

- the interest rates, terms, and conditions.
- the channels through which the products are offered (retail branches or wholesale relationships).
- the expected cash flow repayment ability.
- the expected collateral coverage margins.
- management's objectives, such as profitability, portfolio composition, volumes by product, credit score, and LTV ratios.
- the liquidity, regulatory capital, and ALLL considerations that must be met.

The bank's risk appetite should balance underwriting standards with a reasonable pricing structure to achieve the desired portfolio mix and return.

HELOC programs also should include sufficient periodic reviews of borrowers' financial conditions. The reviews could include quarterly or annual refreshes of borrowers' credit bureau scores. These reviews are particularly important when a line has been inactive for some time and is nearing maturity or conversion from the draw period to the repayment period. In areas or periods of declining real estate values, there should be a process to review the current value of the collateral in relation to the outstanding balance and undrawn line so that the bank can consider renewing or freezing an open HELOC in accordance with the requirements of Regulation Z. A well-documented HELOC risk management program is also necessary to support the 0 percent conversion factor for undrawn line commitments for regulatory capital purposes.

For mortgage loans and closed-end home equity loans, effective oversight should include management's defined criteria for renewals and deferrals, the parameters for loan modifications, and the initiation of foreclosure activities. Policies and procedures for implementing the strategy should include criteria for stopping interest accrual on a loan, classification of a borrower, and appropriate TDR accounting and reporting.

Information Technology

RRE lending can be highly technology dependent. From the time of the loan application through the remaining life of the loan, technology plays a key role in operations, risk management, and regulatory reporting. Information technology (IT) and the IT infrastructure allow bankers to leverage resources and increase both operational and financial efficiency. Additionally, a strong IT culture is needed for high-volume banks because of the high level of MIS and reporting for both investor and regulatory requirements.

Assessment of IT systems for RRE lending activities should include an assessment of the capability of the IT systems to support operational, risk management, and risk control functions within an RRE operation. The assessment also should consider continuity planning for IT as well as the overall resiliency of business processes. IT systems should be compatible and able to process the high volume of data generated during the life of a mortgage loan.

Loan Policies and Real Estate Lending Standards

Section 304 of the Federal Deposit Insurance Corporation Improvement Act (12 USC 1828(o)) directs national banks and FSAs to prescribe formal written policies that establish acceptable terms and underwriting standards for real estate loans. The act's requirements are implemented at 12 CFR 34, subpart D, for national banks, and at 12 CFR 160.101 for FSAs.

These respective regulations require banks to adopt and maintain written policies that establish appropriate limits and standards for real estate loans, including RRE loans. Policies must be consistent with safe and sound banking practices, consistent with bank compliance requirements, appropriate to the bank's size and the nature and scope of its operations, and approved by the board of directors at least annually.

The approved lending policies must also specifically establish

- loan portfolio diversification standards.
- prudent, clear, and measurable underwriting standards, including LTV limits.
- loan administration procedures for the bank's real estate loan portfolio.
- documentation, approval, and reporting requirements to monitor compliance with the bank's real estate lending policies.

Additionally, under the regulations each bank must monitor conditions in the real estate market in its lending area to ensure that its real estate lending policies continue to be appropriate for current market conditions.

More information on the regulatory expectations for an appropriate real estate lending policy is in the "Interagency Guidelines for Real Estate Lending Policies." These guidelines can be found in appendix A to 12 CFR 34, subpart D, and in the appendix to 12 CFR 160.101.

The guidelines do not require specific LTV ratios for the types of real estate loans but do establish supervisory LTV limits.

Higher-Risk RRE-Secured Loans

A bank's loan policy requirements should effectively limit or preclude the origination of loans with higher risk characteristics. The policy should also effectively address situations when a loan becomes problematic after origination. An RRE loan is generally viewed as having higher risk if

- it is not a covered transaction under Regulation Z and its approval relies predominantly on the liquidation or sale of the underlying real estate collateral. (**Note:** Regulation Z prohibits banks from making RRE loans that are covered transactions based predominantly on the bank's realization of the foreclosure or liquidation value of the borrower's collateral, without regard to the borrower's ability to repay the loan according to its terms.[56])
- the amount of the loan is large relative to the appraised value of the property.
- the ability of the obligor to pay is questionable. (**Note:** A creditor shall not make a loan that is a transaction covered by TILA unless the creditor makes a reasonable and good faith determination at or before consummation that the consumer will have a reasonable ability to repay the loan according to its terms.[57])

---

[56] Refer to 12 CFR 1026.43.

[57] Refer to 12 CFR 1026.43(c)(1).

- other elements, such as interest, hazard insurance, and tax arrearages, are significant when not included in an escrow account arrangement.

In cases in which arrearages are significant and there is no escrow account,[58] the bank may make payments for the borrower through additional extensions of credit. While such arrangements can effectively protect the bank's security interest in the real estate collateral, the inability of the borrower to make such payments as required is indicative of possible deterioration in the borrower's creditworthiness. The loan policy should contain specific guidance on making insurance, property tax, and HOA payments on behalf of the borrower as well as on the appropriate accounting for those advances. The guidance in the loan policy may recommend, for example, the establishment of a separate credit agreement with the obligor or the addition of the advance to the principal balance of the loan. The policy also should require evaluation of the relationship for possible classification.

Many banks have jeopardized their regulatory capital structures by granting ill-considered RRE loans. Poorly considered RRE loans can cause significant losses to occur during periods of economic stress. Apart from unusual, localized, adverse economic conditions that could not have been foreseen, resulting in a temporary or permanent drop in real estate values, the principal errors made in granting RRE loans have included inadequate regard for

- normal real estate values during periods when real estate is in great demand, thus inflating the price structure.
- appropriate mortgage or home equity loan amortization.
- the maximum debt load and paying capacity of the borrower.

Potential Predatory Practices

Some RRE lending practices that have been identified as potentially predatory or abusive include the following:

- **Equity stripping and fee packing:** Repeat refinancings in which a borrower's equity is depleted because of financing excessive fees for the loan or ancillary products.
- **Loan flipping:** Repeat refinancing under circumstances in which the relative terms of the new and refinanced loan and the cost of the new loan do not provide a tangible economic benefit to the borrower.
- **Refinancing of special mortgages:** Refinancing of a special subsidized mortgage that contains terms favorable to the borrower (e.g., 3-2-1 rate buy-down loans), when the refinanced loan does not provide a tangible economic benefit to the borrower.
- **Encouragement of default:** Encouraging a borrower to breach a contract and default on an existing loan before and in connection with the consummation of a loan that refinances all or part of an existing loan.

---

[58] If an escrow account has been established for payment of hazard insurance, Regulation X requires timely payment of the hazard insurance premiums, even if the borrower's mortgage payment is more than 30 days overdue. Refer to 12 CFR 1024.17(k)(5).

These practices may disadvantage unsophisticated borrowers in particular.

In some circumstances, certain loan terms, conditions, and features may be deemed to be abusive, predatory, unfair, or deceptive practices. Changes in regulatory requirements, effective in January 2014, prohibit or restrict many of the features or practices that were evident in many loans originated before 2008.[59] Some features or practices that may be found to be abusive, predatory, unfair, or deceptive, or that are now restricted by regulation, include

- collection through financing of up-front, single-premium credit insurance—life, disability, or unemployment.
- pricing and terms, whether interest rates or fees, that far exceed the true risk and cost of making the loan.
- inadequate disclosure of the true costs and risks of loan transactions.
- padding or packing of fees by charging customers unearned, concealed, or unwarranted fees.
- flipping practices that require frequent and multiple refinancings of mortgage loans, which result in additional fees and erosion of the owner's equity.
- loan terms and structures designed to make it more difficult or impossible for borrowers to reduce their indebtedness.
- balloon payment loans that may conceal the true burden of the loan financing and may force borrowers into costly refinancing or foreclosure situations.
- prepayment penalties that are not limited to the early years of the loan, particularly in subprime loans.
- interest rate increases upon default at a level not commensurate with risk mitigation.
- call provisions permitting the bank to accelerate payment of the loan under circumstances other than the borrower's default under the credit agreement or to mitigate the bank's exposure to loss. These are prohibited for high-cost loans (12 CFR 1026.32(d)(8)) and for HELOCs (12 CFR 1026.40).
- absence of an appropriate assessment and documentation of the consumer's ability to repay the loan in accordance with its terms, commensurate with the type of loan. This is prohibited under the ATR rule, 12 CFR 1026.43(c) (closed-end mortgages, with certain exceptions), and 12 CFR 1026.34(a)(4) (high-cost, open-end mortgages).[60] mandatory arbitration clauses or agreements. This practice is prohibited for all dwelling-secured consumer transactions (12 CFR 1026.36(h)).
- original principal balance in excess of appraised value.

---

[59] Refer to Regulation Z, 12 CFR 1026.

[60] Regulation Z's provisions regarding creditor determinations of the borrower's ability to repay a loan generally require that the determinations (and DTI calculations) not be based on teaser rates and that the determinations be based on fully amortizing, substantially equal payments unless an exception to this requirement is stated (for example, for certain balloon payment loans). With respect to IO loans, the creditor must consider, before consummation of a loan, the borrower's ability to repay substantially equal monthly payments of P&I that repay the loan amount over the full term of the loan remaining, even after the IO period expires.

- payment schedules that consolidate more than two periodic payments and that call for them to be paid in advance from the loan proceeds.
- payments to home improvement contractors under a home improvement contract from the proceeds of an RRE-secured loan other than by an instrument payable to the consumer, jointly to the consumer and the contractor, or through an independent escrow agent. This practice is prohibited for high-cost loans (12 CFR 1026.34(a)).

Examiners must evaluate not only individual RRE loans but also the overall RRE lending and administrative policies of the bank to ascertain the relative soundness of the RRE loan operations. Specifically, the examiner must determine if the risk management activities used by bank management, including the loan policy, are commensurate with the risk profile articulated for and ultimately achieved within the portfolio of RRE loans.

For further details, refer to the OCC's "Guidelines Establishing Standards for Residential Mortgage Lending Practices," codified in 12 CFR 30, appendix C.

Supervisory LTV Limits and High LTV Loans

To clarify the regulations and interagency guidelines governing real estate lending standards, the bank regulatory agencies issued "Interagency Guidance on High LTV Residential Real Estate Lending" in October 1999 (OCC Bulletin 1999-38, "Interagency Guidelines for Real Estate Lending Policies: Treatment of High LTV Residential Real Estate Loans"). This high LTV (HLTV) guidance clarifies the "Interagency Guidelines for Real Estate Lending" found in both 12 CFR 34, subpart D, appendix A, which contains the OCC codification of the guidelines for national banks, and the appendix to 12 CFR 160.101, which contains the OCC codification of the guidelines for FSAs, and the supervisory LTV limits for loans on one- to four-family residential properties.[61] A bank's MIS reports for RRE lending should accurately track the volume of HLTV loans, including HLTV home equity and residential mortgages, and report the aggregate and trend of such loans to the bank's board of directors. Specifically, banks are reminded that

- loans in excess of the supervisory LTV limits should be identified in the bank's records. The aggregate of HLTV one- to four-family residential loans should not exceed 100 percent of the bank's total regulatory capital.
- in calculating the LTV and determining compliance with the supervisory LTVs, the bank should consider all senior liens. All loans secured by the property and held by the bank are reported as an exception if the CLTV ratio of a loan and all senior liens on an owner-

---

[61] For purposes of the "Interagency Guidelines for Real Estate Lending," HLTV one- to four-family residential property loans include (1) a loan for raw land zoned for one- to four-family residential use with an LTV ratio greater than 65 percent; (2) a residential land development loan or improved lot loan with an LTV ratio greater than 75 percent; (3) a residential construction loan with an LTV ratio greater than 85 percent; (4) a loan on non-owner-occupied one- to four-family residential property with an LTV ratio greater than 85 percent; and (5) a permanent mortgage or home equity loan on an owner-occupied residential property with an LTV ratio equal to or exceeding 90 percent without mortgage insurance, readily marketable collateral, or other acceptable collateral.

occupied one- to four-family residential property equals or exceeds 90 percent and if there is no additional credit enhancement in the form of either mortgage insurance or readily marketable collateral.

- for the LTV calculation, the loan amount is the legally binding commitment (that is, the entire amount that the bank is legally committed to lend over the life of the loan).
- all real estate loans in excess of supervisory LTV limits should be aggregated and reported quarterly to the bank's board of directors.

Insurance companies have introduced products to help banks mitigate the credit risks of HLTV residential loans. Insurance policies that cover a pool of loans can be an efficient and effective credit risk management tool. If a policy has a coverage limit, however, the coverage may be exhausted before all loans in the pool mature or are paid off. The OCC considers pool insurance as a sufficient credit enhancement to remove the HLTV designation if the policy (1) is issued by an acceptable mortgage insurance company (reviewed as part of the bank's third-party relationships program); (2) reduces the LTV ratio for each loan to less than 90 percent; and (3) remains in effect over the life of each loan in the pool.

Banks with HLTV concentrations as well as higher-risk portfolios are encouraged to perform sensitivity analysis or stress testing on key portfolio segments and to generate MIS reports of the results. This type of analysis identifies possible events that could increase risk within a portfolio segment or for the portfolio as a whole. Banks should consider stress tests that incorporate interest rate increases and declines in home values. Because these events often occur simultaneously, the OCC recommends testing for these events together. Banks should also periodically analyze and report on markets in key geographic areas, including identified "soft" markets. Management should consider developing contingency strategies for scenarios and outcomes that extend credit risk beyond internally established risk tolerances and performance expectations. These contingency plans may include increased monitoring, tightening of underwriting, limiting growth, and selling loans or portfolio segments.

Examiners assess the quantity and quality of MIS against the size and nature of the RRE lending activities. MIS found to be inadequate in relation to a bank's RRE lending strategies and operations are communicated as a deficiency that requires corrective action.

Appraisals and Evaluations

National banks and FSAs are required under 12 CFR 34, subpart D, and 12 CFR 160.101, respectively, to adopt and maintain written real estate lending policies. Pursuant to the "Interagency Guidelines for Real Estate Lending Policies," these policies should include a real estate appraisal and evaluation program. Such programs are designed to ensure that reliable appraisals and evaluations are obtained when required under 12 CFR 34, subpart C. Additionally, in 2010, the bank regulatory agencies published the "Interagency Appraisal and Evaluation Guidelines." (Refer to OCC Bulletin 2010-42, "Sound Practices for Appraisals and Evaluations.") These guidelines describe the elements of a sound program for conducting appraisals and evaluations to support real estate-related financial transactions. The guidelines also provide direction to examining personnel and supervised institutions on procedures, practices, and standards.

Reliable appraisals and evaluations, which banks use to determine the market value of real estate collateral for mortgage loans and other RRE-secured loans, are an integral part of the bank's lending activities.

Complex RRE-secured transactions and nonresidential real estate transactions, other than those involving one-to four-family residential properties, with a transaction value of $250,000 or more, and all transactions with a transaction value of $1 million or more require an appraisal prepared by a state-certified appraiser. All other RRE-secured transactions, subject to the exceptions in 12 CFR 34.43, require an appraisal prepared by either a state-certified appraiser or a state-licensed appraiser. Many states have two state-certified credentials—state-certified residential and state-certified general. A state-certified residential appraiser may appraise one- to four-family residential units without regard to transaction value or complexity. This classification does not include the appraisal of subdivisions. A state-certified general appraiser may appraise all types of real property regardless of transaction value. For RRE-secured transactions of $250,000 or less, an appropriate evaluation of the real property collateral ("evaluation") is allowed in lieu of an appraisal.

The guidelines issued by the bank regulatory agencies in 2010 built on the existing federal regulatory framework and reaffirmed long-standing regulatory expectations. The guidelines also incorporated the agencies' previous supervisory issuances and, in response to advances in IT, clarified standards for the industry's appropriate use of analytical methods and technological tools if such tools are a component in the development of appraisals or evaluations.

The guidelines emphasize that banks are responsible for selecting appraisers and people performing evaluations based on their competence, experience, and knowledge of the market and type of property being valued. Competency is an essential element in the selection and engagement process. Competency is not determined by whether an appraiser is state-certified or state-licensed. State certification and state licensure are credentialing prerequisites but do not determine competency for a given appraisal assignment. Competency is determined on a case-by-case basis. In addition to competency, a bank's appraisal and evaluation program for obtaining a property's market value must ensure appropriate appraiser and evaluator independence from the loan approval functions. Additionally, there must be standards for appropriate communication and information sharing between the personnel responsible for the lending function and the appraisers and people performing evaluations.

The appraiser selection and engagement function is the most important part of a bank appraisal program. If a bank chooses to outsource the appraiser selection and engagement process to a third-party AMC, the bank should provide detailed instructions to the AMC on how to perform that function on its behalf. OCC Bulletin 2013-29, "Third-Party Relationships: Risk Management Guidance," states, "The OCC expects bank management to engage in a robust analytical process to identify, measure, monitor, and control the risks associated with third-party relationships and to avoid excessive risk taking that may threaten a bank's safety and soundness." As discussed in greater detail in this booklet and in other guidance, if a bank uses the services of an AMC for any part of the bank appraisal and evaluation program, the bank should provide significant and ongoing oversight of the AMC's practices. According to OCC Bulletin 2013-29, "Performing ongoing monitoring of the third-party relationship once the contract is in place is essential to the bank's ability to manage risk of the third-party relationship."

In promoting sound credit decisions, the guidelines also emphasize the importance of banks maintaining strong internal controls to ensure reliable appraisals and evaluations. Banks are also responsible for monitoring and periodically updating valuations of collateral for existing real estate loans and for subsequent transactions, such as modifications and workouts.

Finally, the guidelines state that a bank's real estate appraisal and evaluation policies and procedures must be reviewed as part of the bank's overall real estate-related activities. Examiners consider the size and nature of the bank's real estate-related activities when assessing the appropriateness of the program. Banks that fail to comply with regulatory appraisal requirements or to maintain a sound appraisal and evaluation program consistent with supervisory guidelines may be cited in supervisory letters and examination reports. Deficiencies may be criticized as unsafe or unsound banking practices that require corrective action.

The remainder of this section discusses more specifically certain regulatory expectations for an appropriate RRE lending appraisal and evaluation program.

Appraisal and Evaluation Program

As outlined in the 2010 "Interagency Appraisal and Evaluation Guidelines," a bank's board of directors or designated committee is responsible for adopting and reviewing policies and procedures that establish an effective real estate appraisal and evaluation program. Such a program should encompass RRE lending activities and should

- provide for the independence of the persons ordering, performing, and reviewing appraisals or evaluations.
- establish criteria for the selection and engagement of an appraiser based on competency.
- establish procedures to evaluate and monitor the ongoing performance of appraisers and people who perform evaluations.
- ensure that appraisals comply with the agencies' appraisal regulations and are consistent with supervisory guidelines.
- ensure that appraisals and evaluations contain relevant information and, more importantly, sufficient analysis to support the credit decision.
- maintain criteria for the content and appropriate use of evaluations consistent with safe and sound banking practices.
- provide for the receipt and review of the appraisal or evaluation report in a timely manner to facilitate the credit decision.
- develop criteria to assess whether an existing appraisal or evaluation may be used to support a subsequent transaction.
- implement internal controls that promote compliance with these program standards, including those related to monitoring third-party arrangements.
- establish criteria for monitoring collateral values.

- establish criteria for obtaining appraisals or evaluations that are not otherwise covered by the appraisal requirements of the agencies' appraisal regulations. (Such criteria should effectively address the useful lives of appraisals and evaluations as well as standards for reappraising or reevaluating a residential property when the borrower's financial condition deteriorates and the bank is becoming more dependent on the collateral as a potential source of repayment).

Independence of the Appraisal and Evaluation Program

The 2010 interagency appraisal guidelines emphasize the need to maintain high standards of independence as part of an effective collateral valuation program. Subsequent rules under Regulation Z also set forth specific appraiser independence requirements.

Specifically, collateral valuation activities are an integral component of the credit underwriting process and must be isolated from influence by the bank's loan production staff and any other party with a direct or indirect interest in the transaction. Independence of the appraisal and evaluation program is a critical concern. Consequently, a bank should establish appropriate reporting lines independent of loan production for the staff that administers the bank's collateral valuation activities. This independence should be established at every step in the valuation process, including selection of appraisers or persons performing evaluations, ordering, reviewing, and acceptance of appraisals and evaluations. Appraisers and others performing valuations or a valuation management function must be totally independent of the loan production and collection processes and have no direct, indirect, or prospective interest, financial or otherwise, in the property or transaction.

For community banks active in RRE lending, it may not always be possible to separate the collateral valuation activities from the loan production process. Regulation Z (12 CFR 1026.42(d)(3)) sets forth compliance requirements for creditors with assets of $250 million or less. Under the interagency appraisal guidelines, if absolute lines of independence cannot be achieved, the small or rural bank or branch must be able to clearly demonstrate that it has prudent safeguards to isolate its collateral valuation activities from influence or interference from the loan production process. In such cases, another loan officer, other officer, or director of the bank may be the only person qualified to analyze the RRE collateral. To ensure their independence, such lending officials, officers, or directors must abstain from any vote or approval involving loans on which they ordered, performed, or reviewed the appraisal or evaluation.

To facilitate the appraisal and evaluation program, some banks have chosen to use third-party AMCs. Such companies, in selecting and engaging an appraiser for an appraisal assignment, act as agents of the bank. If an AMC is used for any portion of the bank's program, the bank's board and management remain ultimately responsible and accountable for ensuring that any services performed by a third party comply with all applicable laws and regulations, including that a bank and its agent must compensate fee appraisers at a rate that is customary and reasonable for appraisal services performed in the market area of the property being appraised. Therefore, additional resources and expertise may be necessary to perform appropriate and ongoing oversight of these third-party arrangements. In addition to information in OCC Bulletin 2010-42, "Interagency Appraisal and Evaluation Guidelines," refer to OCC Bulletin 2013-29, "Third-Party Relationships: Risk Management Guidance."

Evaluation Development and Content

With the technological advances of the 1990s and 2000s, many banks in their RRE lending activities began to make extensive use of AVMs, property inspection reports, desktop appraisal reports, and BPOs. These tools often did not provide sufficient information about various aspects of the property's location, condition, or local market conditions that affect value. More importantly, they may have lacked a reasonable analysis that reconciled the factual information in a manner that supported the value conclusion consistent with the regulatory expectations for an acceptable evaluation.

The 2010 interagency guidelines provide recommendations for content to ensure that an evaluation meets the regulatory expectations for acceptability. Specifically, an evaluation must contain sufficient information detailing the analysis, assumptions, and conclusions to support the credit decision. An evaluation's content should be documented in the credit file or be reproducible. The evaluation of real estate property, including an RRE property, must at a minimum

- identify the location of the property.
- provide a description of the property and its current and projected use.
- provide an estimate of the property's market value in its actual physical condition, use, and zoning designation as of the effective date of the evaluation (the date the analysis was completed), with any limiting conditions.
- describe the method(s) the bank used to confirm the property's actual physical condition and the extent to which an inspection was performed.
- describe the analysis that was performed and the supporting information used in valuing the property.
- describe the supplemental information that was considered when using an analytical method or technological tool.
- indicate all source(s) of information used in the analysis, as applicable, to value the property, including
  - external data sources such as market sales databases and public tax or land records.
  - property-specific data such as previous sales data for the subject property, tax assessment data, and comparable sales information.
  - evidence of a property inspection.
  - photos of the property.
  - description of the neighborhood.
  - local market conditions.
- include information on the preparer when the evaluation is performed by a person, such as the name and contact information, and signature.

The evaluation document should be a cohesive and complete document that allows a reader to understand the data used and analysis performed. Evaluations must contain sufficient information and analysis in order to support the bank's decision to engage in the transaction.

Both the evaluation report and review report should be in the credit file. As part of the examination process, examiners review a sample of evaluations and reviews of evaluations to determine the quality of analysis and adherence to content expectations. Additionally, examiners assess the process for developing evaluations to ensure that it is independent and commensurate with the nature and size of the bank's RRE lending activities.

Reviewing Appraisals and Evaluations

Similar to the processes for ordering appraisals and evaluations, the 2010 interagency guidelines strongly emphasize the need for qualified and independent reviews of appraisals and evaluations received. The review process should ensure that appraisals and evaluations used in the credit approval process comply with the appraisal regulations, supervisory guidelines, and internal policies of the bank. A competent review is not a box-checking exercise. Appraisers do not always have plentiful sales of truly comparable properties that "fit" the GSE guidelines for things like "distance from subject to comparable" or amount of "net and gross adjustments." Appraisers may, of necessity, use data in an appraisal assignment under circumstances in which data may be imperfect or scarce. An important part of an adequate review is that the reviewer exercises qualitative judgment in assessing the appraiser's analysis considering the availability, or lack of availability, of data. Because qualitative judgment is required, reviewers should have experience and competency to perform reviews. Therefore, the background and training of reviewers may be different from the qualifications of people who perform a review that looks for alignment with GSE guidelines. At a minimum, a bank's policies and procedures for reviewing appraisals and evaluations should

- address the independence, educational and training qualifications, and role of the reviewer.
- establish criteria for determining the depth of the review in each case, based on collateral risk.
- establish a process for resolving any deficiencies in appraisals or evaluations.
- set forth documentation standards for reviews, including documenting the resolution of any deficiencies that were found during the review process, if applicable.

Reviewers of appraisals and evaluations should possess the requisite education, expertise, training, experience, and competence to perform a review that is commensurate with the complexity of the transaction, type of residential property, and market. Reviewers should be independent of the loan production function and any party with a vested interest in the outcome of the valuation and review process. Furthermore, reviewers should be capable of assessing whether the appraisal or evaluation contains sufficient information and quality of analysis to support the bank's decision to engage in the transaction. The independence standards, including Regulation Z requirements, apply to the reviewer and any other person performing a valuation management function.

It may not be possible or practical in some small banks or branches to separate the collateral valuation process from the loan production function. In these cases, a bank should be able to demonstrate clearly that it has prudent safeguards to isolate its collateral valuation program from influence or interference from the loan production process. In such cases, examiners sample completed reviews and assess the valuation policies and practices in order to determine the degree of competence and independence achieved by the bank or branch.

The 2010 guidelines also specifically address the review process for one- to four-family RRE lending activities. Per the guidelines, the reviews for RRE transactions should reflect a risk-focused approach that is commensurate with the size, type, and complexity of the underlying credit transaction, as well as loan and portfolio risk characteristics. These risk factors could include DTI ratios, LTV ratios, level of documentation, transaction dollar amount, or other relevant factors.

Appraisals for Higher-Priced Mortgage Loans

Regulation Z and 12 CFR 34 establish appraisal requirements for HPMLs. For HPMLs subject to the rules, the rules require, in part, that creditors generally obtain, before consummation, a written appraisal by a licensed or certified appraiser who conducts a physical inspection of the interior of the property that secures the transaction.[62] The rules also require creditors to specifically disclose to applicants the purpose of the appraisal within a specified time frame and to provide consumers with a free copy of any written appraisal report. The rules also require a second written appraisal from a different appraiser who conducts an interior inspection of the property when the seller acquired the property at a specified time before the pending sale and there is a specified price differential (90 or fewer days with a more than 10 percent increase; or 91 to 180 days with a 20 percent or more increase).[63] The creditor is permitted to charge the consumer for only one of the appraisals. The specific rules are codified in 12 CFR 34, subpart G.

Copies of Appraisals and Other Valuations

Regulation B (12 CFR 1002) requires creditors to disclose to applicants within a specified time frame that they have the right to receive copies of appraisals and written evaluations. The rule also requires creditors to automatically send the applicants a free copy of home appraisals and other written valuations (including evaluations) promptly after they are completed, regardless of whether credit is extended or denied, or the application is considered incomplete or withdrawn within specified time frames. The rule applies to all written valuations (not just appraisals) developed by a creditor in connection with an application for credit that is to be secured by a first lien on a dwelling. The rule covers all first liens on dwellings, including closed-end mortgage loans and open-end loans.

---

[62] The rules exempt the following transactions from their scope: QMs, loans under a certain threshold ($25,000 in 2014), certain streamlined refinances, temporary loans, loans for the initial construction of a dwelling, reverse mortgages, certain manufactured homes, and transactions secured by a mobile home, boat, or trailer.

[63] Refer to 12 CFR 1026.35 for a list of transactions that may be exempt from these additional requirements.

A creditor making an HPML may comply with both the Regulation B and HPML appraisal requirements by providing one disclosure that meets the timing and content requirements of both rules.

Evaluation and Selection of PMI Providers

Lenders use PMI to mitigate the elevated risk of loss associated with residential mortgages with LTV ratios of 80 percent or more. Banks should report HLTV one- to four-family mortgage loans with LTV ratios of 90 percent or more to their boards of directors and limit exposure for all HLTV loans to no more than 100 percent of their total regulatory capital. HLTV one- to four-family mortgage loans with mortgage insurance are exempt from such mortgage reporting requirements and exposure limits, based on the reliability of loss coverage provided by PMI.

Times of financial stress may introduce unexpectedly high levels of delinquencies and losses from residential mortgage loans of all types. Mortgage insurance providers are also susceptible to significant losses and deterioration of their capital and reserves. The potential for loss underscores the need for robust due diligence when banks select and monitor PMI providers to insure residential mortgages. Sufficiently prudent policies and procedures should define expectations that

- management perform a thorough analysis of each insurer it plans to use to assess the insurer's viability, regulatory capital and reserves, profitability, and overall financial condition.
- the board of directors (or a board committee) and senior management are responsible for overseeing the bank's overall risk management processes, including the approval of PMI provider contracts that involve critical activities.
- management periodically monitor PMI providers for their financial soundness and viability.
- the board and management ensure that the bank adheres to all loan underwriting, documentation, recording, collection, and record-keeping requirements of the PMI insurer so that the insurance remains in force. An independent review should be conducted periodically to ensure compliance.
- when insurance is not maintained on HLTV mortgage loans, those loans are risk-weighted appropriately in regulatory capital computations and no longer exempt from reporting requirements and exposure limits.
- management should escalate to the board any significant issues with PMI providers.

Ability-to-Repay and Qualified Mortgages

Effective January 10, 2014, Regulation Z requires creditors to make a reasonable and good faith determination that the consumer will have a reasonable ability to repay a covered transaction[64] at or before consummation (12 CFR 1026.43). Banks have three options for complying with the ATR rule. They may (1) comply with the general ATR standards, (2) refinance a "non-standard" mortgage into a "standard" mortgage, or (3) make a QM.

Under the general ATR standards, a bank must consider the following eight ATR underwriting factors:

- Current or reasonably expected income or assets (other than the value of the property that secures the loan) that the consumer will rely on to repay the loan.
- Current employment status (if the creditor is relying on employment income when assessing the consumer's ATR).
- Monthly mortgage payment for the loan. This is calculated using the introductory or fully indexed rate, whichever is higher, and monthly, fully amortizing payments that are substantially equal.
- Monthly payment on any simultaneous loans secured by the same property.
- Monthly payment for property taxes and insurance that is required by the creditor, and certain other costs related to the property, such as homeowners association fees or ground rent.
- Debts, alimony, and child support obligations.
- Monthly DTI ratio or residual income that the creditor calculated using the total of all the mortgage and nonmortgage obligations, as a ratio of gross monthly income.
- Credit history.

The creditor may evaluate additional factors as part of the loan origination process, but these eight factors must be considered to comply with the general ATR standards. The creditor must verify the information on the eight factors using reasonably reliable third-party records as provided in the regulation. The creditor cannot rely on stated or oral representations of the applicant. If the loan is a QM, the ATR rule still requires that creditors consider most of the same factors, but how the creditor must take these factors into account may differ.

For a loan to be a QM, it must meet certain underwriting requirements. QM lenders must maintain records for three years after consummation showing compliance with ATR and other provisions of the rules. The rules provide that QM creditors receive either a conclusive or a rebuttable presumption that they complied with ATR requirements. The presumption is rebuttable if the loan is higher priced.

---

[64] Unless otherwise exempt, a "covered transaction" is a closed-end consumer credit transaction secured by a dwelling (including any real property attached to a dwelling). Refer to 12 CFR 1026.43(b)(1). HELOCs and time-share plan loans are not subject to 12 CFR 1026.43. The following are also not subject to 12 CFR 1026.43 except for the prepayment penalty provisions in 12 CFR 1026.43(g): (1) reverse mortgages; (2) temporary or bridge loans with a term of 12 months or less; (3) the construction phase of 12 months or less of a construction-to-permanent loan; (4) loans made by a creditor designated as a community development financial institution; (5) an extension of credit made pursuant to federal emergency economic stabilization programs, including Home Affordable Modification Program and Home Affordable Refinance Program transactions; (6) certain other community housing assistance programs (including credit extended pursuant to a program administered by housing finance agencies); and (7) loans made by 501(c)(3) nonprofit entities, subject to conditions. Refer to 12 CFR 1026.43(a).

There are five types of QMs under the rule. All creditors can originate two types—general and temporary QMs. Only small creditors can originate the other three types—small creditor portfolio, balloon payment, and temporary balloon payment QMs. The QM requirements generally focus on prohibiting certain features and practices that proved to be more risky. These include IO periods, negative amortization, and loan terms longer than 30 years. Additionally, for all types of QMs, points and fees generally may not exceed 3 percent of the total loan amount (higher thresholds are provided for loans less than $100,000) and prepayment penalties are limited. For general QMs, the consumer's total DTI/back-end ratio must be calculated according to the regulation's requirements and may not exceed 43 percent.

For further information on QMs, examiners should contact compliance examiners and the Compliance Policy Division as well as refer to the "Truth in Lending Act" booklet (for Regulation Z) of the *Comptroller's Handbook*.

Mortgage Pricing

Residential mortgage loans are primarily priced as either a fixed-rate loan (interest rate fixed for the life of the loan) or as an adjustable or variable rate loan (interest rate adjusted by predetermined amounts at predetermined intervals). Several hybrid structures have also emerged that employ a fixed interest rate for a predetermined amount of time at the beginning of the mortgage loan and then an adjustable rate for the remainder of the mortgage loan's life. Alternatively, the mortgage loan could be an IO structure for the first several years and then convert to an interest and principal repayment structure with sufficient principal amortization to extinguish the loan at maturity. Additionally, ARMs can be offered with low introductory or teaser rates that eventually adjust up to a market rate. ARMs also can have terms that defer principal amortization and even allow negative amortization of principal. The ATR rule affects how ARMs, IO loans, and other forms of nontraditional lending may be offered.

Certain hybrid structures developed before 2014 are now subject to new rules and guidance. Thus, in pricing any residential mortgage loan, a creditor should consider both the guidance discussed in this booklet and the applicable mortgage rules under Regulations Z and X.

Fixed-Rate Mortgage Loans

Interest rates are determined by market conditions as well as factors based on credit risk, such as the applicant's credit score or credit history, the loan's purpose (purchase, refinance, or cash-out refinance), the term of the loan, the LTV ratio, the loan's size, and the nature of residential property offered as collateral (primary residence, second home, or investment property). In smaller banks, pricing is influenced by local competition as well as the national secondary-market prices available from various investors. The bank's asset and liability management process or committee also helps determine loan pricing. In larger banks, especially those with secondary-market activities, the secondary-marketing unit establishes pricing to ensure consistency with the bank's earnings objectives and ability to sell the loans with servicing retained or released. Regardless of the operation's size, pricing should take into account the bank's strategic plans with key inputs from the finance and accounting departments. Pricing should not be overly influenced or dominated by the compensation structure for loan originators or loan officers whose compensation is based primarily on loan volume versus loan quality.[65]

With regard to incorporating risk-based criteria into the pricing decision, management should ensure that no unlawful disparate treatment or impact occurs on a prohibited basis. Additionally, the Fair Credit Reporting Act (15 USC 1681g(g)) requires any person who makes or arranges loans and who uses a consumer credit score in connection with an application by a consumer for a closed-end loan or an open-end consumer purpose loan secured by one- to four-family residential real property to provide to the consumer his or her credit score information. The information must be provided to the consumer as soon as reasonably practical. Further, it must include (1) the same credit scoring information it obtained from a credit reporting agency that the agency otherwise would be required to disclose to the consumer upon request (with special provisions for automatic underwriting systems); and (2) a notice specified in the statute that explains the bank's use of credit scores, how credit scores are generally calculated, and how the consumer may contact the consumer reporting agency or lender with questions.

Banks that allow overages or rate concessions must have effective policies and monitoring procedures to limit and control such activity in order to prevent violations of TILA, ECOA, the Fair Housing Act, HOEPA, and RESPA. Additionally, to the extent that overages and concessions are legally accomplished, management should understand the potential impact on profitability and reputation. RRE lending standards should outline the acceptable practices and tolerances as well as the types of controls and MIS necessary to properly supervise the activity. Finally, customer complaint resolution processes should actively track and report pricing-related complaints.

Banks subject to the Home Mortgage Disclosure Act must publicly report the pricing information for certain loans with higher annual percentage rate (APR). Reporting for high-cost mortgage loans is required for home purchase originations, secured home improvements, and refinancing.

Adjustable Rate Mortgages

The authority and requirements for national banks and FSAs to offer ARMs are codified in 12 CFR 34, subpart B, and 12 CFR 160.35, respectively. Additionally, the ability of banks to adjust interest rates on their ARMs is also governed by the Alternative Mortgage Transaction Parity Act as implemented in 12 CFR 1004 (Regulation D).

Unlike fixed-rate mortgages, in which the interest rate does not change over the life of the loan, the interest on an ARM is based on the movement of a predetermined index (for example, prime rate, London interbank offered rate, monthly Treasury average, or a cost of

---

[65] 12 CFR 1026.36(d) generally prohibits loan originators from receiving compensation based on the terms of that individual loan originator's transactions or the terms of transactions by multiple loan originators.

funds index). The rate is set as a function of the predetermined index plus an incremental amount established at the initiation of the loan. This incremental amount is commonly referred to as the margin. The combination of the index rate and the margin is referred to as the fully indexed rate. Depending on the type of index on which the ARM is based, the interest accrual rate can change monthly or annually. Some ARMs are structured so there are limits on the amount of increases and decreases in the interest accrual rate due to changes in the underlying rate index. These limits are called interest rate caps, ceilings, and floors.

One feature commonly associated with some ARM products is the teaser interest rate. This rate arises in situations when borrowers receive a short-term subsidy or "buy down" on the loan rate from the seller or lender. Teaser rates reduce the initial interest accrual and monthly payment while the teaser rate is in effect, usually 12 to 36 months. At the expiration of the teaser-rate term, the borrower's monthly interest accrual is calculated at the fully indexed rate.

Loans that have adjustments to higher interest rates may lead to steep increases in payment burden and subsequent delinquencies if borrowers have high DTI burdens. This concern is compounded if other elements of credit risk are layered in through higher LTV ratios, lower credit qualifications (score or history), or limited documentation. Regulation Z adds new requirements for how to consider the borrower's ability to repay loans with teaser rates. (Refer to 12 CFR 1026.43 and associated commentary.) When evaluating an applicant's repayment capacity to qualify for a teaser-rate ARM product, the underwriting lender must consider the greater of the fully indexed rate or the introductory interest rate and, if IO, use substantially equal monthly payments of P&I that will repay the loan amount over the term of the loan remaining as of recast. A creditor must comply with the ATR provisions of Regulation Z, which not only require that a creditor determine the borrower's to repay as if the loan did not have a teaser rate but also require verification of certain borrower information, including income and assets.

The pricing of ARM products should be competitive and provide sufficient yield to cover the operating expenses, funding costs, expected losses, and a reasonable risk-adjusted return on the invested funds. The pricing of ARM products also should facilitate safe and sound RRE lending. Some lenders may incorrectly price ARMs because of a lack of understanding of the options or risks associated with ARMs. Banks should price promotional mortgage loans, such as adjustable teaser-rate mortgages, to yield a sufficient return over the life of the loan. To gauge the appropriateness of a bank's ARM pricing, examiners may compare the points and fees charged to originate ARMs with the discount required by the secondary market to accept the risks of a similarly structured loan. If the required discount is larger than the fees received, the pricing of ARMs should be further evaluated.

ARM documents should precisely identify the index used, the margin to the index, and the ability of the bank to change the rates. The initial disclosure requirements for ARMs, as well as the requirements for disclosures that must be made when the rate adjusts, are governed by TILA and are implemented through Regulation Z. Under HOEPA, banks are subject to special disclosure requirements for high-cost mortgage loans. An ARM loan may be a high-cost loan subject to the restrictions under the HOEPA rule when the APR is calculated—for the purpose of determining compliance with HOEPA only—using the maximum margin permitted at any time during the term of the loan and the index rate in effect. The HOEPA restrictions and disclosure requirements apply when the APR at consummation exceeds specified thresholds, when total points and fees payable by the consumer exceed a specified percentage in relation to the average prime offer rate, or when the lender may charge prepayment penalties with certain characteristics.[66]

Nontraditional Mortgages

Nontraditional mortgage products, which became more widespread between 2000 and 2010, generally represent hybrids of traditional ARMs in that they allow borrowers to defer payment of principal and sometimes interest.[67] In the mid-2000s, the OCC joined other agencies in issuing guidance about these products.[68] In addition, the 2014 mortgage rules issues by the CFPB affect the underwriting of such products.[69]

From 2000 to 2010, the most common nontraditional mortgages were IO mortgages and payment option ARM mortgages. With IO mortgages, the borrower is required to pay only the interest on the loan for a specific number of years. The interest rate during this period may be fixed or variable. After the IO period, the loan recasts, so payments include principal and interest and are designed to fully amortize the loan by its maturity. After the loan recasts, the interest rate may be fixed or variable.

With the payment option ARM mortgages, the borrower chooses from several payment options. For example, each month, the borrower may choose a minimum payment option based on a teaser rate, an IO payment option based on the fully indexed rate, or a fully amortizing P&I payment based on a 15-year or 30-year loan term, plus any required escrow payments. The minimum payment option can be less than the interest accruing on the loan, resulting in negative amortization. The IO option avoids negative amortization but does not

---

[66] The definition of a high-cost mortgage can be found in 12 CFR 1026.32.

[67] Interagency guidance defines nontraditional mortgage loans as "closed-end residential mortgage loan products that allow borrowers to defer repayment of principal and, sometimes, interest. …[This includes] such products as 'interest-only' mortgages where a borrower pays no loan principal for the first few years of the loan and 'payment option' adjustable-rate mortgages (ARMs) where a borrower has flexible payment options with the potential for negative amortization." Refer to OCC Bulletin 2006-41 ("Guidance on Nontraditional Mortgage Product Risks," adopted by the OCC, FRB, FDIC, OTS, and NCUA and as published in 71 Fed. Reg. 58609 (October 4, 2006)). HELOCs and home equity loans are not covered by this guidance; instead, they are covered separately by OCC Bulletin 2005-22 ("Home Equity Lending: Credit Risk Management Guidance," adopted by the OCC, FRB, FDIC, OTS, and NCUA).

[68] Refer to OCC Bulletin 2006-41 ("Guidance on Nontraditional Mortgage Product Risks") and OCC Bulletin 2007-28 ("Nontraditional Mortgage Products: Illustrations of Consumer Information"). Refer also to OCC Bulletin 2005-22 ("Home Equity Lending: Credit Risk Management Guidance") (addressing HELOCs and home equity loans).

[69] All institutions must comply with the CFPB rules. To the extent that the nontraditional mortgage guidance is inconsistent with the requirements in Regulation Z, Regulation Z supersedes the guidance. Nonetheless, much of the agency guidance, particularly with respect to risk management, remains relevant.

---

provide for positive principal amortization. After a specified number of years, or if the loan reaches a certain negative amortization cap,[70] the required monthly payment amount is recast so that the payments include both principal and interest and are designed to fully amortize the loan by its maturity date.

Loan Terms and Underwriting Standards

For all nontraditional mortgage loan products, a bank's analysis of a borrower's repayment capacity should include an evaluation of his or her ability to repay the debt by final maturity at the fully indexed rate,[71] assuming a fully amortizing repayment schedule.[72]

A primary concern with the terms of nontraditional mortgages is that they may allow a very low monthly payment at the beginning of the term with higher payments required later. Therefore, the mortgages subject the borrower to a potential "payment shock" that should be well understood and disclosed. The risks of payment shock can be exacerbated by combining nontraditional mortgages with certain features (e.g., teaser or low introductory rates), reduced documentation, and simultaneous second-lien loans. A bank's standard for qualifying applicants for nontraditional mortgages should recognize the potential impact of payment shock, especially for borrowers with layered credit risks such as high LTV and DTI ratios and low credit qualifications (scores or history).

Most mortgages, including closed-end consumer transactions secured by a dwelling, such as subordinate lien home equity loans,[73] must be underwritten so that the creditor considers, at the time the loan closes, the borrower's ability to repay both principal and interest according

---

[70] The balance that may accrue from the negative amortization provision does not necessarily equate to the full negative amortization cap for a particular loan. The spread between the teaser rate and the accrual rate determines whether a loan balance has the potential to reach the negative amortization cap before the end of the initial payment option period (usually five years). For example, a loan with a 115 percent negative amortization cap but a small spread between the teaser rate and the accrual rate may only reach a 109 percent maximum loan balance before the end of the initial payment option period, even if only minimum payments are made.

[71] The fully indexed rate equals the index rate prevailing at origination plus the margin that applies after the expiration of an introductory interest rate. In different interest rate scenarios, the fully indexed rate for an ARM loan based on a lagging index (for example, monthly Treasury average rate) may be significantly different from the rate on a comparable 30-year fixed-rate product. In these cases, a credible market rate should be used to qualify the borrower and determine repayment capacity.

[72] The fully amortizing payment schedule should be based on the term of the loan. For example, the amortizing payment for a loan with a five-year IO period and a 30-year term would be calculated based on a 30-year amortization schedule. For balloon mortgages that contain a borrower option for an extended amortization period, the fully amortizing payment schedule would be based on the full term the borrower may choose. When a bank does not give the borrower an option to extend the amortization period, underwriting standards for IO and variable rate HELOCs should include an assessment of the borrower's ability to amortize the fully drawn line over the loan term and to absorb potential increases in interest rates.

[73] Refer to 12 CFR 1026.43. Underwriting standards for high-cost open-end mortgages are addressed in 12 CFR 1026.34.

---

to the loan's terms, including after the nontraditional loan recasts (i.e., the end of the IO or negative amortization period). Specifically, under the ATR rule

- for an IO loan, the payment considered must be based on the higher of the introductory or fully indexed rate and substantially equal, monthly payments of P&I that will repay the loan amount over the term of the loan remaining as of the date the loan is recast.
- for negative amortization loans, the payment considered must be based on the fully indexed rate or any introductory interest rate, whichever is greater, and substantially equal, monthly payments of P&I that will repay the maximum loan amount over the term of the loan remaining as of the date the loan is recast.

For both types of loans, the payment must be sufficient that there is no balloon payment at loan maturity.

In addition, the ability to add risky features to nontraditional mortgages is further limited because the creditor must consider and verify eight underwriting factors described in the "Ability-to-Repay and Qualified Mortgages" section in this booklet. Further, mortgage loans that have IO or negative amortization periods cannot be QMs.[74] Finally, a creditor must disclose the maximum payments on nontraditional loans both at the end of five years and at any time over the life of the loan.[75]

Risk Management for Nontraditional Mortgage Loans

Given the potential for heightened risk levels inherent in nontraditional mortgage products, interagency guidance focused on ensuring that a bank's management carefully considered and appropriately mitigated exposures created by such lending. Specifically, to address effectively the risks associated with nontraditional mortgage loans, management should

- ensure that loan terms and underwriting standards are consistent with prudent lending practices, including consideration of the borrower's ATR.
- recognize that many nontraditional mortgage loans, particularly those that have risk-layering features, warrant strong risk management standards, regulatory capital levels commensurate with the risk, and an ALLL that reflects the collectability of the portfolio.
- ensure that customers have sufficient information to clearly understand loan terms and associated risks before making a product choice.

With regard to portfolio and credit risk management practices, banks should ensure that risk management keeps pace with the growth and changing risk profile of the nontraditional

---

[74] QMs are deemed to comply with the ATR requirements and receive a presumption of compliance under the ATR rule if certain underwriting criteria are met. Unlike QMs, loans with IO or negative amortization periods are not eligible for the presumption of compliance.

[75] Refer to 12 CFR 1026.18(s), 1026.19, 1026.37, and 1026.38. Note that the illustrations suggested in OCC Bulletin 2005-22, "Home Equity Lending: Credit Risk Management Guidance," were largely incorporated into these provisions, and that the illustrations were *not* model forms.

---

mortgage loan portfolio and changes in the marketplace. Active portfolio management is especially important for banks that project or have already experienced significant growth resulting in concentrations. Banks should maintain regulatory capital and appropriate concentration limits measured as a percentage of total capital commensurate with the risk characteristics of their nontraditional mortgage portfolios. Banks that originate or invest in nontraditional mortgage loans should adopt more robust risk management practices that effectively manage such exposures in a thoughtful, systematic manner. To meet these heightened regulatory expectations, banks should

- develop written policies that specify acceptable product attributes, production and portfolio limits, sales and securitization practices, and risk management expectations.
- design enhanced performance measures and management reporting standards that provide early warning for increasing risk.
- establish appropriate ALLL levels that consider the credit quality of the portfolio and conditions that affect collectability.
- maintain regulatory capital at levels that reflect portfolio characteristics and the effect of stressed economic conditions on collectability.

More detail on specific risk management expectations can be found in the interagency guidance and in the mortgage rules. Banks found to have nontraditional mortgage lending programs that reflect higher risk profiles and deficient risk management practices relative to the product's structure and underwriting requirements, as well as the nature and size of the bank's RRE lending activities, may be cited in supervisory letters and examination reports. Deficiencies may be criticized as unsafe or unsound banking practices that require corrective action.

Home Equity Lending

Interagency guidance on credit risk management for home equity lending generally promotes sound credit risk management practices at banks with home equity lending programs (both open-end lines of credit and closed-end loans).[76] The specific product, risk management, and underwriting risk factors and trends that attracted regulatory scrutiny were

- IO features that require no amortization of principal for a protracted period.
- limited or no documentation of a borrower's assets, employment, and income (known as low-doc or no-doc lending).
- higher LTV and DTI ratios.
- lower credit risk scores for underwriting home equity loans.
- greater use of AVMs and other collateral evaluation tools for the development of appraisals and evaluations.
- an increase in the number of transactions generated through a loan broker or other third party.

---

[76] Refer to OCC Bulletin 2005-22, "Home Equity Lending: Credit Risk Management Guidance."

Interagency guidance directs banks to adopt sound practices that fully address marketing, underwriting standards, collateral valuation management, individual account and portfolio management, and servicing. To that end, the guidance specifically describes sound credit risk management systems for

- product development and marketing.
- origination and underwriting.
- third-party originations.
- collateral valuation management.
- account management.
- portfolio management.
- operations, servicing, and collections.
- secondary-market activities.
- portfolio classifications, ALLL, and regulatory capital.

Moreover, under Regulation Z for closed-end transactions secured by a dwelling, a creditor must consider and verify the information relied upon, including income or assets, mortgage obligations, mortgage-related obligations, and other debt obligations. Closed-end home equity loans are also subject to the same Regulation Z ATR provisions that apply to nontraditional mortgage loans (discussed earlier).

In addition, if a HELOC would be an open-end high-cost mortgage,[77] the creditor must consider a consumer's ATR as of account opening. The creditor must consider and verify the consumer's current and reasonably expected income, assets, and current debt obligations (including any mortgage-related obligations that are required by another credit obligation undertaken prior to or at account opening). The rules also provide a presumption of compliance with the rules if the creditor takes into account the borrower's ability to pay when payments adjust and there are no balloon payments at maturity.[78]

Consistent with the Dodd–Frank amendments to TILA, the HOEPA rule was revised to expand HOEPA's coverage to purchase-money mortgages and open-end credit plans, amend the existing trigger tests, and add or revise consumer protections.[79] For instance, a creditor may not extend a high-cost mortgage without receiving certification from a homeownership counselor that the consumer received counseling on the advisability of the mortgage.

---

[77] Refer to 12 CFR 1026.32 (defining high-cost mortgages).

[78] Refer to 12 CFR 1026.34. A creditor is presumed in compliance with the rule if

- it considers the largest required minimum periodic payment, assuming that (1) the borrower borrows the full amount at account opening with no additional extensions of credit; (2) the creditor makes only required minimum periodic payments during the draw period and any repayment period; and (3) the maximum interest rate under the contract will apply at account opening and thereafter;
- it considers DTI (including payment on all loans secured by the same dwelling); and
- the loan will be fully amortized at maturity.

[79] Regulations primarily affected by these revisions include 12 CFR 1026.31, 1026.32, 1026.34, and 1026.36.

From a supervisory perspective, home equity lending programs that reflect higher risk profiles and deficient risk management relative to the product's structure and underwriting requirements, as well as the nature and size of the bank's RRE lending activities, may be cited in supervisory letters and examination reports and require corrective action. Deficiencies may be criticized as unsafe or unsound banking practices.

Additional Counseling Requirements

Dodd–Frank amendments to RESPA and TILA added new homeownership counseling requirements. First, a bank may not make a mortgage loan with a negative amortization feature until it obtains documentation establishing that the borrower received homeownership counseling. Second, the bank must provide all applicants for federally related mortgages with a written list of homeownership counseling organizations within three business days of receiving the application. A lender may fulfill the requirement in one of two ways: The lender may obtain the counselor lists through the CFPB's Web site (www.consumerfinance.gov/find-a-housing-counselor) or use the counselor information made available by the CFPB or HUD, provided that the data is used in accordance with instructions provided with the data.

Risks of Brokered and Purchased Loans

Banks should be aware of potential risks when they obtain loans through brokers or through purchase transactions that contain terms or reflect practices that may be characterized as discriminatory, abusive, unfair, deceptive, or predatory.[80] Such loans present significant legal, reputation, and other risks, in addition to the heightened credit risk assumed in cases when the borrower lacks the ability to repay the loan without resorting to liquidation of the collateral.

Supervisory expectations relating to risks of brokered and purchased loans apply to

- traditional broker transactions, in which a mortgage broker refers an application to the bank and the loan is closed in the bank's name.
- "table funded" loans, which are closed in the name of a third party, but in which the bank provides the loan funds and immediately acquires the loan.
- loan purchase transactions, in which the loan is initially made and funded by a third party that subsequently sells the loan to the bank (whether or not the bank performs or participates in the underwriting of the loan).

---

[80] For additional guidance regarding potentially abusive or predatory lending, refer to 12 CFR 30, appendix C, and OCC Bulletin 2005-3, "OCC Guidelines Establishing Standards for National Banks' Residential Mortgage Lending Practices: Appendix C to 12 CFR Part 30." The guidelines incorporate, but do not replace, Advisory Letter 2003-2, "Guidelines for National Banks to Guard Against Predatory and Abusive Lending Practices" (February 21, 2003), and Advisory Letter 2003-3, "Avoiding Predatory and Abusive Lending Practices in Brokered and Purchased Loans" (February 21, 2003). These advisory letters apply to both national banks and FSAs.

Although the specific nature and degree of the risks presented may vary among these different categories of transactions, the general principle articulated in this section—that banks should maintain strong and appropriate controls over all loan origination and purchase functions, including loan sourcing, processing, underwriting, and closing—pertains to them all.

This section summarizes those risks and conveys the OCC's expectation that supervised banks take affirmative steps to avoid such risks. Failure to do so could raise serious supervisory concerns and result in supervisory or other actions directed against the banks, their operating subsidiaries, and the third-party brokers and originators involved in the transactions.

Credit Risk

As noted previously, abusive lending generally arises from a departure from fundamental principles of loan underwriting—lending without a determination that a borrower can reasonably be expected to repay the loan from resources other than the collateral security for the loan and relying instead on the foreclosure value of the borrower's collateral. A loan made without regard to the borrower's ability to service and repay the loan in accordance with its terms presents significant safety and soundness and compliance concerns. Making or purchasing such loans on a regular basis likewise is inconsistent with safe and sound banking practices and contrary to Regulation Z. Such loans may pose both a higher risk of default and a higher potential loss exposure at default.

Because of the less intensive supervision of mortgage brokers and other intermediaries, as well as other factors (such as the fact that intermediaries do not take on the ultimate credit risk of the loan), there is a risk that those intermediaries will be tempted to engage in practices that are inconsistent with existing regulations, such as lending without regard to repayment ability. Thus, mortgage broker and loan purchase transactions may present a heightened risk that banks will acquire loans that are made without a reasonable determination that the borrower will be able to repay the loan as structured.

Legal Risk

Loans originated through brokers or by third-party lenders, which may have features associated with predatory, abusive, unfair, or deceptive lending, also present a wide range of heightened legal risks for supervised banks and could subject them to both supervisory action and civil liability. Dodd–Frank amended TILA and RESPA to include new penalties for violations, which may apply, for example, as a defense to foreclosure if the original creditor failed to consider the borrower's ability to repay the loan. In addition to the liability provisions adopted in Dodd–Frank, borrowers affected by oppressive loan terms or other unscrupulous conduct of a mortgage broker or loan originator may have remedies against the ultimate creditor under common law theories of fraud or unconscionability.

In addition to other legal risks based on safety and soundness standards, consumer protection-based legal risks associated with brokered or purchased loans include the following:

TILA and RESPA: Mortgage lending activities are generally subject to the disclosure requirements and substantive protections of TILA and RESPA. Under TILA, the failure to provide timely and accurate disclosures of the cost of mortgage credit or to comply with the provisions of the new mortgage rules may result in reimbursement of excess finance charges, statutory damages and other civil liability, or the borrower's right to rescind the entire transaction. TILA provides that actions generally may be brought against assignees if the violation for which the action is brought is apparent on the face of the disclosure statement. For example, if the bank purchased a loan from a third party that prepared a TILA disclosure statement on behalf of a bank, and that disclosure understates the finance charge (for example, by failing to reflect the broker's fee accurately), the bank would be subject to a restitution order, civil liability, and potential rescission of the loan. Violating RESPA's ban on kickbacks and certain other types of payments and charges would expose the bank to extensive civil liability (three times the amount of the charge for the settlement service in question) and criminal sanctions. Thus, if a broker engages in fee-splitting or gives or accepts referral fees in violation of these provisions, and is found to be acting as an agent for or in conjunction with a bank, the bank may be subject to these legal risks.

HOEPA: High-cost mortgage loans, including those originated through brokers or by third-party lenders, must comply with the substantive protections and disclosure requirements set forth in HOEPA. HOEPA's substantive protections also restrict many of the other loan terms and structures cited in discussions of predatory lending practices, including refinancing that may constitute loan flipping, payments to home improvement contractors, balloon payments, prepayment penalties, and negative amortization. Civil liability for HOEPA violations may include restitution of all the finance charges and fees paid by the consumer. HOEPA provides that assignees are subject to all claims and defenses that could be brought against the original creditor, unless the assignee can demonstrate "that a reasonable person exercising ordinary due diligence, could not determine, based on the documentation required by TILA, the itemization of the amount financed, and other disclosure of disbursements,"[81] that the mortgage was covered by HOEPA.

Fair lending laws: Certain lending practices by brokers or third-party lenders also can raise fair lending concerns. For example, predatory lenders often target identifiable groups of consumers that are (or are perceived to be) less financially sophisticated, may have less access to mainstream lenders, or are otherwise vulnerable to abusive practices. If this targeting is based on age, race, national origin, gender, or other prohibited bases under the law, the abusive practices may represent violations of ECOA or the Fair Housing Act. Even if such targeting has been performed directly by a mortgage broker in soliciting applications, the creditor making the loan could be subjected to civil lawsuits and government enforcement actions. ECOA also provides for successor liability by defining the term

---

[81] 15 USC 1641(d).

"creditor" to include "any assignee of an original creditor who participates in the decision to extend, renew, or continue credit."[82]

FTC Act: The FTC Act makes "unfair or deceptive acts or practices" unlawful. Lending practices involving fraud, misleading conduct, or material omissions of information concerning costs, risks, or other terms and conditions of a loan may violate the prohibition against deception. Under relevant precedents, this prohibition is violated, for example, by representations, omissions, acts, or practices that are material and are likely to mislead a reasonable consumer in the audience targeted by the advertisement or other practice. Loans with unconscionable terms may also involve violations of the prohibition against unfair acts or practices. Evidence of practices such as loan flipping, equity stripping, or the refinancing of loans made under governmental or nonprofit programs with terms unfavorable to the borrower may be indicative of unfair or deceptive practices that violate the FTC Act.

Other Risks

Abusive loans have generated concern and criticism because of the harm they may cause for families and communities and because such loans are perceived to be inconsistent with national policies on predatory lending practices. Predatory lending creates the risk that a bank will be perceived unfavorably in its community, in the marketplace, and by the general public. Even though the practices in question may have been perpetrated by a third party, the bank that makes, purchases, or services the loans may be tarnished and seen as a bank that does not consistently treat its customers fairly. When a mortgage loan has been underwritten without regard to the borrower's ability to repay the loan, the bank holding the loan at the time of foreclosure may face significant reputation risk.

Discriminatory or other illegal lending practices, including those that violate the fair lending laws, the FTC Act, the consumer protections in HOEPA, or TILA's rescission provisions, also may adversely affect a bank's rating under the CRA. Because CRA performance must be considered with various applications for depository facilities, including access to FHLB funding, branch applications, and bank merger transactions, these types of illegal lending practices may impede a bank's strategic plans to expand its operations or to combine with another organization.

Safety and soundness concerns may also arise when lending practices effectively foreclose access to a secondary market. For more information, refer to the "Mortgage Banking" booklet of the *Comptroller's Handbook*.

Recommended Practices

Banks should take affirmative steps to mitigate the risks of acquiring discriminatory, predatory, unfair, deceptive, or abusive loans through broker or purchase transactions. A bank's policies and procedures relating to brokered and purchased loans should ensure that the loans it obtains comport with the bank's lending policies applicable to loans that the bank

---

[82] 15 USC 1691a(e).

makes directly and with applicable safety and soundness standards and consumer protection laws.

Guidance in OCC Bulletin 2013-29, "Third-Party Relationships: Risk Management Guidance," sets out measures banks should employ to implement effective risk management processes. In addition to implementing this guidance, banks should take the following specific steps to address the risks of obtaining discriminatory, predatory, unfair, deceptive, or abusive loans in broker or purchase transactions.

Establishment of Policies and Procedures

Banks should have clear procedures for entering into and continuing relationships with third-party mortgage loan brokers and originators and standards that delineate underwriting and appraisal requirements and unacceptable characteristics for brokered and purchased loans. These policies should also delineate, if applicable, the circumstances under which the bank makes through a broker, or acquires in a purchase transaction, loans with features that have been associated with lending practices that raise consumer protection concerns. As appropriate, a bank's policies should address specific practices in which it engages (to the extent these practices are permitted by applicable law), such as

- frequent, sequential refinancings.
- refinancings of special subsidized mortgages that contain terms favorable to the borrower.
- negative amortization.
- financing points, fees, penalties, and other charges.
- interest rate increases upon default.
- acquisition of loans subject to HOEPA.

In addition, policies should address the maximum points and other charges that may be imposed on brokered and purchased loans. In the case of brokered loans, these policies should address total compensation to the broker and the lender, and bank management should consider establishing limits on broker compensation.[83] Banks also should have policies to help ensure that interest rates and other pricing terms for brokered and purchased loans reasonably reflect the costs and risks of making such loans.

Finally, bank RRE lending policies and procedures should reflect strong and appropriate controls over all mortgage origination functions, including loan sourcing, appraisals and other aspects of loan processing, underwriting determinations, and loan closings. These controls vary, of course, with the risks presented by different types of transactions. In developing policies and procedures, banks should carefully consider the strengths, capabilities, and incentives of the third parties with whom they may do business. In mortgage broker transactions, for example, banks may well determine that it is appropriate to restrict

---

[83] 12 CFR 1026.36(j) requires banks to have loan originator policies addressing compensation that apply regardless of whether the loan officer is internal or a contractor.

brokers to loan sourcing functions, and to require and ensure that processing functions, underwriting determinations, and loan closings be conducted independently. Similarly, for loan purchase transactions, bank policies should establish clear standards for the degree of the bank's involvement in the underwriting decision, and appropriate controls may vary in accordance with this involvement. If a bank has not made the initial underwriting decision, it should take the steps necessary and appropriate to determine that such loans have been underwritten consistently with the bank's policies.

Due Diligence

Banks also should perform thorough due diligence, including background checks, before entering into relationships with mortgage brokers or third-party originators. These efforts should include a review of the third party's

- general competence.
- business practices and operations, including potential conflicts of interest.
- reputation.
- financial capacity and condition.
- internal controls.
- record of compliance with applicable licensing, consumer protection, and other laws and regulations.

In addition, these reviews should include an assessment of any litigation, enforcement actions, or pattern of customer complaints. The due diligence process also should include a risk assessment and plans to address identified risks. Based on this due diligence, a bank should develop approved lists of brokers and originators with whom it may transact business.

Broker and Originator Agreements

Banks should have written agreements with third-party brokers and originators that specifically and clearly delineate the rights and responsibilities of each party and fully address changes to the CFPB's mortgage rules, including those relating to loan originator compensation. Risks identified in the due diligence process should be addressed in these agreements, and, if such risks cannot be adequately mitigated, the agreement should not be consummated.

In addition, agreements with brokers and originators should specifically explain the bank's lending policies with regard to loan features and should contain the third party's express agreement to abide by those policies. Brokers and originators also should specifically agree to (1) comply with all applicable laws, including safety and soundness regulatory standards applicable to banks, and laws prohibiting lending discrimination and unfair or deceptive practices; and (2) make best efforts to ensure that the loans offered to borrowers are consistent with their needs, objectives, and financial situations. The bank should reserve the right not to make or purchase, and to put back to the broker or originator,[84] any loans failing to comply with these standards.

Agreements also should protect banks against risk by

- ensuring that no inappropriate compensation incentives exist to induce brokers or originators to treat borrowers in a discriminatory manner, or otherwise unfairly.
- providing for indemnification to the bank upon breach of the agreement.
- enabling banks to exit the arrangement through clear termination rights and procedures.
- providing for the bank's (and the OCC's) ability to access all records of the third party necessary to enforce and ensure compliance with the agreement and to audit the third party's operations.

If necessary, existing agreements with brokers and originators should be revised to protect banks from these risks. In addition, agreements should stipulate clear minimum performance standards and service levels.

Individual Loan Review (QC Review)

Banks should verify that brokers and originators have established policies and procedures sufficient to ensure that loans obtained from a broker and originated or purchased by the bank comply with applicable laws and the bank's policies. In appropriate circumstances—for example, at the outset of the third-party relationship or after a particular risk has been identified—banks should conduct a documentation review to confirm that transactions comply with the bank's policies and legal requirements. As a general matter, banks also should periodically perform a documentation review on a random sampling of broker and purchase transactions. When banks do not re-underwrite each loan, this file sampling should be adequate to ensure that loans are being underwritten consistently with the bank's policies. Loan reviews also should be sufficient to protect against potential fraud in these transactions.

In addition, with respect to brokered loans, the bank should have in place a process for the review of written agreements between the borrower and the broker to ensure that the agreements conspicuously (1) disclose the fees to be paid to the broker for its services, (2) contain a specific request for such broker services at that fee, and (3) include a signed and dated acknowledgment of receipt by the customer before the broker commences services. The bank should retain copies of this documentation.

Monitoring and MIS

RRE lenders need effective MIS to monitor the performance of brokers and originators from whom they acquire loans. Banks should be able to carefully monitor, track, and evaluate a third party's compliance with the terms of its contract, including minimum performance standards and service levels. Banks should follow OCC guidance, as applicable, on

---

[84] Repurchase or recourse agreements may result in the purchase of loans being deemed an extension of credit to the broker/originator and subject to the legal lending limits under 12 CFR 32.3(b)(2).

monitoring the financial condition, operations, and internal controls of third-party brokers and originators with whom they establish relationships. They also should carefully monitor the third parties' record of compliance with applicable laws and policies.

In addition to such general monitoring, banks should adopt criteria and procedures for additional targeted reviews, as appropriate, of brokers or originators whose loans exhibit unacceptable default, foreclosure, or complaint rates; broker fees that significantly exceed market rates or that do not comply with bank policies; potential violations of law or bank policies; or other risks. Targeted reviews may also be appropriate for brokers or originators whose concentrations suggest that borrowers may have been targeted on the basis of age, race, national origin, or gender. MIS should be adequate to identify brokers or originators whose loans show these risk characteristics.

Corrective Action

When brokers or originators are found to have violated bank policies, applicable laws, or the provisions of their agreements, other than on a clearly isolated and inadvertent basis, banks should take prompt and appropriate corrective action, including modification of loan terms and termination of the relationship with the third party in question.

Control Functions

MIS and Reports

The bank's MIS should provide timely, accurate, and detailed information for prudent decisions. MIS reports should enable management and the board of directors to assess the performance of the RRE loan portfolios in aggregate and on a segmented basis. From the MIS, management and the board should be able to discern if the performance and credit risk profile achieved is consistent with the risk appetite articulated in policies and procedures for loan origination, servicing, and collections. Finally, the intensity of data collection, the level of detail in data reporting, and the quality of data analysis within the MIS should be commensurate with the size and nature of the RRE lending activities. Banks should periodically assess the adequacy of their MIS in relation to significant growth in their operations or changes in their articulated risk appetite and strategies.

Appropriate MIS reporting for RRE lending begins with loan origination activities and the characteristics of approved loans segmented by product type. Commensurate with the volume and nature of origination activities, the MIS should provide monthly information about the volume of new originations by various significant characteristics, such as application or credit score, originating office or channel, loan officer, geographic location, DTI or other borrower capacity measure, LTV, appraisal type, lien position, documentation requirement, loan terms, and loan pricing. The MIS reports also should highlight originations obtained through brokers or correspondents when these channels generate strategically important volumes or products that may adversely affect the bank's reputation. Finally, MIS reports for new originations should also effectively highlight the volume and trend of loans approved and booked as exceptions to underwriting requirements because these could reflect a deviation from the approved level of risk appetite and tolerance. Analysis of this information may be helpful in identifying correlations between certain types of exceptions and subsequent delinquency and loss performance.

In RRE lending operations in which management does not systematically capture and report pertinent loan origination information—such as credit bureau score, repayment capacity measures, and LTV ratio measures—some type of manual collection, compilation, and review process should be established. In a larger and more automated origination environment, it is more likely that management can effectively capture and report loan origination statistics. Additionally, greater sophistication in an operation should result in more timely and relevant analysis of reported statistics, such as the performance of loans by origination vintage.

Portfolio performance MIS reports are derived primarily from the loan servicing system and the collection servicing system (in smaller banks, this may be the same system with two separate components).[85] From these systems, management and the board should be able to obtain predefined reports of loan positions and performance, appropriate accounting information, and single loan data elements downloaded into databases or spreadsheets for analysis. The reporting process should be able to report on each primary product as well as significant subsegments. If the RRE lending activities include the origination, sale, and servicing of loans and lines, the reporting should be able to distinguish between owned loans and lines and serviced loans and lines. For HELOCs, the MIS should accurately report total commitments to lend, the present balance, and the unused amounts. The MIS should also be able to detail any HELOCs permitted to exceed their assigned amount.

In smaller RRE lending operations, the MIS reports often focus on lagging indicators of risk such as delinquency and losses. In larger, more sophisticated operations, the MIS reports are more appropriately focused on the current and prospective risk profile of the portfolio(s) as gleaned from refreshed credit or behavior scores and refreshed collateral valuations using some type of AVM. Sophisticated reporting also provides information on potential and identified credit concentrations by product, market, property type, geography, score band, and adjusted LTV.

From the collection servicing system or platform, management and the board should have up-to-date information on the volume and status of delinquent loans by the number of days past due. Such systems may also be able to report the volume of delinquent loans that roll from one delinquency status to another each month. To the extent that management and the board actively designate RRE loans as nonaccruing assets, the MIS should report this information. Additional MIS reports for loans experiencing repayment problems should include the volumes of extensions, deferrals, and renewals for closed-end loans and re-ages for HELOCs. The MIS reports should also be able to track and monitor the effectiveness of these servicing activities by reporting the performance of the loans and lines after these actions in relation to expectations. The volumes of residential loans under review for modification or

---

[85] Except for small servicers, 12 CFR 1024.38 requires servicers to retain documents for at least one year after discharge or transfer and to be able to compile a complete servicing file within five days.

receiving modification should be reported as well as any modifications determined to be TDRs. Portfolio reporting should include reports detailing the volumes of modified loans and TDRs and the performance of these loans in relation to the modified terms and expectations.

Collections-related MIS reports should include information about the volume of loans in bankruptcy, in the process of foreclosure, or foreclosed and transferred to OREO. Reports for loan losses taken should refer to significant portfolio segments. The volume and nature of RRE loans subject to the bank's classification standards should be reported. Classification of RRE-secured loans and lines must conform to the interagency regulatory guidance "Uniform Retail Classification and Account Management Policy," issued by the Federal Financial Institutions Examination Council (FFIEC) in June 2000.

In some banks, periods of financial stress may result in a large volume of RRE loans that are subject to Chapter 7 bankruptcy liquidation proceedings. In many cases, the borrower may continue to make timely payments on the mortgage or home equity loan to avoid foreclosure actions. The borrower, however, may not re-affirm his or her obligation to repay the underlying note, and the borrower's personal liability may be discharged as part of the bankruptcy action. In these cases, the bank now holds a nonrecourse loan such that collection can occur only through foreclosure and sale of the collateral. A bank's MIS reports for RRE lending should be able to identify the volume of and performance of such loans, including their current repayment status, accrual status, internal classification, and loss reserve analysis. Refer to OCC Bulletin 2014-4, "Secured Consumer Debt Discharged in Chapter 7 Bankruptcy: Supervisory Expectations."

Loan Reviews

Periodic loan reviews should be independent and risk-based with a focus on both determining adherence to approved policies and procedures, including those for appraisal and evaluations of collateral, and assessing the quantity of risk inherent in the portfolio(s) based on sampling results, MIS reports, and trends in portfolio risk profile and performance. Loan reviews should include all RRE lending activities, including originations for investment and for sale, as well as loan purchases from others, the servicing of loans and lines (owned and sold), and collection activities. Coverage should be statistically valid for less complex portfolios and should specifically target portfolios concentrated in nontraditional, subprime, or other unusual RRE loan products. Additionally, the loan review procedures should strive to assess

- the quality of the risk management activities performed by lending personnel, including the level and performance of loans approved as exceptions to policies.
- the quality and integrity of loan information within the automated systems or platforms for evaluating applications, servicing loans and lines, and collecting delinquent or charged-off loans.
- the integrity and reliability of management portfolio reports for originations, servicing, and collections, including reports for deferrals, renewals, re-ages, modification of loans, classification of loans, and TDRs.

- any relevant trends in credit risk characteristics that may affect the collectability of the portfolio or ALLL calculations, including any reports of refreshed credit scores and real estate collateral values.

Quality Control

The purpose of a QC function is to monitor and evaluate the integrity of the origination process and to provide feedback to the organization about its loan originations. If a bank's RRE lending activities are of sufficient size and nature to warrant a QC function, the board should ensure that the function is sufficiently independent of the loan production process to provide meaningful information about the quality of RRE lending activities. Reports from the QC function should identify and highlight transactions not completed in accordance with loan policies and procedures, investor requirements, or regulatory requirements. The reports should also provide information about trends in the quality of decisions by lending personnel, for example, whether the volumes of identified issues are increasing or decreasing. Finally, the QC function should identify training needs or personnel performance problems whenever these issues are consistently noted over time.

Internal and External Audits

The board of directors should require risk-based periodic audits and loan reviews of the bank's RRE lending activities. Audit procedures should include regular testing of the credit underwriting function for compliance with board-approved policies as well as applicable laws, regulations, and regulatory guidance. Audit procedures should also review operational controls for proper segregation and independence of duties between loan personnel who assist the customer and facilitate the application process and staff members who disburse funds, collect payments, and provide the timely receipt, review, and follow-up on necessary loan documentation, including appraisals and evaluations. Audits of compliance with the many consumer laws and regulations governing RRE lending activities also should be conducted. Depending on the bank's size, these audits may be conducted by internal or external auditors or separate compliance management or compliance audit functions.

Because of the variety of risks inherent in RRE lending activities, internal audit coverage should include an evaluation of all the risks and controls in the bank's RRE lending operations. The scope and frequency of these audits should be based on the risk of associated controls and activities for the bank. Audits should assess strategic business risks and the overall risk management framework, including compliance with bank policies or approved practices, limits, investor criteria, federal and state laws, and regulatory issuances and guidelines. Internal audit staff should be independent and knowledgeable about RRE lending activities. Staff should report audit findings, including identified control weaknesses, directly to the board or the audit committee. Refer to the "Internal and External Audits" booklet of the *Comptroller's Handbook*.

The board and management should ensure that the internal audit staff has the necessary qualifications and expertise to review RRE activities, including all related IT environments, or should mitigate voids with qualified external sources.

Examination Procedures

This booklet contains expanded procedures for examining specialized activities or specific products or services that warrant extra attention beyond the core assessment contained in the "Community Bank Supervision," "Large Bank Supervision," and "Federal Branches and Agencies Supervision" booklets of the *Comptroller's Handbook*. Examiners determine which supplemental procedures to use, if any, during examination planning or after drawing preliminary conclusions during the core assessment. Examiners can tailor the examination request items found in appendix A, "Suggested Request Items for RRE Lending Activities," and the request letter found in appendix B, "HELOC End-of-Draw Request Letter," to assist in their examinations.

Scope

These procedures are designed to help examiners tailor the examination to each bank and determine the scope of the RRE lending examination. This determination should consider work performed by internal and external auditors and other independent risk control functions and by other examiners on related areas. Examiners need to perform only those objectives and steps that are relevant to the scope of the examination as determined by the following objectives. Seldom will every objective or step of the supplemental procedures be necessary.

Objective: To determine the scope of the examination of RRE lending and identify examination objectives and activities necessary to meet the needs of the supervisory strategy for the bank.

1. Review the following sources of information and note any previously identified problems related to RRE lending that require follow-up:

    -   Supervisory strategy
    -   Examiner-in-charge (EIC) scope memorandum
    -   OCC's information system
    -   Previous ROEs and work papers
    -   Internal and external audit reports and work papers
    -   Bank management's responses to previous ROEs and audit reports
    -   Customer complaints and litigation

2. Obtain the results of such reports as the Uniform Bank Performance Reports and Canary.

3. Obtain and review policies, procedures, and reports bank management uses to supervise RRE lending, including internal risk assessments.

4. Before going on-site or within the first week on-site, discuss the bank's RRE lending activities with management. Focus on changes made since the previous examination or planned for the future, including

- growth in RRE lending activities overall or in the individual products offered.
- changes in the portfolio product mix.
- changes in the terms of existing products.
- new products offered or planned.
- loan origination or acquisition channels (retail branches, correspondents, brokers, Internet, telemarketing, or direct mail).
- expansion into new market or trade areas.
- new or expanded third-party loan origination, servicing, or collection arrangements.
- changes to underwriting, risk selection criteria, and targeted portfolio quality.
- changes in policies, practices, or personnel relating to activities, systems, and collection processes.
- risk management monitoring processes and associated MIS.
- score models or other models used to underwrite or manage RRE products and portfolios.
- operating platforms for RRE loan origination (application and underwriting), servicing, and collections.
- any other changes in internal or external factors that could affect RRE lending activities and operations.

5. Determine the type of RRE loan products offered, the nature of the RRE lending (risk appetite), and the scale and structure of the RRE lending activities (portfolio lender, departmental lender, large lender).

6. Discuss examination goals and objectives with the EIC or loan portfolio manager examiner.

7. Obtain and review a copy of the EIC's request letter to the bank for information to use during the examination. Highlight items related to RRE lending activities. From the requested examination materials,

- review copies of board-level reports for RRE lending activities.
- identify any board or management committees responsible for the supervision of RRE lending activities and review minutes or reports from their meetings.
- determine whether there is any litigation, filed or anticipated, associated with the bank's RRE lending activities, and the expected cost or other implications.
- review copies of any issued internal or external audit reports covering any RRE lending activities (such as originations, servicing, portfolio management, and collections).
- review copies of any issued loan review reports covering any RRE lending activities or portfolio performance.

8. Using call report data downloaded through FINDRS, perform an analysis to determine

   - the volumes and trends in outstanding one- to four-family first-lien real estate loans, one- to four-family junior-lien loans, and revolving HELOCs over the past eight quarters.
   - the volumes and trends in delinquency, nonaccrual, TDRs, foreclosures and charge-offs, and recoveries for one- to four-family first-lien real estate loans, one- to four-family junior-lien loans, and revolving HELOCs over the past eight quarters.
   - the volumes and trends in adjustable rate closed-end loans secured by first liens on one- to four-family residential properties over the past eight quarters.
   - the volumes and trends in reverse mortgages outstanding and held for investment over the past eight quarters.
   - the volume and trends of activities reported in Schedule RC-P, "1-4 Family Residential Mortgage Activities," over the past eight quarters.
   - any significant growth in the portfolios (greater than 10 percent in one quarter or 25 percent in one year), significant changes in the portfolio mix, or significant changes in credit performance (delinquency volumes and rates, nonaccrual volumes and rates, or net charge-off volumes and rates) as compared to aggregated performance data for all banks.

9. Review the OCC's Customer Assistance Group database for the bank and determine the volume and nature of any customer complaints related to RRE lending products and services.

10. From the Interagency Loan Data File provided by the bank, use the OCC's National Credit Tool application to generate pre-formatted retail loan reports for the RRE loan portfolios. Review the reports to discern if there are any examiner concerns that may warrant additional review or targeted transaction testing.

11. Form a preliminary working premise regarding the nature and risks inherent in the bank's RRE lending activities. Specifically, determine what risk appetite is suggested by the reviewed information (low risk, moderate risk, and high risk). Additionally, determine whether the bank's activities are primarily those of a portfolio lender, a departmental lender, or a large lender. The primary characteristics of each type of lender are listed in this section. Refer to appendix C for a more detailed listing of RRE lending characteristics (mortgage and home equity) and the risk management processes associated with each.

   Portfolio lender (may have small volume of activities reported on call report Schedule RC-P):

   - Primary products are conventional and conforming mortgage loans as well as home equity loan and line products with very basic terms.
   - Primary channel of origination is main office and branches.
   - Bank primarily services and collects only the loans and lines made by the bank.

- Bank may serve as a correspondent originator for a larger bank's mortgage banking activities.

Departmental lender (could have activities reported on call report Schedule RC-P):

- Primary products are conventional and conforming mortgage loans but may also have government-insured mortgages, jumbo mortgages, and other nonconforming mortgages. Home equity loans and lines are first lien or subordinate lien to a portfolio loan or a loan from another lender.
- Primary channel of origination is main office and branches but may also have some wholesale originations through brokers and correspondents.
- Bank primarily services and collects only the loans and lines made by the bank but may also service and collect loans sold to secondary-market investors.

Large lender (likely to have activities reported on call report Schedule RC-P):

- Primary products are a full menu of conventional, conforming mortgage products and government-insured products, and a significant volume of jumbo mortgages or other nonconforming mortgage products. May also have nontraditional mortgage products. Home equity loans and lines may have higher LTVs and longer terms. Home equity products may be offered as a piggy-back loan to a first-mortgage position.
- Bank may have full-scale retail originations through the bank's locations as well as a significant volume of wholesale lending activities with correspondents and brokers.
- Bank services and collects the loans and lines held by the bank as well as those held by secondary-market investors.

12. Based on findings resulting from the previous steps and in consultation with the EIC and other appropriate supervisors, determine if the scope of the RRE lending examination as set out in the EIC's examination scope memo remains appropriate or should be adjusted, including the nature and volume of transaction testing performed, to meet supervisory objectives. Discuss any recommended adjustments with the EIC. Select from the following procedures, internal control questions, and verification procedures necessary to meet the examination objectives.

Note: If the bank is a larger operational lender with active secondary-market positions reported in call report Schedule RC-P, the examiner must determine the applicability of the OCC's mortgage banking procedures as detailed in the "Mortgage Banking" booklet of the *Comptroller's Handbook*. Appendix D of the "Mortgage Banking" booklet provides additional discussion on the "Common Mortgage Banking Structures" that exist in banks. Expansion of the examination's scope and use of the mortgage banking procedures should be considered if the RRE lending activities are heavily weighted toward wholesale originations and purchases made for sale to secondary-market investors and include an active secondary-market unit for pricing and hedging activities.

Procedures

These procedures are grouped by functional and product-specific areas. They guide examiners' assessments of the quantity, aggregate level, and direction of credit, operational, strategic, and reputation risk, and the quality of risk management. The primary procedures provide the steps used for completing a comprehensive RRE lending examination for portfolio lenders and serve as the base procedures for larger or more complex operations.

The scope of the review may be expanded when the bank offers new or significantly changed products, when a particular concern exists, or for larger, more complex operations. In these situations, examiners should select the appropriate supplemental procedures to augment the primary procedures. Examiners are also encouraged to refer to other *Comptroller's Handbook* booklets, including "Community Bank Supervision," "Large Bank Supervision," "Allowance for Loan and Lease Losses," "Concentrations of Credit," "Internal and External Audits," "Internal Control," and "Loan Portfolio Management." In addition, examiners may refer to appropriate booklets in the *Consumer Compliance* series of the *Comptroller's Handbook*.

The primary examination procedures comprise "Management and Supervision," "Internal and External Audits," "Information Technology," "Loan Production," and "Servicing," and apply to all RRE lending activities. These functional areas also contain supplemental procedures. In addition, the supplemental procedures should be used based on the bank's activities: "Collections and Default Management," "HELOC End of Draw," "Third-Party Management," and "Nontraditional Mortgages."

Examiners can use appendix D, "Quantity of Credit Risk Indicators"; appendix E, "Quality of Credit Risk Management Indicators"; and appendix F, "Appraisal and Evaluation Questionnaire," to help formulate their RRE lending activity conclusions.

Management and Supervision

Conclusion: Based on the responses to procedures, the quality of risk management for the bank's management and supervision activities is (strong, satisfactory, or weak).

Objective: To assess the effectiveness of management and board supervision of RRE lending operations.

Primary Examination Procedures

1. Determine the level of compliance with or divergence from strategic business plans through risk assessments and impact analysis. (**Note:** Significant deviation from plans may lead to a change in the quantity and quality of products, services, controls, management supervision, and technology. Management should have a clear and demonstrable understanding of the anticipated strategic changes' impact on the financial condition of the operation.)

2. Review staffing levels and expertise relative to origination volume, servicing size, or complexity of operations. (**Note:** Insufficient staffing levels, experience, and operational efficiency can lead to high error rates and pose significant risk to the bank.)

3. Assess the nature and number of customer complaints relative to the amount of production and servicing. Determine whether the bank has accurately assessed the reasons for such complaints and instituted appropriate steps to provide relief to existing customers and prevent further events from occurring.

4. Review the key risk limits for each of the major functional areas. (**Note:** Absence of meaningful risk limits is usually indicative that the bank does not understand the nature of the risk and is vulnerable to unwittingly accepting excessive risk, such as credit, operational, or interest rate risk and all of the attendant negative results.)

5. Assess the depth and timing of MIS reporting. (**Note:** Insufficient and lagging reporting efforts suggest a high level of management and oversight risk. Management is not able to effectively integrate appropriate risk management processes without a clear knowledge of profitability, servicing values, and production expectations by type and channel.)

6. Review the functional organization dynamics and assess the separation of duties among the primary operating functions (origination, underwriting, servicing, and finance). (**Note:** Insufficient functional independence may lead to conflicts of interest and expose the bank to various risks, such as credit, operational, and liquidity risk.)

7. Review the volume of mortgage originations, portfolio size and turnover rate, and the amount of the servicing portfolio. (**Note:** Significant changes may indicate management's desire to accelerate earnings or an absence of appropriate management oversight.)

Supplemental Examination Procedures

Policies and Control Systems

1. Review policy and procedural guidelines for the RRE lending operation. Determine whether they are communicated to relevant staff and how compliance is monitored. Ascertain whether guidelines have been established to

   - define permissible RRE lending activities (including loan originator and servicing policies, as applicable).
   - identify individual responsibilities.
   - define reasonable risk limits and monitor compliance.
   - require segregation of duties.

2. Review corporate or bank plans, policies, procedures, and systems for asset-liability management, operational risk management, and consumer compliance. Determine the extent to which the policies, procedures, and systems incorporate RRE lending activities.

3. Review the strategic plan for RRE lending activities. Determine whether

    - the plan is reasonable and achievable in light of the bank's capital position, physical facilities, data-processing systems, capabilities, size and expertise of staff, market conditions, competition, and current economic forecasts.
    - the goals and objectives of the RRE business are compatible with the overall business plan of the bank or its holding company.

4. Review the budget process and financial performance of the RRE lending unit(s). Determine

    - whether bank executive management and the board have communicated performance goals to the RRE lending unit(s).
    - whether staff periodically compares current financial results to the unit's financial plan and past performance.
    - how staff analyzes and documents significant deviations from the financial plan.

5. Determine whether management has established a system that reflects all risk characteristics to ensure that sufficient capital is maintained for RRE lending operations.

6. Determine whether the risk management process is effective and based on sound information. Evaluate the comprehensiveness of the risk management process and whether it adequately addresses significant risks in each functional area of the RRE operation.

7. Determine whether comprehensive procedures are in place to ensure compliance with laws and regulations.

8. Review the RRE lending unit's new product development process to ensure that it considers all applicable risks (credit, interest rate, liquidity, operational, compliance, strategic, and reputation). (Refer to OCC Bulletin 2004-20, "Risk Management of New, Expanded, or Modified Bank Products and Services.") Determine whether management

    - considers customer needs and wants.
    - prepares financial projections and risk analyses.
    - considers accounting and regulatory requirements applicable to the product.
    - obtains legal opinions.
    - considers technology and MIS requirements' risk impact.

Note: Before implementing any marketing initiative, including the rollout of a new product or change to an existing product, management should review all marketing materials, customer disclosures, and product features and terms for compliance with laws and regulations and to identify and address potentially unfair, deceptive, abusive, and predatory lending practices that may adversely affect reputation and compliance risk.

Personnel

9. Assess the expertise and experience of the RRE lending unit's management team and key staff. Review management succession plans and determine whether designated successors have the necessary background and experience.

10. Review the organizational chart for RRE lending activities. Determine

    - whether decision making is centralized or decentralized.
    - which individuals are responsible for major decisions and who makes final decisions.
    - whether sufficient independence exists among the various functional areas.

11. Review compensation plans, including incentive components, for RRE lending managers and staff (and, as appropriate, brokers or correspondents). Determine whether the plans

    - comply with applicable laws, regulations, and internal standards designed to mitigate risk and reward qualitative factors, not just the quantity of loans originated.
    - comply with applicable laws, including Regulation Z and Regulation X.
    - have been reviewed and approved by the board of directors.
    - consider qualitative factors rather than just production volume.
    - include controls to ensure that originators are not improperly encouraged to direct borrowers to particular products in a discriminatory, predatory, or otherwise unlawful manner.
    - include systems to ensure that overages, if allowed, have sufficient controls and monitoring.
    - are designed to recruit, develop, and retain appropriate talent.
    - discourage employees from taking risks that are incompatible with the bank's risk appetite or prevailing rules or regulations.
    - are consistent with the long-term strategic goals of the bank.
    - include compliance with bank policies, laws, and regulations.
    - consider performance relative to the bank's stated goals.
    - consider competitors' compensation packages for similar responsibilities and performance.
    - consider individual overall performance.

Management Information Systems

12. Evaluate the systems for managing risk within the RRE lending unit(s). Determine to what extent the bank uses simulation modeling to assess the impact of interest rate changes or other economic variables on the mortgage operation.

13. Review MIS and determine management's capacity for evaluating and monitoring RRE lending activities. Evaluate MIS reports for detail, accuracy, and timeliness. Determine whether

- MIS and operating systems are adequate to monitor current operations and handle future product growth.
- the board receives MIS reports on profitability, monthly production volume, delinquencies, foreclosures, status of reserves, operational efficiency, and policy exceptions.
- current MIS allocates all revenues and costs (including overhead and administrative support) by functional area (production, servicing, etc.) and production channel (retail, wholesale, and correspondent), and how management uses this information to administer mortgage operations.
- management has adequate knowledge of product profitability, including production, servicing costs, and whether that knowledge is incorporated into the overall risk management process.

14. Assess the extent to which the board and management use the data obtained from MIS in their decision-making process.

15. Assess the adequacy of physical facilities, data-processing systems and platforms, and human resources capabilities. Determine adequacy relative to

- current business volume.
- future business plans, including strategic initiatives to meet any shortcomings.

Internal and External Audits

Conclusion: Based on the responses to procedures, the quality of risk management for the bank's internal and external audit activities is (strong, satisfactory, or weak).

Objective: To determine whether a comprehensive audit program has been implemented and whether the board or audit committee has established effective audit guidelines and processes for RRE lending activities.

Primary Examination Procedures

1. Determine whether an audit review has been performed since the last examination.

2. Assess the scope and frequency of internal audits. Consider statutory requirements and regulatory guidelines, purpose and objectives of audits, control and risk assessments, audit cycles, and reporting relationships and requirements.

3. Determine whether audit staff and related functions have a direct reporting line to the board of directors to reduce the possibility of managerial pressure and preserve the integrity of the audit process.

4. Determine whether management takes appropriate and timely action on the audit findings and recommendations and whether it reports the action to the board of directors or its audit committee.

5. Evaluate the independence and competence of those who manage and perform the audit functions. Determine the level of experience of bank auditing personnel, specifically in the areas of RRE lending and capital markets.

6. Determine whether audit personnel actively review appropriate MIS to assist in targeted audit programs. Optimally, audit staff should have access to all systems such that they can create their own MIS reporting independent of the targeted area for review.

7. Determine whether the nature and depth of the relationship between the internal and external audit function is promoting a thorough review of the targeted area and detailing all pertinent areas of concern. Areas of review might include the contract outlining the scope of the work to be performed, fees, and the protocol for changing terms of engagement for increased work assignments.

8. Review the board or audit committee minutes as well as audit information packages submitted to the board or audit committee to determine whether the audit findings are reviewed, discussed, and acted on by the board of directors. Actions that suggest active participation by the board of directors might include the review and approval of audit strategies, policies, programs, and compensation structures for external auditors.

Supplemental Examination Procedures

Policies and Control Systems

1. Review the bank's internal audit program for RRE lending activities. Determine whether it includes adequate objectives, procedures, scheduling, and reporting systems.

2. Determine the extent to which the internal audit program covers the following RRE lending areas, as applicable:

- Production
- Servicing
- Internal control
- Financial and regulatory reporting
- Accounting treatment
- Inter-company transactions
- MIS
- IT and IT environment
- Compliance with applicable laws, regulations, and guidance, including assessing whether any lending practices are unfair, deceptive, abusive, or predatory

3. Determine whether the audit program specifically targets those RRE lending activities exhibiting higher risk, including risks from nontraditional mortgage products.

4. Determine whether auditors periodically review and verify

- accuracy of data input, record keeping, and related MIS.
- appropriate accounting for and financial reporting of operations.
- information security processes and requirements (refer to the "Information Security" booklet of the *FFIEC Information Technology (IT) Examination Handbook*).
- system architecture and performance.
- loan documentation management.
- outsourcing arrangements and services (refer to the "Outsourcing Technology Services" booklet of the *FFIEC IT Examination Handbook*).
- continuity of operations, including backup and recovery (refer to the "Business Continuity Planning" booklet of the *FFIEC IT Examination Handbook*).

Personnel

5. Review the education, experience, and ongoing training of the internal audit staff and draw a conclusion about its expertise in auditing RRE lending activities.

6. Evaluate the independence of the internal audit staff by considering whether it has necessary authority and access to records and to whom it reports audit findings.

Management Information Systems

7. Determine whether the internal auditors periodically verify the accuracy of MIS reports.

8. Determine whether the internal audit function itself has sufficient MIS to report and monitor significant findings for appropriate management resolution.

Audit Coverage

9. Determine whether the board and management have established internal and external audit coverage for the RRE lending unit and its associated IT environment.

10. Determine whether internal or external audit provides adequate audit coverage of primary income- and expense-related activities most likely to have a significant impact on earnings or capital. Consider any significant recommendations from other examination areas that were not addressed by internal or external audit findings.

11. Review internal audit working papers. Evaluate the effectiveness of the audit by considering the scope, frequency, and working paper documentation as well as the conclusions reached.

12. Review the criticisms and recommendations in the internal audit report. Determine whether, and the extent to which, management changes operating and administrative procedures as a result of report findings. Evaluate how the internal audit unit assesses the appropriateness of management's corrective action.

13. Review the results of the most recent engagement letter, external audit report, and management letter for potential issues or concerns to ascertain the consistency and thoroughness of issues identified related to the RRE lending operation.

14. Determine to what extent the external auditors rely on the internal audit staff and the internal audit report.

15. Determine whether the external auditors review all functional RRE lending areas.

16. Review the findings in the external audit report. Determine whether the auditors rendered an opinion on the effectiveness of internal controls and assessed the overall condition of the RRE lending operation.

17. Determine whether management promptly and effectively responds to the external auditor's recommendations, and whether management makes appropriate changes to operating and administrative procedures as a result of the report's finding(s).

Information Technology

Conclusion: Based on the responses to procedures, the quality of risk management for the bank's IT activities is (strong, satisfactory, or weak).

Objective: To assess the adequacy of the RRE lending function's IT structure, operating environment, and control practices.

Note: These procedures are intended to provide an overview of IT in the RRE lending function. The procedures are not all-inclusive and should be adjusted accordingly. Refer to the *FFIEC IT Examination Handbook* as needed.

Primary Examination Procedures

1. Determine whether the bank adopted new Internet-based systems for mortgage loan origination, processing, pricing, or delivery, or enhanced existing usage of such systems. (**Note:** Significantly increasing broker or correspondent relationships through an electronic application exposes the bank and customers to multiple forms of fraud.)

2. Assess the level of remote access for independent agents (e.g., mortgage brokers, correspondents, credit repositories, title insurance companies, and settlement firms) and information walls to assure third-party confidentiality.

3. Review the number and nature of outsourcing relationships. (**Note:** Vendors can be problematic for a bank to manage given the technical challenges of connecting to each third party and the potential for increased electronic threats.)

4. Determine whether the bank uses a third party to process mortgage applications and the safeguards in place to ensure the security of the customers' personal information.

5. Assess the level of access controls over customer information from internal as well as external threats.

6. Review the bank's incident response process to system problems. (**Note:** Rapid identification and mediation are imperative to recovery and monitoring for future events.)

7. Determine whether the bank has properly segregated IT duties. Failure to appropriately segregate IT duties from the production process can expose the bank to fraud schemes and, ultimately, affect its earnings and capital.

8. Determine the existence, testing, and updating of the business continuity processes. Examine the assumptions, change control processes, data synchronization procedures, crisis management methodologies, and incident response times for level of continuity.

Supplemental Examination Procedures

1. Review internal and external IT audit comments and reports issued that address the technology supporting the RRE lending business. (**Note:** IT-related audit comments and reports may be issued by a specialized IT audit group or integrated with general internal or external audit comments and reports.)

2. Review internal IT risk assessments of the technology systems that support RRE lending activities.

3. Obtain and review technology management reports to assess performance issue trends of key RRE lending systems.

4. Obtain and review a listing of recent RRE Lending IT projects, e.g., new systems, enhancements, and upgrades.

5. Review meeting minutes from the board of directors or designated committee overseeing RRE lending activities. (**Note:** The IT examiner should coordinate this review with the LPM.)

6. After reviewing the above information and discussion with the LPM, determine the scope of the IT examination.

7. Determine whether key RRE lending systems are operated internally or by a third- party vendor. If the RRE lending system is managed by a third party, review the service contract and assess the effectiveness of the bank's vendor management program. Refer to OCC Bulletin 2013-29, "Third-Party Relationships: Risk Management Guidance," and the "Outsourcing Technology Services" booklet of the *FFIEC IT Examination Handbook.*

8. Assess the effectiveness of the IT control environment managed by the bank's IT department, with emphasis on

   - IT management.
   - IT audit.
   - systems development life cycle.
   - data input, access, processing, and change controls.
   - data and system validation.
   - network performance monitoring.
   - information security.
   - business continuation and disaster recovery planning and testing.
   - user access controls.
   - systems administrator practices.
   - level and quality of IT technical staff.

9. Assess access control and change management policies and procedures for internally developed and off-the-shelf software used by the RRE lending function.

10. Discuss any IT-related issues and concerns with the LPM and bank management.

11. Compile IT conclusions and matters requiring attention (MRA) and communicate to the LPM.

Loan Production

Conclusion: Based on the responses to procedures, the quantity of risks is (low, moderate, or high), and the quality of risk management for the bank's loan production activities is (strong, satisfactory, or weak).

Objective: To assess the risks associated with loan production and determine whether loan production activities are executed in conformity with board-approved strategies and processes and comply with statutory and regulatory requirements.

Primary Examination Procedures

1. Assess the level of wholesale originated (broker or correspondent) mortgage loans relative to overall production. (**Note:** Significant increases or a disproportionate percentage can present the bank with substantial credit, pricing, recourse, and liquidity risk.)

2. Assess the volume of nonconforming, subprime, Alt-A, or nontraditional mortgage loans originated by the bank and by the industry. (**Note:** The bank should have a robust mortgage origination process [i.e., processing and underwriting] and several funding options to avoid potential liquidity issues. Rapid increases in such loans may signal a

significant buildup of credit, operational, and compliance risks within the bank and across the system.)

3. Review the bank's strategy to originate for the portfolio versus originating for sale, and determine the extent to which mortgage loans originated for sale are transferred to the portfolio. (**Note:** Portfolio increases beyond strategic plans may indicate systemic or staffing issues in the origination process. Significant variations in standards used to underwrite loans for sale versus loans for the portfolio may be cause for concern.)

4. Determine whether the bank has a high or increasing level of policy exceptions. (**Note:** The pressure to acquire assets and achieve revenue targets may be driving the bank to ignore characteristics that have been proven to cause higher levels of default and repurchase requests. Institutions should have a repurchase reserve methodology to determine the amount of recourse liability for loans sold. For more information, refer to the "Mortgage Banking" booklet of the *Comptroller's Handbook*.)

5. Determine whether the bank is loosening underwriting standards without other compensating factors and adequate funding sources. (**Note:** Excessive underwriting flexibility without investor or senior management approval is likely to prove harmful to the bank at different levels.)

6. Determine whether the bank has a high level of missing documents on closed loans. (**Note:** High volumes and poorly defined pre-funding review processes can lead to high levels of rejections or repurchase requests.)

7. Review the number and nature of QC, audit, and consumer compliance findings. (**Note:** Banks should ensure that customers have clear and balanced information about the menu of products being offered by the bank. Failure to do so may be in violation of federal and state laws and regulations.)

8. Determine whether the bank has sufficient policies, procedures, and staff to comply with requirements related to the origination of mortgage loans set forth in federal law (including Regulations X and Z), state law, and investor requirements. The bank should pay particular attention to the assessment of consumers' ability to repay the loan, appraisal requirements, loan originator registration and licensing obligations, loan originator compensation limitations, and disclosure requirements.

Supplemental Examination Procedures

Policies and Control Systems

1. Determine whether the board or its RRE lending committee, consistent with its duties and responsibilities, has adopted adequate loan production policies. Determine whether policies adequately address

   - the types of loans the bank will originate or purchase.

- loan sources.
- underwriting guidelines.
- pricing methodologies.
- compliance activities.
- documentation standards.
- real estate appraisal and evaluations.

2. Determine whether management recognizes the risks of nontraditional and subprime mortgages and whether appropriate portfolio and risk management practices are in place. Determine

- whether policies have been developed that specify acceptable product attributes, production and portfolio limits, and risk management expectations. Consider whether the bank
  - manages risk appropriately by means of operating practices, accounting procedures, and policy exception limits and reporting.
  - uses appropriate MIS to identify risk layering and establish appropriate limits on risk layering.
  - establishes growth and volume limits by loan type, especially for products and product combinations requiring heightened attention due to easing terms or rapid growth.
- whether concentrations of nontraditional or subprime mortgage products exist and, if so, whether they are effectively monitored. Consider concentration limits on
  - loan types.
  - third-party originations.
  - geographic area.
  - property occupancy status.
  - key portfolio characteristics, such as loans with high CLTV and DTI ratios, loans with potential for negative amortization, loans to borrowers with credit scores below established thresholds, and nontraditional mortgage loans with layered risks.

3. Determine whether the bank's policies and procedures provide adequate guidance to avoid unfair, deceptive, abusive, or predatory lending practices, including the following:

- Lending predominantly based on the liquidation value of collateral rather than on the borrower's ATR as required under Regulation Z
- Refinancing loans frequently and sequentially
- Refinancing special subsidized mortgages that contain terms favorable to the borrower into a loan with less favorable terms

4. Determine whether policies and procedures address, if applicable, the circumstances (and associated controls and monitoring processes) in which the bank may make loans involving features or actions that may raise concerns regarding compliance with

applicable law or discriminatory, unfair, deceptive, abusive, or predatory lending practices. Such features or actions include the following:

- Financing single-premium credit life insurance or similar products[86]
- Allowing negative amortization
- Requiring balloon payments in short-term transactions[87]
- Charging prepayment penalties in contravention of Regulation Z[88]
- Increasing interest rates upon default[89]
- Inserting mandatory arbitration clauses[90]
- Making high-cost mortgage loans (e.g., loans subject to HOEPA)

Note: If weaknesses or concerns are found relating to compliance with applicable laws or discriminatory, unfair, deceptive, abusive, or predatory lending practices, consult the bank's EIC or compliance examiner.

5. Evaluate management oversight of origination, processing, and underwriting functions to ensure supervisor accountability for the quality and timeliness of production functions. Consider the following:

- Benchmarking standards for the production function
- Processes to detect and prevent errors before closing and delivery

Personnel

6. Review the organizational chart and reporting structure for the loan production area. Determine whether

- responsibilities and reporting structure for the origination, processing, underwriting, and closing functions are clearly defined.
- each function is sufficiently independent and not unduly influenced by sales and origination.
- the QC unit is independent of the origination function.

7. Review the qualifications, any required licensing or registration, experience levels, and training programs for originators, processors, underwriters, closers, and QC staff for adequate abilities to execute their respective responsibilities in a safe and sound manner.

---

[86] Refer to 12 CFR 1026.36(i).

[87] Refer to 12 CFR 1026.32.

[88] Refer to 12 CFR 1026.43(g).

[89] If the loan is high cost, refer to 12 CFR 1026.32.

[90] Refer to 12 CFR 1026.36(h).

Management Information Systems

8. Assess the quality of the MIS used to monitor and administer loan production functional areas, including the adequacy of source document(s) to process application reconcilement procedures.

9. Evaluate the disaster recovery plan to determine whether it covers all major production functions performed in-house. Consider whether backup systems exist in case primary systems fail, and assess the existence of any unnecessary risk exposure.

Processes

Origination

10. Assess the bank's credit culture and lending philosophy, including to what degree the bank is willing to relax credit standards or offer below-market pricing to increase mortgage production volume.

11. Determine whether the bank's origination activities are primarily retail- or wholesale-oriented. Determine key differences in the programs, including price and product type.

12. Review the sources and types of mortgage products offered. Examiners should

- evaluate product volume, trends, and concentrations.
- determine the volume of, and growth in, higher-risk or nontraditional products, such as loans
  - with IO features.
  - with payment-option ARMs.
  - with reduced documentation of the borrower's assets, employment, or income.[91]
  - with higher LTV ratios.
  - with simultaneous second liens.
  - with higher DTI ratios.
  - with lower credit risk scores.
  - with longer-term amortization.
  - with negative amortization.
  - secured by non-owner-occupied properties.

Note: When evaluating lending activities, examiners should remain alert for practices and product terms that could indicate unfair, deceptive, abusive, or predatory issues.

---

[91] Regulation Z requires verification of certain information. Refer to 12 CFR 1026.43.

13. Determine whether the bank complies with applicable laws in originating loans, including

- providing accurate initial consumer compliance disclosures (e.g., good faith estimate and informational booklet, homeownership counseling list, and truth-in-lending statement) to the applicant within prescribed time frames.
- providing full and fair product information to customers. Consider
  - the availability of full and fair product descriptions when customers are shopping for mortgages.
  - whether promotional materials and product descriptions provide sufficient information to enable customers to prudently consider the costs, terms, features, and risks of mortgages, including nontraditional and subprime mortgages, in their product selection decisions.
  - whether information regarding payment increases, negative amortization, prepayment penalties, and balloon payments is being disclosed according to the requirements of Regulation Z.
  - whether customers are inappropriately directed to or steered toward consummating any particular transaction.[92]
  - compliance with special rules for certain mortgage transactions (e.g., HOEPA).

Note: Examiners should consult compliance examiners for assistance with these procedures, if needed. Examiners also should consider the asset size of the bank to assess whether the OCC is primarily responsible for assessing compliance with the requirements of federal consumer financial laws.

14. Evaluate controls designed to prevent originators from altering loan pricing parameters.

15. Determine the methods used to evaluate and compensate loan originators. Determine whether

- the bank pays loan officers based on transaction terms and conditions, an action prohibited by loan originator compensation standards set forth in Regulation Z.
- the bank ensures loan originators do not receive prohibited dual compensation or non-deferred profits-based compensation in excess of Regulation Z limits.
- performance and compensation programs consider qualitative factors such as loan quality, completeness of application information, and timeliness and accuracy of initial consumer disclosures, as well as origination volume.
- compensation programs incorporate controls to ensure that originators are not improperly encouraged to direct borrowers to particular products in a discriminatory, predatory, or otherwise unlawful manner.
- management adequately holds originators accountable for quality.

---

[92] Loan originator compensation that could provide incentives for this result is generally prohibited. Refer to 12 CFR 1026.36.

16. Review management's analysis of origination costs. Determine whether all direct and indirect costs are appropriately measured and accounted for. Examiners should

    - determine whether the analysis covers all major product types and sources of production.
    - evaluate management's comparison of key production functions (e.g., origination costs, underwriting efficiency, and processing time) with budget and industry averages.
    - review management's analysis of origination costs within the organization and whether costs are assessed by product unit.
    - determine whether the bank defers loan fees in excess of cost in accordance with Accounting Standards Codification 310 for retained mortgages.

Loan Processing

17. Review management's system for monitoring processor workflow and efficiency. Determine whether industry standards are used as a benchmark.

18. Determine the method used to ensure that all required loan documents are obtained and accurately completed before the scheduled loan closing. Determine

    - how often required loan documents were not obtained and not accurately completed within the bank's prescribed time frames.
    - whether the volume of exceptions is excessive relative to the volume of closed loans.
    - whether the volume of these exceptions is high relative to the bank's internal guidelines.
    - whether management has evaluated the underlying cause of any errors and has taken appropriate corrective action.

Underwriting

19. Review management's process for measuring underwriter efficiency and quality to determine whether performance is measured against objective benchmarks.

20. Review systems in place to ensure that underwriting practices comply with applicable law, bank policy, and the underwriting criteria specified by the purchaser(s) of the bank's mortgage products. Determine

    - whether the bank has a contractual relationship with each purchaser.
    - whether the bank uses automated underwriting systems, AVMs, and other automated underwriting processes.
    - whether mortgage insurance is obtained (if required by policy).
    - number and dollar volume of loans originated that do not conform to policy. Evaluate the process for approving policy exceptions and determine the reasonableness of the volume of loans approved with policy exceptions.

21. Determine whether loan terms and underwriting standards are consistent with prudent lending and the repayment capacity of borrowers.

22. Determine whether a bank's qualifying standards recognize the potential impact of interest rate increases on borrowers. Additional underwriting consideration should be given to borrowers with high LTV ratios, high DTI ratios, low credit scores, reduced documentation, and any combination thereof.

23. Determine whether the analysis of borrower repayment capacity includes a determination of the ability to repay the debt by final maturity that, at a minimum, complies with the general ATR requirements in Regulation Z. For nontraditional and subprime mortgage products, the analysis of repayment capacity is required to be determined at the fully indexed rate, assuming a fully amortizing schedule. For products that permit negative amortization, the repayment analysis is required to be based on the total amount the bank has committed to lend. This would include the initial loan amount plus any balance increase that may accrue from the negative amortization provision.

24. Review the procedure for handling loans that do not conform to policy. Determine whether the bank requires, and obtains, senior management's approval for policy exceptions. Review monitoring systems, reporting, and tracking of performance for loans approved with policy exceptions.

25. Determine whether the bank has developed and deployed processes to mitigate exposures and protect its collateral positions when municipal lending programs are offered that could create a super-senior lien priority. For new mortgage loans, mitigating efforts should include reducing LTV limits to reflect the maximum advance rates offered by the lending program and consideration of the lien's payment requirements in the borrower's financial capacity.

26. Determine whether customers denied credit are provided a proper notice under ECOA and the Fair Credit Reporting Act.

Loan Closing

27. Determine the adequacy of the bank's process for closing and funding loans, including its compliance with applicable law.

28. Determine how management monitors loan closer performance and ensures that loan closers follow the underwriter's instructions.

29. Determine whether there is a process in place to ensure that settlement statements reflect all actual charges and adjustments in connection with the settlement and require that all charges or adjustments subsequent to settlement are disclosed to the lending institution through the preparation of an amended HUD-1.

30. Determine whether insured closing letters from title insurers are used and whether this letter sets forth the title insurance company's responsibilities for negligence, fraud, and errors in closings performed by approved agents or attorneys.

31. Determine whether the bank has formed bona fide affiliated business arrangements (ABA) with third parties to offer real estate settlement services. Determine the volume and nature of these arrangements. Determine whether the ABA disclosure is provided (12 CFR 1024.15).

Appraisal and Evaluation

32. Determine whether there is an effective internal control structure to ensure appropriate collateral valuation policies and procedures that comply with the appraisal provisions of Regulation Z (12 CFR 1026.42), Regulation B (12 CFR 1002.14), OCC appraisal regulations (12 CFR 34), and OCC Bulletin 2010-42, "Sound Practices for Appraisal and Evaluations."

33. Review the appraisal and evaluation function to determine the independence of the function and the competency of the individuals administering the function. Determine whether

- those preparing a valuation or performing a valuation management function do not have a prohibited conflict of interest in the transaction.
- required independence in the appraisal function is fostered through reporting lines and compensation systems in the organizational structure.
- appraisers and evaluators, whether in-house or third-party providers, are appropriately independent from loan production and pressure from other sources that may attempt to influence the outcome of an appraisal or evaluation assignment.
- appraisers and evaluators are selected and engaged on the basis of their competency for valuing property on a case-by-case basis. Geographic and property-type competency, educational background, and experience are important elements to consider in selecting the appropriate provider.
- the bank has a process to ascertain that persons it engages to perform appraisals or provide evaluation services have no direct or indirect interest, financial or otherwise, in the property or transaction.
- the information the bank provides in its engagement of an appraiser or evaluator does not inappropriately influence the appraiser or suggest the property's value.
- persons independent of the loan production function oversee the selection of appraisers and persons providing evaluation services.
- the appraisal review process is appropriately independent of the loan production process.

34. Review the bank's process for establishing and maintaining its list of individuals qualified to perform appraisals, evaluations, and valuation reviews. Determine whether

- the bank has a process for evaluating the quality of work of appraisers and individuals providing evaluation services.
- findings are documented and are used by management in making periodic adjustments to the list.

35. Determine whether appraisal disclosures and copies of appraisals or valuations are provided to applicants in accordance with Regulation B (12 CFR 1002.14) and, as applicable, Regulation Z for HPMLs (12 CFR 1026.35(c)(6)).

36. Review the types of appraisals and evaluations that are in use. Determine whether management has established criteria for determining that the valuation methodology is appropriate to the risks associated with a particular transaction.

- If applicable, determine whether the valuation tools meet the GSE or third-party investor valuation standards pertaining to that category of real estate. In the case of a GSE, for a loan using the appraisal exemption section (12 CFR 34.43(a)(10)(ii)), determine whether the loan was sold to the GSE.
- If AVMs are used as a part of the evaluation process, a thorough review of the use of AVMs in the evaluation process is necessary. Refer to OCC Bulletin 2010-42, "Sound Practices for Appraisal and Evaluations," for more information. The following is a starting point for the review and is not meant to be all-inclusive:
  - Determine whether the bank did a thorough validation of models and continues to validate (and document) results periodically.
  - Consider (1) documentation of the validation's analysis, assumptions, and conclusions; (2) back-testing a representative sample of the valuations against market data on actual sales; and (3) whether the validation process covers properties representative of the geographic area and property type for which the tool is used.

Portfolio Management

37. Review monitoring systems for the credit quality of loan production. Determine

- the number and dollar volume of existing past-due loans, first and early payment default, and loans repurchased since the last examination by each retail and wholesale source.
- how the bank's credit quality compares with bank trends as well as against industry comparative data.
- whether the bank has any significant concentrations (product type, underwriting criteria, geography, etc.) and whether management is monitoring this exposure.

38. Determine whether the bank monitors loan documentation and underwriting exceptions by loan production source.

39. Assess the effectiveness of credit risk management and determine whether management is effectively supervising and analyzing the cause of delinquencies. Determine whether

- key financial statistics (e.g., credit score, LTV ratio, housing, and total debt coverage ratios) and their relationship to credit quality are tracked and analyzed.
- management is obtaining and analyzing past-due information on mortgages.
- management assesses the impact on delinquencies from changes in underwriting practices, origination channels, and new products.
- management is employing vintage analysis to actively track and monitor delinquencies, foreclosures, and losses.
- products and sources of production are compared over comparable periods of seasoning.

40. Determine whether management has sufficient MIS to detect changes in the risk profile of nontraditional mortgages and analyzes potential portfolio performance in a stressed environment. Consider whether

- the bank's MIS provides early warning reporting and vintage analysis to detect changes in the portfolio's risk profile.
- reporting systems allow management to isolate key loan products, layered nontraditional loan features, and borrower characteristics to allow early identification of performance deterioration.
- portfolio volume and performance results are tracked against expectations, internal lending standards, and policy limits.
- sensitivity analysis is performed on key portfolio segments to identify and quantify events that can increase risks within a segment or the entire portfolio.

Production Quality Control

41. Consider whether the QC plan covers all

- channels of production.
- mortgage products.
- underwriting methods.
- employees involved in the origination process.
- vendors or contractors involved in the origination process.

42. Review a sample of reports issued by the QC unit. Determine whether QC reports

- are analyzed according to mortgage broker, loan officer, underwriter or processor, branch office, builders, appraisers, settlement agents, product, geographic area, and other identified concentrations.
- are presented to personnel outside the production unit.

- accurately identify noncompliance with underwriting standards or procedures, whether underwriters properly refer suspected fraudulent loan activity, and whether reappraisal requests are properly initiated.
- provide qualitative analysis and make conclusions regarding trends, common deficiencies, and deficiency concentrations by branch, underwriter, broker, or correspondent.
- adequately document findings and conclusions.
- require corrective action for noted material exceptions.

43. Review the adequacy of the bank's QC program and determine whether it is independent of the production process (determining whether the bank performs the program internally or uses an outside vendor). Determine whether

- the QC unit tests a sample of closed loans from all origination channels to verify that underwriting and closing processes comply with bank policies, government regulations, and private mortgage insurers' policies (if applicable).
- if discretionary sampling is used, it is based on the lender's specific needs, such as sampling of specific offices, brokers and correspondents, staff persons, appraisers, higher-risk loans, nontraditional loans, and loans that may involve fraud.
- QC findings are effectively communicated and whether corrective action or response is required for significant deficiencies.
- management takes timely corrective action to resolve adverse QC findings.

44. Determine whether the bank has any material exposure to mortgage insurance providers. Ensure that management has a process in place to quantify the exposure and assess the credit risk of the insurance providers. Assess and determine

- PMI providers the bank uses as credit enhancements to the bank's portfolio (currently and in the past).
- aggregate exposure report by number and dollar for each provider.
- aging reports on claims submitted and the disposition of those claims.
- list of deferred payment obligations, if any.
- ALLL assessment and methodology.
- internal and external audit with management responses.

Fraud Detection

45. Determine the number of mortgage fraud referral cases identified since the last examination. Discuss significant cases with management to assess root causes and corrective actions taken.

46. Determine the number of suspicious activity reports relating to mortgage fraud submitted since the previous examination. Ensure that the bank's suspicious activity report submission process is effective.

47. Determine whether the individual or group responsible for fraud risk management

  - adequately trains originators, processors, underwriters, and servicing personnel to help identify loans with a higher risk for fraud, fraud schemes, and inconsistencies in borrower and property data that indicate potential fraud.
  - investigates fraud referral cases and resolves them promptly and effectively.
  - tracks loans repurchased because of fraud or misrepresentation.
  - identifies and communicates to the accounting unit fraud losses considered "operational losses" (as distinct from those considered "credit losses").

48. Determine whether effective systems, such as timely MIS, are in place to detect possible fraud.

49. Determine whether the bank uses pre-funding QC in addition to post-funding QC reviews for loans that are at higher risk for fraud. If so, determine the following:

  - Whether an appraisal and evaluation compliance review process is incorporated into any pre-funding QC program.
  - If a bank determines there is a high risk for inflated appraisals in certain loans, whether the bank uses a second valuation method (such as an AVM, BPO, or another appraisal) as a validation tool.
  - Whether the bank tracks all loan participants in instances of suspected fraud and determines each participant's involvement in the incident.
  - Whether the bank organizes data so that patterns of fraud can be recognized.
  - Whether management uses automated tools to help detect mortgage fraud, such as
    - information databases.
    - AVMs.
    - mortgage fraud databases—industry or internal.
    - fraud scoring models.

50. Determine whether adequate systems are in place to report mortgage fraud to appropriate authorities. Determine whether

  - required suspicious activity reports are promptly submitted to the appropriate authorities and whether investors are appropriately notified of fraudulent activity, as required by investor agreements.
  - processes are in place to report fraud to title insurers and the bank's insurer.
  - there is a process in place to make a referral to the appropriate state appraiser board if suspected fraud involves a state-licensed appraiser.

Servicing

Conclusion: Based on the responses to procedures, the quantity of risks is (low, moderate, or high), and the quality of risk management for the bank's loan-servicing activities is (strong, satisfactory, or weak).

Objective: To assess risks associated with mortgage servicing and determine whether servicing activities are executed in compliance with applicable laws, rulings, regulations, guidance, and board-approved strategic mandates.

Primary Examination Procedures

1. Determine whether the bank has sufficient policies, procedures, and staff to comply with all federal regulations (e.g., Regulations X and Z) and state law. The bank should pay particular attention to practices surrounding disclosures, escrow management, error resolution procedures, borrower information requests, force-placed insurance, default management, including loan modification and foreclosure processes, and continuity of contact practices.

2. Review the delinquency, default, or foreclosure rates for loans in the bank's portfolio with industry data. As a part of this exercise, evaluate the bank's servicing portfolio concentrations (agency, nonconforming, or nontraditional product type, subprime mortgages, high CLTV ratio, low credit score, high DTI, property types, geography, etc.). Ongoing reviews defined by clearly established risk assessment procedures should measure the need for additional staff, systems, and, potentially, a sub-servicer.

3. Review default management procedures for proper implementation of collection strategies on early-, mid-, and late-stage delinquency accounts. The bank should be employing consistent policies, procedures, and practices in its collection techniques to ensure compliance with applicable law (Regulations X and Z).

4. Determine whether the bank is experiencing a high or rapidly increasing cost to service. (**Note:** Current and projected profitability may need to be adjusted based on management's analysis of profitability on a product-by-product basis and how that analysis drives strategic business decisions.)

Supplemental Examination Procedures

Policies and Control Systems

1. Determine whether the board of directors, consistent with its duties and responsibilities, has adopted policies that adequately cover all facets of the servicing operation, including servicing nontraditional loan products or loans to subprime borrowers. Policies and internal controls should be in place to ensure compliance with applicable law (e.g., RESPA [12 CFR 1024] and TILA [12 CFR 1026] have requirements in connection with these types of actions), including the prevention of predatory servicing practices such as the following:

   - Failure to properly credit mortgage payments that are made on time, as a pretext for imposing unjustified late fees, and knowingly reporting borrowers to credit bureaus for the resulting false delinquencies.

- Force-placing high-cost insurance coverage on borrowers despite documentary evidence that satisfactory insurance is in effect. (When escrow accounts are insufficient to make these higher insurance premiums, monthly mortgage payments are increased, leading to further delinquencies and late fees.)
- Charging fees for services not specifically sanctioned in loan documents or in excess of what is normal and customary.
- Failure to inform borrowers about available loan modification options and to evaluate loan modification applications in a timely manner.
- Threatening borrowers with unjustified foreclosures (e.g., those caused solely by the servicer's own servicing practices).
- Failure to respond to customer inquiries and complaints about these practices adequately or in a timely manner.
- Failure to pay insurance or taxes (on loans with escrowed funds) in a timely manner, which could subject borrowers to unnecessary penalties.

2. Review policies and procedures in place to ensure the accuracy and integrity of information furnished to consumer reporting agencies.

3. Review the organizational chart for the servicing unit. Evaluate the qualifications and experience of senior management and key staff for major functional areas. Determine whether staff members have the special skills required to service nontraditional loan products or other special categories of loans or borrowers (e.g., service members), if applicable.

Personnel

4. Review the organizational chart and reporting structure for the servicing department. Determine whether

- overall responsibilities for all servicing marketing functions are centralized or otherwise meaningfully structured.
- personnel assigned to provide continuity of contact have adequate training and experience to provide loss mitigation information and evaluation of loss mitigation applications.
- responsibilities for investor accounting and reporting, document custodianship, escrow account administration, collections and default management, loan setup and payoff, OREO administration, and customer service are clearly defined.

Management Information Systems

5. Review the most recent management reports in which the operating results for the servicing unit are described. Determine whether the amount of detail provided is sufficient to supervise each servicing function.

Processes

Portfolio Supervision and Assessment

6. Determine the characteristics of the servicing portfolio, paying specific attention to the following:

    - Types of products (30-year fixed, 15-year fixed, ARMs, balloons, jumbos, hybrids)
    - Types of borrowers (prime versus nonprime)
    - Level of nontraditional mortgages, such as IO or payment-option ARMs
    - Level of mortgage loans with risk-layering features, such as reduced-documentation and simultaneous second-lien loans
    - Servicing portfolio reports may include
      - geographic dispersion and concentration of borrowers.
      - lien priority of loans in which municipal lending programs are available.
      - range of interest rates on the loans.
      - projected life of the loans.
      - average loan size.
      - average age of the loans.
      - delinquency level.
      - foreclosure level.
      - bankruptcy level.
      - loss experience.
      - amount of OREO.

7. Determine whether the bank has a QC program covering the major functional areas of the servicing unit. If so, assess its scope and effectiveness.

8. Evaluate the disaster recovery plan to determine that it covers all major servicing functions performed in-house. Consider whether

    - backup systems exist in case primary systems fail.
    - any unnecessary risk exposure exists.

9. Review the list of outside sub-servicers and vendors employed by the bank to perform servicing functions.

    - Verify that management assesses the financial condition of each sub-servicer and vendor.
    - Evaluate the bank's contingency plan to ensure that it addresses servicing responsibilities if sub-servicers or vendors fail to perform.
    - Assess the quality of work performed by sub-servicers and vendors and any associated risk(s).
    - Confirm that sub-servicers and vendors are complying with applicable law and the bank's policies and procedures.

Loan Setup

10. Determine how management ensures that loans, including nontraditional loan products, are set up accurately and in a timely manner (normally within 15 days of loan closing).

11. Determine the volume of loans not set up on the bank's servicing system before the first payment due date. Determine

    - reason(s) loans were not set up in a timely manner.
    - whether adequate systems are in place to notify the mortgagor where to send note payments.
    - impact on the servicing unit's operating performance.

Document Custodianship

12. Evaluate the procedures for safeguarding loan documents. Determine whether

    - loan documents are stored in a secured and protected area.
    - the bank's safekeeping facilities are appropriate.
    - the bank maintains a log of documents held in safekeeping.
    - the log identifies which documents have been removed and by whom.
    - copies of critical documents are stored separately from original documents.
    - processes for loan file imaging are adequate.
    - records are retained for the time periods required under Regulations X and Z.

Escrow Account Administration

13. Review the effectiveness of the system for ensuring the timely payments of taxes, insurance, and other obligations of borrowers.

14. Determine whether escrow account administration complies with 12 USC 2609 (RESPA) and its implementing regulation, Regulation X (12 CFR 1024.17):

    - Evaluate the process for establishing the required escrow account balance at loan inception.
    - Determine whether the bank sends each borrower an annual statement itemizing the elements required by 12 USC 2609(c) and 12 CFR 1024.17(i).
    - Determine whether the bank accurately analyzes each escrow account annually.
    - Evaluate the appropriateness of the bank's calculation method and assumptions.

15. Determine whether the bank sends the borrower a statement showing the amount of any overage or shortage in the account and an explanation of how the bank will correct it in a timely manner.

    - Review the method for correcting shortages and surpluses in escrow accounts.

- Ensure that overages and shortages in escrow accounts are administered in accordance with requirements of RESPA (12 USC 2609 and 12 CFR 1024.17(f)).

16. Review the method for substantiating that insurance is in place for each property. Determine whether the bank uses a blanket insurance policy or forced-placement flood insurance (a bank-purchased policy covering a specific property or a portfolio of properties) for borrowers with expired insurance. Consider whether

- force placement of hazard insurance complies with 12 CFR 1024.17(k)(5) and 1024.37.
- force placement of flood insurance complies with 12 CFR 22.5 or 172.5.
- sufficient notice to borrowers is given if evidence of insurance is not provided, consistent with 12 CFR 1024.37 for hazard insurance and 12 CFR 22.7 and 172.7 for flood insurance.
- force-placed insurance is required and if the bank has policies in place to reduce the impact of payment shock.
- controls exist for a process to ensure accurate identification of insurance shortfall and the timely cancellation of a force-placed insurance policy once the borrower provides evidence that adequate insurance coverage is obtained.[93]

17. Review the method for substantiating that required flood insurance is in place for each property including review of revisions to flood maps. Determine the adequacy of management's process to force-place flood insurance on loans lacking required flood insurance and loans with an insufficient amount of flood insurance, pursuant to 12 CFR 22.7 and 172.7, as appropriate.

18. Review the procedures for ensuring that tax and insurance payments are made on delinquent loans. Evaluate their effectiveness.

19. Evaluate the adequacy of systems in place for preventing the use of escrow custodial balances to meet other bank obligations.

20. Determine the volume of serviced loans that do not have an escrow requirement.

21. Evaluate how the bank documents that tax and insurance payments are current for these loans.

22. Review management reports to determine the number and dollar volume of loans for which the bank does not have a hazard insurance policy in place. Determine how management protects the bank against losses on those loans.

23. Review management reports detailing loans lacking required flood insurance and loans with an insufficient amount of flood insurance. Determine how management protects the

---

[93] Refer to 42 USC 4012a(e)(3) (flood insurance) and 12 CFR 1024.37(g) (hazard insurance).

bank against losses on these loans. Coordinate findings with OCC consumer compliance examiners.

24. Determine the number and dollar volume of loans with a delinquent tax bill.

25. Determine how management monitors delinquent taxes on non-escrowed accounts.

26. Determine how management protects the bank and investor's lien position on those properties.

Customer Service

27. Determine the level of customer complaints the bank has received since the previous examination. Determine whether

   - any customer complaints may indicate predatory or abusive servicing practices.
   - customer service segregates complaints on nontraditional loan products.
   - customer service segregates complaints by servicing process (e.g., inquiries related to general administration inquiries, escrow, loss mitigation, foreclosure, and payoff).

28. Determine whether the customer service unit appropriately informs the bank's senior management of significant and recurring complaints. Determine whether

   - customer complaints are appropriately resolved.
   - processes and reporting history of dropped calls indicate whether system or staffing is sufficient to handle call volume during peak periods.
   - specific training needs are identified and implemented.

Collections and Default Management

These supplemental examination procedures should be used when a bank has significant exposure to collections and default management activity.

Conclusion: Based on the responses to procedures, the quantity of risks is (low, moderate, or high), and the quality of risk management for the bank's collection and default management activities is (strong, satisfactory, or weak).

Objective: To evaluate the quantity of risks associated with collections and default management and whether activities are executed in compliance with applicable laws, rulings, regulations, guidance, and board-approved strategic mandates.

Supplemental Examination Procedures

1. Review key reports for collection and default management. Consider whether reports include key performance indicators for the collection department and for individual collectors against established standards. Consider

- daily and monthly metrics for inbound and outbound collection calls.
- reporting systems to track and monitor loss mitigation activities, bankruptcies, and foreclosures.

2. Review collection strategies for early-, mid-, and late-stage delinquent accounts. Consider whether

- call programs are appropriately prioritized by risk (e.g., high-risk and large-balance accounts). (**Note:** Regulation X early intervention and continuity of contact may require good faith effort for live contact by 36th day of delinquency, written notice, and assigned personnel by 45th day of delinquency.)
- staffing plans adequately address peak calling periods. This could vary depending on the geographic location and concentration of the servicing portfolio.
- collection calls are initiated in a timely manner for first and early payment defaults, consistent with the requirements of 12 CFR 1024.39.
- systems identify accounts with no contact within a specified time frame.

3. Review procedures for collecting delinquent loans, including nontraditional loans and subprime loan products. Determine whether

- collection efforts follow applicable laws, including RESPA, Regulation Z, and the Fair Debt Collection Practices Act.
- the bank documents all attempts to collect past-due payments, including the date(s) of borrower contact, the nature of the communication, and the borrower's response or commitment.
- the bank conducts appropriate property inspections for delinquent loans.
- the bank engages in nonabusive collection practices.
- management uses adequate methods to ensure that the bank complies with applicable state and federal laws and regulations.

4. Determine whether

- early contact is made with borrowers who have nontraditional loan products subject to payment shock.
- early contact is made with borrowers who have other kinds of loans whose low initial start rates have not yet reset.
- early contact is made with borrowers after increased payment requirements go into effect.
- records are retained for the time periods required under Regulations X and Z.
- early intervention processes that comply with Regulation X are in place for delinquent customers.

5. Determine whether a behavior-scoring modeling is used in the collection process. Consider whether

   - behavior-scoring models are subject to model validation or review by internal audit.
   - behavior scores provide appropriate portfolio segmentation by risk (e.g., low-, medium-, and high-risk accounts).
   - sufficient attention is paid to collecting high-risk accounts.
   - customers' payment patterns are considered in the behavior-score model.
   - refreshed credit scores are periodically obtained for the portfolio and are appropriately included in the behavior-score model.

6. Evaluate the collection unit's call monitoring program, whether performed internally or outsourced, to monitor the quality and effectiveness of collection calls. Consider whether monitoring processes include identifying

   - consistency of collection techniques used across portfolio risk segments.
   - effective and efficient use of time in administering collection calls.
   - compliance with collection policies and procedures and regulatory requirements.
   - collectors with performance issues.
   - specific training needs.

7. Evaluate the collection unit's risk management process, including

   - monthly review of delinquencies, including roll rate analysis.
   - refreshing credit scores.
   - review of extension reports.
   - review of first and early payment defaults
   - third-party vendor agreements that include performance standards.
   - internal QA process.

8. Review outstanding investor advances and advances to cover borrowers' escrow account obligations for taxes and insurance,[94] and determine whether there are advances with uncollectible balances that should be charged off.

9. Determine whether effective policies, procedures, and workflows have been established to administer loss mitigation, bankruptcy, and foreclosure activities in accordance with Regulation X and supervisory guidance. Consider the bank's use of the following loss mitigation techniques:

   - Reinstatement or repayment plans
   - Partial mortgage insurance advance claim payments
   - Forbearance agreements

---

[94] 12 CFR 1024.17(k)(5) generally requires the bank to make advances to cover taxes and insurance payments from escrow even though a borrower is delinquent.

- Mortgage modifications
- Loan assumptions
- Pre-foreclosure or short sales
- Deed in lieu of foreclosures

10. Determine the number of foreclosure actions that have not been completed within the time periods allowed by investors and GSEs. Determine the reasons for delay and whether the bank has notified the investors.

11. Review the list of delinquent loans for which foreclosure action is delayed because of forbearance.[95] Select and review a sample of forbearance files. As appropriate, determine whether

- the bank has sound reasons for delaying foreclosure action.
- forbearance actions comply with bank policy.
- the bank appropriately documents the reasons for forbearance consistent with Regulation X restrictions on foreclosure referrals and foreclosure sales.

12. Consider the average foreclosure costs for each product type. Assess the adequacy of foreclosure reserves relative to the volume of loans currently in foreclosure and those severely delinquent, as well as average historical foreclosure costs.

- Confirm that the bank makes charge-offs, recoveries, and provision expenses directly to the foreclosure reserve.

13. Review loan delinquency reports. Select and review a sample of files for borrowers delinquent 121 days or more. Assess the bank's foreclosure process. Determine whether

- the bank initiates foreclosure proceedings in a timely manner and properly notifies borrowers of the initiation of foreclosure actions.
- the methods used by management to ensure that foreclosure procedures comply with applicable state and federal laws and regulations are effective.
- the bank has established a foreclosure reserve.

14. Assess the bank's process for handling delinquent loans in forbearance status. Determine whether

- the bank has sound reasons for delaying foreclosure action.
- forbearance actions comply with bank policy and loss mitigation requirements in 12 CFR 1024.41.
- the bank documents the reasons for forbearance.

---

[95] Refer to RESPA (12 CFR 1024.41) for loss mitigation requirements.

15. Determine whether the bank has incurred fines for failing to file mortgage release and satisfactions in accordance with applicable state laws and whether the amount of fines paid is reasonable.

Administration of OREO

16. When title has been or will be obtained to an OREO property, determine whether the bank follows applicable laws, regulations, and financial reporting rules.

17. Review the list of delinquent loans on which the bank has decided against proceeding with foreclosure or has decided to release the lien. Evaluate whether

    - the bank has accurately determined market value of the property in making a decision not to finalize a foreclosure.
    - the bank has notified the borrower, including required notice language (refer to the "Other Real Estate Owned" booklet of the *Comptroller's Handbook*).
    - the bank has notified local governments (refer to the "Other Real Estate Owned" booklet of the *Comptroller's Handbook*).

HELOC End-of-Draw

These supplemental examination procedures should be used when a bank has significant exposure to HELOC EOD.

Conclusion: Based on the responses to procedures, the quantity of risks is (low, moderate, or high), and the quality of risk management for the bank's HELOC activities is (strong, satisfactory, or weak).

Objective: To evaluate the quantity of risks and whether management is providing adequate oversight of risks associated with HELOC EOD exposure.

Supplemental Examination Procedures

1. Consider whether management has

    - acknowledged EOD as a potential exposure.
    - ensured EOD has the attention of the correct level of management to evaluate exposure and develop alternatives.
    - ensured that all key operating and control functions are involved in EOD program development, approval, and monitoring (audit, compliance, operations, IT, risk, legal, accounting, and business line management).
    - a clear understanding of the range of contract terms and potential alternatives given the composition of the HELOC portfolio (purchased portfolios, origination channels, product evolution, etc.).

- reporting packages that monitor what actually happens at EOD today (temporary extensions, transitions according to contract, full re-underwriting for a new draw period, re-underwriting under retention programs, flow to workout, etc.).
- a stated view of what it expects or prefers to occur at EOD (considering property values, borrower quality, risk appetite, etc.).
- a well-defined protocol and process map for how borrowers receive EOD offers/terms (workflow diagram).
- well-designed and effective borrower outreach programs that ensure all parties have sufficient and timely information to make prudent decisions.
- recognized gaps in information, resources, or systems capacity to either identify exposure or implement action.
- developed a project plan to address identified gaps in analysis or information.
- developed EOD solutions commensurate with the risk and complexity of the portfolio (for example, program terms that vary by balance, borrower quality, and property value; modification terms that are sustainable and improve the loan structure; etc.).
- assigned responsibility for program execution and follow-up.
- established HELOC (and EOD) line cancellation/suspension policies that are consistent with Regulation Z and the individual contracts.
- evidence that EOD policies and procedures are informed and updated through ongoing feedback from loss mitigation and EOD pilots, tests, and program performance results.
- ensured control systems have appropriately scoped-in EOD practices into reviews.

MIS Reports

2. Available information should include the following:

- The size and scope of HELOC origination volumes.
- The size, scope, and timing of EOD volumes.
- The range of contract terms and provisions that must be managed (including volumes under each major contract/provision type).
- The volumes of EOD accounts that have balloon or near-balloon (<= five years) payments rather than full amortization.
- The volume of contracts that allow EOD actions outside of management's preferred result (for example, borrower option to extend IO draw periods).
- Which underwriting criteria are likely to be the most problematic for EOD borrowers (e.g., CLTV, DTI, and geographic concentration limits).
- An approximation of the volume and percent of near- and medium-term EOD populations that would fail current underwriting standards of the bank (in aggregate and by specific criteria).
- Performance reporting that shows overall and segment performance for each post-EOD option (i.e., temporary extensions, transitions according to contract, full re-underwriting for a new draw period, re-underwriting under retention programs, flow to workout, etc.). Reporting should also compare actual performance to management expectations.

Policies and Procedures

3. Consider whether written policies and procedures address the following:

- Clearly articulated underwriting standards for new HELOCs that are consistent with OCC Bulletin 2005-22, "Home Equity Lending: Credit Risk Management Guidance," and Regulation Z if a high-cost mortgage loan.
- Re-age, renewal, and extension policies that are written, explicit, and designed to control the use of extensions, deferrals, renewals, and re-writes. Policies should be consistent with OCC Bulletin 2000-20, "Uniform Retail Credit Classification and Account Management Policy: Policy Implementation."
- Workout-program policies and procedures that require management to track and monitor all loss mitigation programs, including EOD. Reporting should track performance in aggregate and by significant program (loan product; program; borrower characteristic, such as troubled borrowers and troubled collateral; significant underwriting criteria; vintage; etc.), as well as exceptions to internal policies and regulatory guidance.
- Specific responsibility and authority for establishing EOD program terms and making changes to EOD underwriting criteria or modification structures.
- EOD-program re-write qualification criteria, including the expectation that borrowers will qualify under current, existing standards for new "through the door" borrowers if there is a refinancing or new legal obligation (ATR,[96] credit scores, CLTV ratio, etc.).
- EOD-program loan modifications that are consistent with OCC loan modification and accounting guidance, including Supervisory Memorandum 2009-7, "Guidance for the Treatment of Residential Real Estate Loan Modifications."
- Accounting policies that clearly address TDR consideration for all EOD actions.
- EOD-program collateral valuation methods, documentation, and reviews that are well defined and comply with appraisal regulations and interagency guidance.
- When EOD-related policy exceptions are permitted, what approvals are necessary and how exception volumes and performance are tracked.
- Operating policies that require any third parties involved in the EOD process to be subject to a formal program of oversight (such as approval process, control system review, performance reporting).
- ALLL policies that require consideration of EOD exposure and compliance with OCC Bulletin 2012-6, "Interagency Guidance on ALLL Estimation Practices for Junior Liens."

Control Systems

4. Consider whether control systems specifically target the following:

- HELOC re-writes and modifications, including any formal or informal EOD programs or initiatives.

---

[96] Refer to 12 CFR 1026.34 if the HELOC is a high-cost mortgage.

- Annual HELOC credit reviews for risk-based capital and line management purposes (including contract review for actions permissible under Regulation Z).
- Compliance with EOD-related regulatory policy (e.g., HELOC underwriting and account management, modifications, TDRs, and Regulation Z).
- Servicing system and other resource limitations when evaluating EOD programs and planned activities (e.g., ability to handle amortizing payments, workout programs, payment allocations, and contractual features).
- Correspondent and broker contracts for HELOC products to ensure they limit product terms and EOD parameters to bank-specified terms and conditions.
- HELOC/EOD related TDR and reserve/impairment determinations.
- Timely resolution of control deficiencies and open items from business line management for EOD reviews.
- Whether EOD issues are properly reported to appropriate senior management and board levels.
- Whether third parties involved in HELOCs (and EOD) are subject to QC, internal audit, or other independent control system reviews.

Third-Party Management

These supplemental examination procedures should be used when a bank has significant exposure to third-party providers.

Conclusion: Based on the responses to procedures, the quantity of risks is (low, moderate, or high), and the quality of risk management for the bank's third-party management activities is (strong, satisfactory, or weak).

Objective: To evaluate the quantity of risks and whether management is providing adequate oversight of risks associated with third-party management exposure.

Supplemental Examination Procedures

These procedures apply to any arrangements with third parties to provide RRE lending-related services to customers on the bank's behalf. Banks may partially or fully outsource loan originations through brokers and correspondents. AMCs may be used in conjunction with appraisal and evaluation activities. Credit bureaus or other vendors may be used in the development, implementation, and performance monitoring of credit scoring systems. Additionally, banks may outsource collection and foreclosure activities to collection agencies and attorneys.

The terms "third party," "third-party vendors," and "vendors" are used interchangeably throughout this section of procedures. "Vendor management" is the term used to describe the bank's process for overseeing these parties. Refer to OCC Bulletin 2013-29, "Third-Party Relationships: Risk Management Guidance," and OCC Bulletin 2002-16, "Bank Use of Foreign-Based Third-Party Service Providers: Risk Management Guidance," for additional information on OCC expectations.

1. Determine the adequacy of the bank's third-party vendor management program as it applies to RRE-related lending activities. Consider the following:

   - Does the vendor management policy clearly address expected analysis, documentation, and ongoing reporting requirements for vendors used (including appropriate servicing standards, as applicable under Regulation X)?
   - Has management designated an individual to be responsible for the program and delegated the authority necessary for its effective administration to that individual?
   - Does the process require maintenance of a complete list of third-party vendors used for RRE lending activities?
   - Does the process use specific criteria to identify "significant" vendors (for more rigorous reviews), such as the dollar amount of the contract, the importance of the service provided, or the potential risk involved in the activity?
   - Does the process's due diligence activities include requirements
     - for comprehensive, well-documented reviews by qualified staff?
     - for identification of any potential conflicts of interest with institution directors, officers, staff, and their related interests?
     - for addressing compliance with all applicable laws and regulations, including safety and soundness regulatory standards, and laws prohibiting lending discrimination and unfair or deceptive acts or practices?

2. Determine whether management has adequate controls, including policies and procedures and monitoring controls, to avoid becoming involved with a third party engaged in illegal, discriminatory, unfair, deceptive, abusive, or predatory lending practices or practices violating Regulation Z or other compliance regulations. Consider whether the third party is

   - lending predominantly on the liquidation value of collateral rather than the borrower's ability to repay the debt.
   - refinancing loans frequently.
   - refinancing special subsidized mortgages that contain terms favorable to the borrower.
   - requiring single-premium life insurance or similar products.
   - using negative amortization.
   - requiring balloon payments in short-term transactions.
   - charging pre-payment penalties in the later years of a loan.
   - charging high financing points, fees, or penalties.
   - making high-cost loans (for example, loans subject to HOEPA).

3. Determine the adequacy of contract management and focus on the process for ensuring that clauses necessary to effectively manage the vendor are included. Consider the following:

   - Does the bank have a current contract on file for all third-party vendors and does the bank monitor key dates (for example, maturity, renewal, and adjustment periods)?

- Do the contracts with significant vendors (based on a reviewed sample) satisfactorily address
  - the scope of the arrangement, including the frequency, content, and format of the services provided by each party?
  - the need to comply with certification, licensing, and other requirements?
  - adherence to training requirements, if any, imposed by the bank or other entity?
  - outsourcing notifications or approvals required, if the vendor proposes to subcontract a service to another party?
  - all costs and compensation, including any incentives?
  - performance standards, including when and if standards can be adjusted, and the consequences of failing to meet those standards?
  - reporting and MIS requirements?
  - data ownership and access?
  - appropriate privacy and confidentiality restrictions?
  - requirements for compliance with all applicable laws and regulations, including safety and soundness regulatory standards and laws prohibiting lending discrimination and unfair or deceptive acts or practices?
  - requirements that brokers in the mortgage loan origination process make best efforts to ensure that the mortgage loans offered to borrowers are consistent with their needs, objectives, and financial situations?
  - mandatory vendor control functions such as QA and audit, including requirements for submitting audit results to the bank?
  - expectations and responsibilities for business resumption and contingency plans?
  - responsibility for customer complaint resolution and associated reporting to the bank?
  - vendor financial statement submission requirements?
  - appropriate dispute resolution, liability, recourse, penalty, indemnification, and termination clauses?
  - the authority of the bank to perform on-site vendor reviews? Third-party performance of services is also subject to OCC examination oversight if warranted.
- Does the bank's monitoring of vendors' adherence to their contracts (especially to financial terms and performance standards) have sufficient frequency and scope?
- Does the bank's vendor management program have a process to resolve issues identified during monitoring in a timely and effective manner?

4. Determine the adequacy of the monitoring process for significant vendors. Consider the following:

- Does the bank's oversight process incorporate at a minimum
  - reports evidencing the third party's performance relative to service-level agreements and other contract provisions?
  - customer complaints and resolutions for the services and products outsourced?
  - third-party financial statements and audit reports?
  - compliance with applicable laws and regulations?

- Does the process result in an accurate determination of whether the contractual terms and conditions are being met, and whether any revisions to service level agreements or other terms are needed?
- Does management effectively follow up and document any performance, operational, or compliance-related problems in a timely manner?
- Does the relationship manager or other bank staff periodically meet with the vendors to discuss performance and operational issues?
- Does the bank's process adequately determine when on-site reviews are warranted, the scope of those reviews, and the reporting of the results?
- Does the process require management to formally evaluate and document the third party's ability to perform the contracted functions in a satisfactory manner based on reviews of performance and financial condition?

5. For brokers and other third-party mortgage loan originators, determine the adequacy of the process to qualify the third-party originator as an acceptable business partner to the bank. Does the process

- require tracking mechanisms and reports to comprehensively monitor credit performance statistics (e.g., volume of applications submitted, approved, and booked; quality of applications; exceptions; and loan performance)?
- require tracking reports for relationship profitability, including performance and profitability compared with projected performance?
- track and monitor compliance with the bank's RRE lending policies?
- maintain a watch list of problematic originators as well as the timeliness and appropriateness of any actions taken, including termination of the relationship?

6. Determine whether the bank is involved in any significant third-party relationships involving RRE lending activities when deficiencies in management expertise or controls result in the failure to adequately identify and manage the associated risk. Consider the following:

- Should the issue and management's expected corrective action be memorialized in the ROE as an MRA?
- Consult with the EIC and supervisory office to determine if it is appropriate to require that the activity be suspended until satisfactory and effective corrective action is in place.

Nontraditional Mortgages

These supplemental examination procedures should be used when a bank has significant exposures to nontraditional mortgage products or significant planned growth for nontraditional mortgage products. Many of the problematic features of nontraditional mortgages have been prohibited or restricted through changes to Regulation Z.[97]

Conclusion: Based on the responses to procedures, the quantity of risks is (low, moderate, or high), and the quality of risk management for the bank's nontraditional mortgage loan activities is (strong, satisfactory, or weak).

Objective: To evaluate the quantity of risks inherent in the bank's nontraditional mortgage loan activities and the quality of risk management practices in relation to the "Guidance on Nontraditional Mortgage Product Risks" issued in OCC Bulletin 2006-41, "Nontraditional Mortgage Products."[98]

Supplemental Examination Procedures

Procedures with "no" answers indicate potential weaknesses in risk management that need to be discussed with management. Management practices that are insufficiently justified should be discussed with the EIC to determine if an MRA should be included in the ROE to record the findings and management's expected corrective action.

1. Determine if the higher risks inherent in nontraditional mortgage products are appropriately considered by the board and management in conformance with interagency guidance. Do the board (through policy) and management (through procedures)

    -   ensure that loan terms and underwriting standards are consistent with prudent lending practices and regulatory requirements, including a determination of the borrower's repayment capacity consistent with the ATR and HOEPA rules in Regulation Z as applicable?
    -   recognize that many nontraditional mortgage loans, particularly when they have risk-layering features, warrant strong risk management standards, regulatory capital levels commensurate with the risk, and an ALLL that reflects the collectability of the portfolio?
    -   ensure that customers have sufficient information to clearly understand loan terms and associated risks before making a product choice?

---

[97] Examiners may wish to consult compliance examiners with questions on the applicability of Regulation Z and other applicable compliance laws and regulations as they review nontraditional mortgage loans.

[98] To the extent that the practices in the guidance are inconsistent with the requirements in Regulation Z, the requirements in the guidance are superseded by the regulatory requirements.

2. Determine if the loan terms and underwriting standards for nontraditional mortgage loans reflect the risks associated and risk management expected in the interagency guidance. Consider the following:

- Does the bank's analysis of borrower repayment capacity for nontraditional mortgage loan products that permit negative amortization include the initial loan amount plus any balance increase that may accrue from the negative amortization provision?
- Does the bank's analysis of borrower repayment capacity for nontraditional mortgage loan products that permit negative amortization or IO payments include an evaluation of the borrower's ability to repay the debt by final maturity at the fully indexed rate, assuming a fully amortizing repayment schedule?
- Do the bank's underwriting standards for nontraditional mortgage loan products
  - specifically avoid creating a heightened need for the borrower to rely on the sale or refinancing of the property once amortization begins? (Loans to individuals who do not demonstrate the capacity to repay, as structured, from sources other than the collateral pledged are generally unsafe or unsound and inconsistent with Regulation Z's ATR rule.)
  - specifically require that when risk-layering features exist, demonstrated mitigating factors supporting the underwriting decision and the borrower's repayment capacity must be documented?
  - specifically limit the use of reduced documentation and unverified income and require more diligent verification and documentation commensurate with the level of credit risks inherent in the transaction or product and consistent with regulatory requirements?
  - specifically require that any ITIN loans are effectively underwritten and documented and ITIN portfolio concentration limits are established?
  - generally preclude a payment structure that allows for delayed amortization or negative amortization when minimal or no owner equity exists at origination, such as situations with HLTV, simultaneous second-lien loans or lines of credit?
  - specifically address applicable interagency guidance for subprime lending when targeted to subprime borrowers?
  - require that borrowers financing non-owner-occupied investment properties
    - qualify for the loan based on their ability to service the debt over the life of the loan?
    - maintain sufficient borrower equity over the life of the loan through an appropriate CLTV ratio that considers negative amortization?
    - reflect evidence that the borrower has sufficient cash reserves to service the loan, considering the possibility of extended periods of property vacancy and the variability of debt service requirements?
- Do the bank's loan terms and use of introductory interest rates specifically seek to minimize the likelihood of disruptive early recasting of monthly payments, negative amortization, and extraordinary payment shocks at the end of the introductory rate period?

3. Determine if the portfolio and risk management practices for nontraditional mortgage loan products reflect the risks and risk management expected in the interagency guidance. Consider whether the bank has

   - developed written policies that specify acceptable product attributes, production and portfolio limits, sales and securitization practices, and risk management expectations.
   - designed enhanced performance measures and management reporting that provide early warning for increasing risk.
   - established appropriate ALLL levels that consider credit quality of the portfolio and conditions that affect collectability.
   - maintained regulatory capital at levels that reflect portfolio characteristics and the effect of stressed economic conditions on collectability. Banks should hold regulatory capital commensurate with the risk characteristics of their nontraditional mortgage loan portfolios.

4. Determine the adequacy of the bank's governing policy for nontraditional mortgages. Does the policy

   - set appropriate limits on risk layering?
   - include appropriate risk mitigation tools?
   - set growth and volume limits by loan type, with special attention to products and product combinations in need of heightened attention due to easing terms or rapid growth?
   - reference regulatory requirements that prohibit or otherwise limit certain features of nontraditional mortgage loans?

5. Determine if the bank has well-developed monitoring and risk management practices governing concentrations in nontraditional mortgage loans. Does the bank monitor and track concentrations

   - in key portfolio segments such as loan types, third-party originations, geographic area, and property occupancy status?
   - in portfolio characteristics such as loans with high CLTV ratios, loans with high DTI ratios, loans with the potential for negative amortization, loans to borrowers with credit scores below established thresholds, loans with risk-layered features, and non-owner-occupied investor loans?

6. Determine if the bank has well-developed controls to monitor compliance with underwriting standards and exceptions granted for nontraditional mortgage loans. Consider the following:

   - Does the QC function regularly review a sample of nontraditional mortgage loans from all origination channels and a representative number of underwriters to confirm policies are followed?
   - Does the bank hold business-line managers accountable for corrective action when control systems or operating practices are found to be deficient?

- Does the bank have low exception tolerances and strong controls over accruals, customer service, and collections given the borrower's ability to defer P&I payments for extended periods of time?
- Does the bank limit and carefully monitor re-ages, payment deferrals, and loan modifications on nontraditional mortgage loans?
- Does the bank provide customer service and collection personnel with product-specific training on the features and potential customer issues with nontraditional mortgage products?
- Does the bank have adequate early intervention processes in place for delinquent loans?[99]

7. Determine if the bank has strong systems and controls in place for establishing and maintaining relationships with third-party originators of nontraditional mortgage loans. Does the bank

- perform specific due diligence procedures before entering into a third-party relationship that involves originations of nontraditional mortgage products?
- specifically monitor and report on the quality of third-party-originated nontraditional mortgage loans in relation to underwriting standards and compliance with applicable laws and regulations?
- specifically track the quality of loans by origination source and key borrower characteristics in order to proactively identify problems such as early payment defaults, incomplete documentation, and fraud?
- require immediate remedial action (including termination of a relationship) when documentation issues or customer complaints are discovered and uncorrected?

8. Determine if the bank has management information and reporting systems that allow for detection of changes in the risk profile of a nontraditional mortgage portfolio. Consider the following:

- Does the structure and content of MIS allow for the isolation of key loan products, risk-layering features, and borrower characteristics? The following breakdowns reflect minimum expectations:
  - Information by loan type (for example, IO mortgage loans and payment option ARMs).
  - Information by risk-layering features (for example, payment option ARMs with stated income and IO mortgage loans with simultaneous second-lien mortgages).
  - Information by underwriting characteristics (for example, LTV, DTI, and credit score).
  - Information by borrower performance (for example, payment patterns, delinquencies, interest accruals, and negative amortization).
- Does the MIS for portfolio volumes and performance reflect tracking against expectations, projections, internal lending standards, and policy limits? Volume and

---

[99] Required by Regulation X.

performance expectations should be established at the sub-portfolio and aggregate portfolio levels.
- Does the MIS reflect regular variance analyses to identify exceptions to policies and approved limits? Qualitative analysis should occur when actual performance deviates from established policies and limits.
- Does the bank use variance analysis as a critical component in monitoring the nontraditional mortgage portfolio's risk characteristics and as an integral part of establishing and adjusting risk tolerance limits?

9. Determine if the bank's size and complexity warrant appropriate sensitivity analysis or stress testing on key portfolio segments to identify and quantify events that may increase risk in a segment or entire portfolio. Consider the following:

- Does the volume of nontraditional mortgage loans held, sold, or serviced reflect a significant portion of the overall RRE lending activities or a concentration (greater than 25 percent) in regulatory capital?
- Does the scope of stress testing conducted include key performance drivers such as interest rates, employment levels, economic growth, housing value fluctuations, and other factors beyond the bank's immediate control?
- Does the stress testing assume a rapid deterioration in one or more factors and attempt to estimate the potential influence on default rates and loss severity?
- Does the stress testing aid the bank in identifying, monitoring, and managing risk, as well as developing appropriate and cost-effective loss mitigation strategies?
- Does the stress testing provide direct feedback in the determination of underwriting standards, product terms, portfolio concentration limits, and regulatory capital levels?

10. Determine the overall quantity of risk inherent in the bank's nontraditional mortgage loan activities as low, moderate, or high. Consider

- the type of nontraditional mortgage products offered, originated, held, and sold by the bank.
- the volumes of nontraditional mortgage products originated, held, and sold by the bank in relation to the total RRE portfolio, the total volumes of mortgage loans sold, and the bank's regulatory capital position.
- the performance of the bank's nontraditional mortgage portfolios (held and sold) based on delinquency and losses.
- the risk profile of the bank's nontraditional mortgage portfolios based on distribution of balances by credit scores and LTV or current LTV.

11. Determine if the quality of risk management is commensurate with the quantity of risks inherent in the bank's nontraditional mortgage loan activities.

- If the quality of risk management activities is not commensurate with the quantity of risks being assumed by the bank, discuss the results with the EIC.
- From discussions with the EIC, determine if the findings should be recorded in the ROE as an MRA with appropriate management corrective actions.

Conclusions

Conclusion: The aggregate level of each associated risk is (low, moderate, or high).
The direction of each associated risk is (increasing, stable, or decreasing).

Objective: To determine, document, and communicate overall findings and conclusions regarding the examination of RRE lending.

1. Determine preliminary examination findings and conclusions and discuss with the EIC, including

   - quantity of associated risks (as noted in the "Introduction" section).
   - quality of risk management.
   - aggregate level and direction of associated risks.
   - overall risk in RRE lending.
   - violations and other concerns.

Summary of Risks Associated With RRE Lending				
Risk category	Quantity of risk (Low, moderate, high)	Quality of risk management (Weak, satisfactory, strong)	Aggregate level of risk (Low, moderate, high)	Direction of risk (Increasing, stable, decreasing)
Credit				
Interest rate				
Liquidity				
Operational				
Compliance				
Strategic				
Reputation				

2. If substantive safety and soundness concerns remain unresolved that may have a material adverse effect on the bank, further expand the scope of the examination by completing verification procedures.

3. Discuss examination findings with bank management, including violations, recommendations, and conclusions about risks and risk management practices. If necessary, obtain commitments for corrective action.

4. Compose conclusion comments, highlighting any issues that should be included in the ROE. If necessary, compose an MRA comment.

5. Update the OCC's information system and any applicable ROE schedules or tables.

6. Write a memorandum specifically setting out what the OCC should do in the future to effectively supervise RRE lending in the bank, including time periods, staffing, and workdays required.

7. Update, organize, and reference work papers in accordance with OCC policy.

8. Ensure that any paper or electronic media that contain sensitive bank or customer information are appropriately disposed of or secured.

Internal Control Questionnaire

An ICQ helps an examiner assess a bank's internal controls for an area. ICQs address standard controls that provide day-to-day protection of bank assets and financial records. The examiner decides the extent to which it is necessary to complete or update ICQs during examination planning or after reviewing the findings and conclusions of the general assessment.

Policies

1. Has the board of directors, consistent with its duties and responsibilities, adopted written RRE LPM policies and objectives that

   - establish suggested guidelines for aggregate outstanding RRE loans in relation to other loan portfolio balances and balance sheet activities?
   - outline portfolio management objectives for distribution of loans in RRE-secured primary categories of first mortgages, second mortgages, and HELOCs and significant subsegments such as nontraditional mortgages, reverse mortgages, HLTV mortgages, and investor-owned mortgages, that acknowledge
     - concentrations of credit within specific mortgage products, channels of origination, loan characteristics, etc.?
     - the need to employ residential lending personnel with specialized knowledge and experience?
     - community service obligations of affordable housing programs?
     - possible conflicts of interest?
     - possible fair lending risks?[100]
   - establish loan authority of committees and individual lending officers?
   - define acceptable types of RRE loans?
   - define acceptable types of RRE properties to secure loans and lines of credit?
   - establish geographic limits for RRE loans?
   - define maximum maturities for various types of RRE loans?
   - define RRE loan pricing?
   - establish minimum financial information required at inception of RRE loans and lines of credit?
   - establish standards for appraisal and evaluation of RRE properties securing loans and lines of credit?
   - define a maximum advance as a percentage of appraised value or purchase price?
   - define limits on the amount of negative amortization, when allowed, on a mortgage compared with its current market value?
   - define sound review standards for RRE loan applications that require the underwriting analysis and decision to be fully documented?

---

[100] Refer to OCC Bulletin 2013-38, "Statements on Qualified Mortgage Loans."

- define minimum standards for fully documenting an approved RRE loan or line of credit?
- establish limitations on the number or amount of loans involving an individual borrower or investor?
- establish limits and guidelines for purchasing RRE loans from brokers and other third-party originators?
- establish limits and guidelines for selling RRE loans to the GSEs and other third-party investors?
- establish guidelines for RRE loans and lines of credit to the bank's directors, officers, principal shareholders, and their related interests?
- establish minimum standards for the qualification of borrowers for various nontraditional, subprime, or other unique RRE loan products such as ARMs, low introductory rate loans, etc.?
- establish oversight of and limits for exceptions to policy?

2. Are RRE LPM policies and objectives reviewed at least annually to determine if they are compatible with changing RRE market conditions?

3. Does the bank have written collection, loss mitigation, and foreclosure policies and procedures for RRE lending that have been approved by the board of directors?

4. Does the bank have a written schedule of fees, rates, terms, and collateral requirements for all RRE loan and line of credit products offered?

Documentation

1. Does the bank have specific loan documentation procedures and requirements?

2. Does the bank require a written application for RRE loans and lines of credit?

3. Does the bank verify each applicant's income, employment, and financial condition before making a commitment on an RRE loan?[101]

4. Are procedures in effect to ensure compliance with the requirements of government agencies insuring or guaranteeing the RRE loans?

5. Has a system for maintaining adequate loan document files been established, including

- a check sheet to assure that required documents are received and on file?
- inspection performed by internal loan administration personnel?

---

[101] Refer to 12 CFR 1026.34 and 1026.43.

6. Are procedures in effect to protect RRE loan documents from theft, damage, or inappropriate release?

    - Are collateral releases executed only after required payments have been cleared?
    - Are lien releases reviewed and approved by an officer or officers based on the size of the RRE loan?

7. Are all RRE loan commitments issued in written form?

Loan Interest and Commitment Fees

1. Is the preparation of interest earned or loan fee records reviewed by personnel who do not issue checks or drafts or handle cash?

2. Are interest and fee computations made and tested by persons who do not also issue checks or drafts or handle cash?

3. Does the bank properly account for deferred and earned RRE loan fees?

Record Keeping

1. Is the preparation and posting of subsidiary RRE loan records performed or reviewed by persons who do not also issue official checks or drafts or handle cash?

2. Are the subsidiary RRE loan records reconciled daily with the appropriate general ledger accounts and are reconciling items investigated by persons who do not also issue official checks or drafts or handle cash?

3. Are delinquent account collection requests and past-due notices checked to the trial balances used in reconciling RRE loan subsidiary records to general ledger accounts and are they handled by persons who do not also issue official checks or drafts or handle cash?

4. Are contacts with delinquent borrowers and borrowers in the loan modification process documented?

5. Are detailed statements of account balances and activity mailed to mortgagors at least annually, or periodically, if required by Regulation Z?

6. Are inquiries about RRE loan balances received and investigated by persons who do not also handle cash?

7. Are documents supporting recorded credit adjustments checked or tested by persons who do not also handle cash?

8. Is a daily record maintained summarizing RRE loans made, payments received, and interest collected to support applicable general ledger accounts?

9. Are note and liability ledger trial balances prepared and reconciled to controlling accounts by employees who do not process or record loan transactions?

10. Are records and files for serviced RRE loans segregated and identifiable?

11. Is an overdue accounts report generated and distributed to parties responsible for its review on timely basis?

12. Are loan officers prohibited from processing loan payments?

13. Are loan payments received by mail recorded upon receipt independently before being sent to and processed by a note teller?

14. Are advance loan payments adequately controlled if they are not immediately credited to the RRE loan account?

15. Are properties under foreclosure proceedings segregated?

Insurance and Escrow

1. Does the bank require escrow accounts for taxes and insurance, and include such payments when qualifying borrowers?

2. Does the bank have a mortgage blanket hazard insurance policy?

3. Is there an effective, formalized system for determining whether insurance premiums are current on RRE collateral properties?

4. Does the bank require that insurance policies include a loss payable clause to the bank?

5. Are disbursements for taxes and insurance supported by records showing the nature and purpose of the disbursements?

6. If advance deposits for taxes and insurance are not required, does the bank have an effective system for determining whether taxes and insurance have been paid?

Reports

1. Are the following reported to the board of directors or its committees (indicate which) at their regular meetings at least monthly?

   • Past-due RRE loans and lines of credit.
   • Nonaccrual RRE loans and lines of credit.

- RRE loans and lines of credit recommended for charge-off.
- Net losses on RRE loans and lines of credit.
- Total outstanding loan balances and open commitments to lend on HELOCs.
- Newly originated RRE loans and lines of credit, including loans
  - approved as exceptions to approved policies.
  - approved from each major channel of loan production.
  - purchased from correspondents and brokers.
  - originated or purchased for sale that were subsequently determined to be unmarketable.
- Restructured, deferred, re-aged, and modified RRE loans and lines of credit.
- RRE loans and lines of credit requiring special attention or classification.
- Stratification of RRE loan portfolios and lines of credit by current risk grade, credit score, or behavior score.
- Stratification of RRE loan portfolios and lines of credit by LTV ratio (original or updated).
- Stratification of RRE loan portfolios and lines of credit by vintage of origination (including analysis of performance since origination).
- Results of QC reviews (pre-funding and post-funding).
- Results of appraisal reviews.

2. Are reports submitted to the board or its committees rechecked by a designated individual for possible omissions before their submission?

If a bank produces substantial volumes of RRE loans originated or purchased for sale to third-party investors, or services significant volumes of loans for others, refer to the "Internal Control Questionnaire" in the "Mortgage Banking" booklet of the *Comptroller's Handbook* for additional questions.

Loan Review

1. Does the bank have a loan review function or equivalent that reviews the RRE lending activities?

2. Is the loan review function independent of the RRE lending function?

3. Are the initial results of the loan review process submitted to a person or committee who is also independent of the RRE lending function?

4. Do specific criteria and cut-offs exist for determining which RRE loans and lines of credit are reviewed?

5. Do RRE lending officers recommend loans for review?

6. Are internal loan reviews of the RRE lending activities conducted at least annually?

7. In a smaller bank with an officer identification system, are guidelines in effect that define the consequences of an officer withholding a significant RRE loan from the review process?

8. Is the bank's problem loan list periodically updated by residential lending officers to include significant problem RRE loans and lines of credit?

9. Does the bank maintain a list of RRE loans and lines of credit reviewed, the date of the review, and the credit rating?

10. Does the loan review section prepare summary reports detailing the results of the review of RRE lending activities?

11. Are the loan review summations of RRE lending activities maintained in a central location or in appropriate credit files?

12. Are follow-up procedures in effect for significant internally classified RRE loans, including an update memorandum to the appropriate credit file?

13. Is a systematic and progressively stronger follow-up notice procedure utilized for delinquent RRE loans and lines of credit?

Internal and External Audit

1. Has the board established internal and external coverage of the RRE lending activities?

2. Are the scope and coverage of RRE lending activities commensurate with the size, scale, and complexity of the activities?

3. Are the internal and external audit reports submitted to a person or committee who is independent of the RRE lending function?

4. Do specific criteria exist detailing the expectations and time frames for management's responses to internal and external audit findings?

Nontraditional, Non-QM, and Subprime RRE Loans

1. Does the bank have a nontraditional, non-QM, or a subprime RRE loan program?

2. Is the bank tracking performance of the nontraditional, non-QM, and subprime RRE loans based on

   • product type?
   • CLTV ratio?
   • credit score?
   • ATR?

- originating office, channel, or officer?
- broker or correspondent?
- other significant characteristic?

3. Does the bank use the same underwriting standards for sold or held-for-sale nontraditional, non-QM, or subprime RRE loans as it does for its portfolio loans?

4. Does the bank sell nontraditional, non-QM, or subprime RRE loans without any form of implicit or explicit recourse?

5. Are representations and warranties for nontraditional, non-QM, or subprime RRE loans standard and limited to 120 days?

6. When repurchase obligations for nontraditional, non-QM, or subprime RRE loans are significant, does the bank maintain adequate reserve accounts for such contingencies?

7. Has the bank had to repurchase a significant amount of sold nontraditional, non-QM, or subprime RRE loans?

Conclusions for RRE Loans

1. Is the foregoing information considered an adequate basis for evaluating internal control in that there are no significant additional internal auditing procedures, accounting controls, administrative controls, or other circumstances that impair any controls or mitigate any weaknesses indicated during the completion of the ICQ? (Explain negative answers briefly and indicate conclusions as to their effect on specific examination or verification procedures.)

2. Based on answers to the foregoing questions, internal controls for RRE lending activities are considered (strong, satisfactory, or weak).

Verification Procedures

Verification procedures are used to verify the existence of assets and liabilities, or test the reliability of financial records. Examiners generally do not perform verification procedures as part of an examination. Rather, verification procedures are performed when substantive safety and soundness concerns are identified that are not mitigated by the bank's risk management systems and internal controls.

Consideration also should be given to directing the board to contract with an independent auditor to perform these or similar procedures.

1. Reconcile the trial balance(s) to the general ledger. Include loan commitments and any other contingent liabilities in the testing.

2. Using an appropriate sampling technique, select loans from the trial balance and

   - prepare and mail confirmation forms to borrowers. (Loans serviced for other institutions or investors should be confirmed with the other institution, the investor, and the borrower. Confirmation forms should include the borrower's name, loan number, original amount, interest rate, current loan balance, contingency and escrow account balance, and a brief description of the collateral.)
     - After a reasonable time period, mail second requests.
     - Follow up on any no-replies or exceptions and resolve differences.
   - examine notes for completeness and reconcile date, amount, and terms to trial balance.
     - If any notes are not held at the bank, request confirmation with the holder.
     - Confirm that required initials of approving officer are on the note.
     - Confirm that the note is signed, appears to be genuine, and is negotiable.
   - compare collateral property legal description in files with legal description of collateral property in mortgages and deeds of trust. List and investigate all collateral discrepancies.
   - determine that each file contains documentation supporting any guarantees or subordination agreements, when appropriate.
   - determine that any required homeowner's insurance coverage is adequate and that the bank is named as loss payee.[102]
   - review escrow disbursement records, and determine if disbursements are authorized and documented appropriately for payments to property tax-collecting entities and insurance companies.

3. Review the accrued interest accounts and

   - review procedures for accounting for accrued interest and handling of adjustments.

---

[102] Flood insurance may be reviewed during transaction testing of a flood compliance exam.

- scan accrued interest and income accounts for any unusual entries and follow up on any unusual items by tracing to initial and supporting records.

4. Obtain or prepare a schedule showing the amount of monthly interest income and the RRE loan balances at the end of each month since the last examination, and

- calculate or check yield.
- investigate significant fluctuations or trends.

5. Using a list of nonaccruing loans, check loan accrual records to confirm that interest income is not being accrued or is being addressed through financial means (accrued at the account level to maintain integrity of account records but reversed at the general ledger level to preclude overstatement of income).

Appendixes

Appendix A: Suggested Request Items for RRE Lending Activities

1. Copies of board-level reports for all RRE lending activities since the last examination.

2. A list of board and senior management committees that supervise RRE lending activities. Include a list of members and meeting schedules. Provide copies of the minutes for each meeting since the last examination.

3. Copies of all loan policies and procedures that govern RRE lending activities, including copies of any specific underwriting risk acceptance criteria, matrices, or worksheets.

4. Copies of all rate sheets used to evaluate applicants for approval referred to by the loan originator and servicing, as well as record retention policies and procedures.

5. An inventory listing of all key reports used by management to monitor and control all RRE lending activities. Provide the name of each report, the producer(s) of each report, the user(s) of each report, and how often the report is produced for distribution.

6. Copies of the most recent version of each key management report listed in the inventory. Reports would include summary reports showing current volumes and past trends in

   - outstanding balances of products and portfolios.
   - originations and yields.
   - product or portfolio delinquencies.
   - product or portfolio nonaccrual loans or lines.
   - product or portfolio TDRs.
   - product or portfolio extensions, deferrals, modifications, and re-ages.
   - product or portfolio loss write-offs (charge-offs) and recoveries.
   - product or portfolio distributions by original or refreshed credit bureau scores.

7. For larger departmental and operational activities (and portfolio lenders if appropriate), copies of

   - the organizational chart for the department or operation, including each primary functional area.
   - formal job descriptions for principal department or operation positions.
   - résumés of principal officers in the department or operation.
   - compensation plans for managers of the department or operation, including incentive plans.
   - balance sheet and income statements for the department or operation as of the examination date and most recent year-end.

- budget for the department or operation at the beginning of the year and budget revisions as of the examination date. (For balance sheet, income statement, and budget, please provide copies of the materials used by the bank to manage the department or operation.)
- marketing plans for the RRE lending activities as directed through the department or operation.

8. A summary listing of all RRE lending products offered by the bank. Include a brief description that details their characteristics, including pricing.

9. Copies of all internal and external audit reports and loan review reports covering RRE lending activities since the last examination and copies of any management responses.

10. Copies of any internal and external audit or loan review issue tracking logs maintained that reflect the tracking of issues noted for RRE lending activities.

Appendix B: HELOC End-of-Draw Request Letter

Subject: Home Equity Line-of-Credit (HELOC) End-of-Draw (EOD) Transition Review

Dear _____,

We are performing a range-of-practice review to evaluate how lenders are managing HELOCs that are at or near their EOD periods, along with home equity balloons (End of Term). We have noted significant loan volumes that are scheduled to either mature or transition to an amortization phase in the near future, and we would like to ensure that lenders have appropriately considered the issues and risks. We are visiting all our large banks with sizable HELOC portfolios to review planned responses and discuss expectations and alternatives.

We would like to learn more about how your company manages borrower transitions from the credit-line access and lower payments typical during draw periods to the higher payments associated with amortization or maturity. We expect many banks will have issues with refinancing borrowers into new HELOCs (and therefore new interest-only draw periods) since underwriting standards have tightened and housing values are generally lower than when the lines were first granted. Given the challenges, we are particularly interested in how lenders are approaching account management and loss mitigation programs; accounting practices such as troubled-debt restructure recognition, income recognition, and ALLL segmentation; capital and reserve allocations; and risk management issues such as oversight, reporting, and quality control. We also have interest in any other control processes that help management assess and respond to practical or emerging issues, and in identifying best practices and any lessons learned.

A small team of examiners will conduct short reviews at each selected bank over the next six months. We will coordinate dates with your OCC resident team, but we expect to visit your bank on _____ for one to two weeks on-site. The results of this range-of-practice review will be communicated to your resident team and then discussed with you shortly afterward.

The attached list contains information we will need to conduct the review. Please provide the information to _____ (resident team) by _____, along with a list of contact names and phone numbers for each item listed. Requested information should be dated as of _____, or the most recent date available. To protect the confidentiality of the information, all data should be transmitted in a secure manner. _____ (resident examiner) will work with you to determine the most convenient method to exchange the information.

For our on-site work location, please have the following available:

- A conference room with a phone line.
- Computer terminals that allow access to request letter information, and bank systems necessary to review a sample of loan applications and loan modifications.

- Building/floor access cards.
- A locking file cabinet to store work-in-process.
- Printing capabilities from the bank's computer terminals.

Thank you in advance for your assistance. We look forward to working with your staff. Please contact me at (___) ___-____ or at _____ (e-mail address) if you have any questions.

Sincerely,

National Bank Examiner

cc:

Attachment

Appendix C: Categories of RRE Lending Activities

Examiners should consider the following categories when assessing the size, nature, and complexity of a bank's RRE lending activities.

Residential Mortgages

Activity	Portfolio Lender	Departmental Lender	Large Lender
Residential mortgage products	Primarily conforming and conventional residential mortgages, 15-year and 30-year fixed, ARMs, and balloons. Very limited other products or nontraditional products.	Primarily conforming and conventional residential mortgages for up to 30 years fixed, ARMs, and balloons. Some volume of government-insured, jumbo, reverse, or other nontraditional products.	Full menu of conventional and conforming mortgage products and government-insured products. Significant volume of jumbo, reverse, and other nontraditional products.
Residential mortgage channels	Primarily retail channel through bank locations and branches. Limited volume of wholesale originations for sale to others. Very limited volume of purchased originations from brokers or others.	Primarily retail channel through bank locations, branches, and affiliates. Some volume of wholesale activities, primarily originations for sale to others through correspondent activities or direct to investors. Limited volume of purchased originations from brokers or others.	Full-scale retail lending through bank locations, branches, and affiliates. Significant volume of wholesale activities, including purchases of originations by correspondents or brokers for sale to investors.
Residential mortgage application process	Paper-based and automated data capture and disclosure. Primarily a manual approval process. May use Fannie Mae DU or Freddie Mac Loan LP software. Reporting from data capture is limited.	Significantly automated with disclosures to meet compliance requirements. Uses DU or LP regularly as part of application process and decision. Good data capture and good data reporting for application volumes, characteristics, and approvals (including exception approvals and overrides).	Fully automated with disclosures to meet compliance requirements. May include imaged files. Uses DU and LP extensively as part of application process and decision. Strong data capture and strong data reporting on application volumes, characteristics, and approvals (including exception approvals and overrides).
Residential mortgage processing and underwriting	Primarily involves loan officers and related administrative staff reviewing applications and ordering credit bureau, appraisal, and title information. Early truth-in-lending and good-faith-estimate disclosures provided. Loan officer(s) or staff does any required verifications of employment and income. Loan officer(s) approve	Significantly automated process with disclosures automatically generated for delivery to applicant. Automated systems often order needed information such as credit bureau, appraisal, and title information. Staff processors move applications through process and do any required verifications of employment and income. Final underwriting done	Fully automated with disclosures to meet compliance requirements automatically generated for delivery. Automated ordering of credit bureau, appraisal, and title work. Professional staff of processors verifies employment and income or otherwise complete file for decision. Segregated staff of professional underwriters makes a decision for the file based

Activity	Portfolio Lender	Departmental Lender	Large Lender
	loans based on internal standards.	by segregated staff of underwriters or loan officers with specialty expertise.	on internal standards and investor criteria.
Residential mortgage documentation preparation and closing	Primarily involves loan officers and related administrative staff printing and reviewing documents, including preliminary HUD-1 settlement form. Closing may occur at bank offices, title company offices, or an attorney's office. Administrative staff follows up on all filing requirements and trailing documents after closing.	Significantly automated process with documentation and disclosures generated easily. Staff of processors or closers reviews information before closing and ensures delivery of preliminary HUD-1 settlement form. Closing takes place at title company or attorney's office. Staff of processors ensures all filing is complete and tracks trailing documents after closing.	Fully automated process with documentation and disclosures easily updated and generated. Staff of closers reviews information before closing and delivers preliminary HUD-1 settlement form. Closing typically takes place at title company or attorney's office. Staff of closers ensures all filing is completed and tracks and reports trailing documents after closing. Closers ensure delivery to investors.
Residential mortgage QC process	Limited and primarily involves a worksheet or checklist completed by the loan officer or administrative staff. No reports or limited formal reports of results on a loan or aggregated basis.	Specific process completed by limited internal staff or outsourced to a vendor. Usually involves sampling of new originations with individual loan results reported to management. May have reporting of aggregated results. May or may not serve to identify training opportunities.	Robust process completed by internal staff or external vendor using secondary-market investor standards for sampling. Results are reported at the individual loan level as well as in aggregated format. Poorly graded loans are identified and serve to highlight training opportunities.
Residential mortgage appraisal and evaluation ordering processes	Primarily involves loan officers and related personnel and the use of an internally approved appraisers list. Evaluations typically performed by loan officers. May use outside vendors for values and inspections.	Primarily involves loan officers or originators and the use of an internally approved appraisers list. May use the services of an AMC. Evaluations prepared by loan officers or internal appraisers. Typically uses outside vendors for values and inspections.	Primarily involves automated ordering process through the application system. System may categorize appraisal type. Uses an approved appraisers list and services of an AMC (especially for unusual properties or properties outside of the normal market). Evaluations are prepared by internal appraiser(s) with significant use of outside vendors for values and inspections.
Residential mortgage appraisal and evaluation review process	Primarily involves loan officers and related personnel and the use of a checklist that focuses on completion. Independence from loan production may be	Primarily involves loan officers or underwriters and the use of a checklist that focuses on completion. Independence from loan production may be	Involves underwriters with a checklist or an appraisal review function housed within internal appraiser unit. Definitive process exists for appraisal or evaluation

Activity	Portfolio Lender	Departmental Lender	Large Lender
	limited. Feedback on appraisal and evaluation quality is limited.	limited. Escalation process to internal appraiser may exist. Feedback on appraisal or evaluation quality usually exists and results in modifications to the approved appraisers list.	escalation to internal appraiser or AMC for second review process. Feedback on appraisal or evaluation quality exists and results in modifications to approved appraisers list.
Residential mortgage loan servicing activities	Primarily portfolio loans with very limited escrow activities.	Portfolio loans and limited volumes of loans serviced for others (primarily sales with servicing retained). Typically has good escrow capabilities.	Portfolio loans and significant volumes of loans serviced for others through sales with servicing retained or purchased servicing rights. Robust escrow capabilities.
Residential mortgage loan servicing process	Automated servicing platform with limited data capture and reporting for portfolio characteristics (origination scores, DTI ratios, LTV ratios, etc.) and portfolio performance (delinquency and losses).	Automated servicing platform with good data capture and reporting on portfolio characteristics and portfolio performance. Loans serviced for others can be readily identified for segmented reporting.	Automated servicing platform with strong data capture and reporting for portfolio characteristics and performance (including channel, product, vintage, etc.). Loans serviced for others segmented and reported regularly.
Residential mortgage collection process	Primarily conducted by loan officers and administrative staff using bank's loan servicing system reports to determine delinquency status. Policy provides guidance on renewals, deferrals, and initiation of foreclosure proceedings. Manual documentation typically maintained for credit files. Foreclosure activities usually coordinated with local attorney with expertise in local geography and state requirements.	Conducted by loan officers and dedicated staff of collection personnel. Uses either the loan servicing system or a specialty collection loan servicing platform for reports. Policy provides guidance on renewals, deferrals, and initiation of foreclosure proceedings. Servicing system may automatically prompt and queue actions for collectors. Documentation is manual or keyed into servicing system. Foreclosures coordinated with attorneys appropriate to geographic location and state requirements.	Conducted by dedicated staff of collection personnel supervised by head of collections. Uses specialty collection loan servicing platform. Policy requirements are incorporated into an automated servicing system with prompt actions and queue by delinquency status. Documentation is keyed into servicing system. May have imaged paperwork. System can differentiate between portfolio loans and loans serviced for others to ensure investor requirements are met. Foreclosures coordinated with several legal service vendors and attorneys based on geographic location of property and state requirements.
Residential mortgage credit risk manager	Primarily the senior lending officer for real estate lending activities or executive vice president (EVP) of lending.	Executive or senior manager for mortgage lending operations with oversight from EVP of lending. Could delegate some responsibilities to	Executive or senior manager for mortgage lending operations with oversight from EVP of lending. May also employ credit risk officers within

Activity	Portfolio Lender	Departmental Lender	Large Lender
		specific product managers.	the line of business for underwriting, QC, servicing, and collections.
Residential mortgage MIS	Primarily monthly board-type reporting that details balances, delinquencies, yields, and net losses. May also include some new origination reports that detail applications, approvals, scores, LTV ratios, etc.	Monthly board-level reporting that details portfolio performance characteristics (balances, delinquencies, yields, and net losses) in aggregate as well as new origination activities. Within line of business, daily, weekly, or monthly reports that detail new originations and collection activities.	Comprehensive daily, weekly, and monthly line of business reporting of origination and collection activities. Monthly reporting of portfolio risk profile and performance metrics. Monthly board-level reporting that details new originations' risk profile, portfolio risk profile, and performance.
Residential mortgage audit and loan review coverage	Limited internal audit coverage focused on ensuring compliance with board-approved policies. Loan review, if any, limited to small sampling of completed loans and review of portfolio performance statistics.	Risk-based internal audit coverage of primary activities to ensure compliance with board-approved policies and integrity of automated processes. Loan review limited to sampling of loans to determine compliance with polices. Review of portfolio performance may result in discussions with line management.	Risk-based internal audit coverage of all activities to ensure compliance with policies and procedures as well as integrity of automated processes. Annual loan review coverage samples new loans and loans in collection process for compliance with policies. Portfolio performance is evaluated against forecasts and risk appetite.

Home Equity Loans and Lines

Activity	Portfolio Lender	Departmental Lender	Large Lender
Home equity products	Primarily home equity-secured loans with fixed rates. Typically up to 20-year maturities. May have variable rates. Home equity-secured lines of credit with variable rates. Repayment terms may be IO during draw period or interest plus some principal. Lines typically have a draw period that converts to a repayment period until overall maturity (there are balloon loans that examiners must review closely). Term is usually 10 to 15 years.	Primarily home equity-secured loans and lines of credit. Loans typically have fixed rates and terms up to 20 years. May have variable rates. Lines of credit typically have variable rates, IO, or interest with principal repayment terms. Draw periods typically last five years but may go a second five years for 10 years total. Repayment periods typically 10 to 15 years when draw period ends.	Home equity-secured loans and lines of credit. Loans may be fixed or variable rate. Products with CLTV ratios up to 100 percent may exist. Lines are typically variable rate and may have multiple IO draw periods that eventually convert to repayment with up to 25 years total term. CLTV ratios up to 100 percent may exist. Loans and lines may be piggybacked onto a first mortgage secured loan at origination.
Home equity channels	Primarily retail channel through bank locations and branches. Very limited, if any, volume of wholesale originations for sale to others or purchased originations from brokers or others.	Primarily retail channel through bank locations, branches, and affiliates. Small volume of wholesale activities such as originations for sale to others or purchased originations from brokers may be present.	Full-scale retail lending through bank locations, branches, affiliates, and correspondents. Some wholesale activities, including originations for sale to others or purchases from brokers, could be present.
Home equity application process	Paper-based and automated data capture. Manual or automated decision approval process. May use credit bureau scores as a primary approval criteria. Data capture and reporting is limited.	Significantly automated application and decisions process. May include use of customer application scores in addition to credit bureau scores as primary approval criteria. Good data capture and good data reporting for application volumes, characteristics, and approvals (including exception approvals and overrides).	Fully automated applications and decisions process that includes the use of custom applications scores and credit bureau scores. May include imaged files. Strong data capture and strong data reporting on application volumes, characteristics, and approvals (including exception approvals and overrides with their performance compared to standard approvals).
Home equity processing and underwriting process	Primarily involves loan officers and related administrative staff reviewing applications and ordering credit bureau, appraisal and evaluation, and title information. Early truth-in-lending and other disclosures provided. Loan officer approves loan and line based on	Partially automated process with disclosures automatically generated for delivery to applicant. Automated systems often order needed information such as credit bureau, appraisal and evaluation, and title work. Administrative staff moves application through the process.	Highly automated with disclosures automatically generated for delivery to applicant. Automated systems order needed information, and a dedicated staff of processors compiles file for decision. Segregated staff of underwriters or loan officers who make a decision about the file

Activity	Portfolio Lender	Departmental Lender	Large Lender
	internal standards.	Final underwriting typically done by loan officers with specialty expertise.	based on internal criteria or investor criteria if sale of loan and line is expected.
Home equity documentation preparation and closing	Primarily involves loan officers and related administrative staff printing and reviewing documents, including any preliminary closing forms. Closing may occur at bank offices, title company offices, or attorney's office. Administrative staff follows up on any trailing documents after closing.	Partially automated process with documents and disclosures generated for review and delivery. Administrative staff processes and reviews information before closing. Closing takes place at bank offices, title company offices, or attorney's office. Administrative staff or closers follow up on any trailing documents after closing.	Highly automated process with documents and disclosures generated for review and delivery. Specialty staff of processors reviews before closing. Closing takes place at bank offices, title company offices, or attorney's office. Specialty staff of processors follows up and reports on trailing documents and ensures delivery to investors when sales of originations occur.
Home equity appraisal and evaluation ordering process	Primarily involves loan officers and related personnel and the use of an internally approved appraisers list. Evaluations typically performed by loan officers and may use outside vendors for values and property inspections.	Primarily involves loan officers or originators and the use of an internally approved appraisers list. May have nature and depth of valuation determined by risk-based policy. May use the services of an AMC. Evaluations typically prepared by loan officers or internal appraiser(s). Usually use outside vendors for values, including AVMs and property inspections.	Primarily involves automated ordering process through the application system. System may determine nature and depth of valuation required based on imbedded risk-based policy parameters. Usually uses internally approved appraisers list or services of an AMC (especially for unusual properties or properties outside of normal market). Evaluations prepared by internal appraiser(s) and typically use outside vendors for values (including AVMs) and property inspections.
Home equity appraisal and evaluation review process	Primarily involves loan officers and related personnel and the use of a checklist for completeness. Independence from loan production is limited. Feedback on appraisal or evaluation quality usually limited.	Primarily involves loan officers or underwriters and the use of a checklist for completeness. Independence from loan production often limited. Escalation process to internal appraiser or AMC for second review process may exist. Feedback on appraisal or evaluation quality is limited but usually results in modifications to approved appraisers list.	Primarily involves underwriters with checklist for completeness or an appraisal review function housed within the internal appraisal unit. Definitive process exists for appraisal and evaluation escalation to internal appraiser or AMC for second review process. Complete independence from loan production may or may not be achieved. Feedback on appraisal and evaluation quality

Activity	Portfolio Lender	Departmental Lender	Large Lender
			exists and results in modifications to approved appraisers list.
Home equity servicing activities	Primarily portfolio loans and lines only.	Portfolio loans and lines with limited volumes of loans or lines serviced for others.	Portfolio loans and lines and a significant volume of loans and lines serviced for others due to sales with servicing retained or purchases of servicing rights.
Home equity loan servicing processes	Automated servicing platform with limited data capture and reporting on portfolio characteristics (origination scores, DTI ratios, LTV ratios, etc.) and performance (delinquency and loss). Limited, if any, use of updated credit bureau scores or property valuations for account management purposes such as line exposure changes.	Automated servicing platform with good data capture and reporting on portfolio characteristics and portfolio performance. Any loans and lines serviced for others can be identified for reporting. Some use of updated credit bureau scores and property valuations for account management purposes.	Automated servicing platform with strong data capture and reporting on portfolio characteristics and performance. Reporting broken down by owned versus serviced. Regular use of updated credit bureau scores and property valuations for account management purposes.
Home equity collection processes	Primarily conducted by loan officers and administrative staff using bank's loan servicing system reports to determine delinquency status. Policy provides guidance on renewals, extensions, and deferrals for loans and re-ages for lines. Policy provides guidance on evaluating foreclosure decision and initiating a foreclosure. Paper-based credit files typically used. Foreclosure activities, if initiated, usually coordinated with local attorney with expertise in local geography and state requirements.	Conducted by loan officers or dedicated staff of collection personnel. Uses either the loan servicing system or a specialty collection servicing platform for reports. Policy provides guidance on renewals, extensions, and deferrals for loans and re-ages for lines. Servicing system may automatically prompt and queue actions for collectors. Policy provides guidance on evaluating foreclosure decision and initiating a foreclosure. Files may be paper-based or imaged. Foreclosures, if initiated, coordinated with local attorneys with expertise in local geography and state requirements.	Conducted by dedicated staff of collection personnel supervised by head of collections. Typically uses specialty collection loan servicing platform. Policy requirements automated, and servicing system prompts and queues actions by delinquency status. Notes typically keyed into system, and files may be paper or imaged. System can differentiate between any loans and lines owned versus serviced for others. Foreclosures, if initiated for portfolio or serviced loans and lines, coordinated with several legal services vendors and attorneys based on geographic location of property and state requirements.
Home equity credit risk manager	Primarily a senior lending officer for real estate or consumer lending activities or EVP of lending.	Executive or senior manager for non-mortgage real estate or consumer lending department with oversight from EVP of lending. Could delegate	Executive or senior manager for non-mortgage consumer lending operations with oversight from EVP of lending. May also employ credit risk officers with

Activity	Portfolio Lender	Departmental Lender	Large Lender
		some responsibilities to home equity product manager.	the line of business for underwriting, servicing, and collections.
Home equity MIS	Primarily monthly board-type reporting with details on balances, delinquencies, yields, and net losses. May also include some new origination reports that detail applications, approvals, credit bureau scores, LTV ratios, etc.	Monthly board-level reporting that details portfolio performance characteristics (balances, delinquencies, yields, and net losses) in aggregate as well as new origination activities. Within the department, there may be daily, weekly, or monthly reports that provide more details on new origination and collection activities.	Comprehensive daily, weekly, and monthly line of business reporting of origination and collection activities. Monthly reporting of portfolio risk profile and performance metrics. Monthly board-level reporting that details new originations risk profile, portfolio risk profile, and portfolio performance.
Home equity audit and loan review coverage	Limited internal audit coverage with a focus on ensuring compliance with board-approved policies. Loan review, if any, limited to small sampling of completed loans and lines and review of portfolio performance reports.	Risk-based internal audit coverage of primary activities to ensure compliance with board-approved policies and integrity of automated processes. Loan review typically limited to sampling of loans and lines to determine compliance with policies. Review of portfolio performance may result in discussions with management.	Risk-based internal audit coverage of all activities to ensure compliance with policies and procedures and integrity of automated processes. Annual loan review coverage samples new loans and lines in collection processes for compliance with policies and loss recognition. Portfolio performance reports reviewed and evaluated against approved risk appetite and previously reported expectations for performance.

Appendix D: Quantity of Credit Risk Indicators

Examiners should consider the following indicators when assessing the quantity of credit risk of RRE lending activities.

Low	Moderate	High
The level of RRE loans outstanding is low relative to total capital.	The level of RRE loans outstanding is moderate relative to total capital.	The level of RRE loans outstanding is high relative to total capital.
Residential loan growth rates are supported by local, regional, or national economic trends. Growth, including off-balance-sheet activities, has been planned for and is commensurate with management and staff expertise as well as operational capabilities.	Residential loan growth rates exceed local, regional, or national economic trends. Growth, including off-balance-sheet activities, has not been planned for or exceeds planned levels and may test the capabilities of management, lending staff, and MIS.	Residential loan growth rates significantly exceed local, regional, or national economic trends. Growth, including off-balance-sheet activities, has not been planned for or exceeds planned levels and stretches the experience and capability of management, lending staff, and MIS. Growth may also be in new nonconforming or nontraditional products, in new channels such as broker purchases, or from outside the bank's traditional lending area.
Interest and fee income from RRE lending activities is not a significant portion of loan income.	Interest and fee income from RRE lending activities is an important component of loan income; the bank's lending activities, however, remain diversified.	The bank is highly dependent on interest and fees from RRE lending activities. Management may seek higher returns through higher-risk product or consumer types. Loan yields may be disproportionate relative to risk.
The bank's RRE portfolios are well diversified with no single large concentrations or a few moderate concentrations. Concentrations are well within reasonable internal limits. The RRE loan portfolio mix does not materially affect the risk profile.	The bank has a few material RRE loan concentrations that may be approaching internal limits. The RRE portfolio mix may increase the bank's credit-risk profile.	The bank has large RRE loan concentrations that may exceed internal limits. The RRE portfolio mix increases the bank's credit-risk profile.
RRE loan underwriting is conservative. Policies and procedures are reasonable. Residential loans with underwriting exceptions are occasionally originated; the weaknesses, however, are effectively mitigated.	RRE loan underwriting is satisfactory. The bank has an average level of residential loans with exceptions to underwriting standards. Exceptions are reasonably mitigated and consistent with competitive pressures and reasonable growth objectives.	RRE loan underwriting is liberal and policies are inadequate. The bank has a high level of residential loans with underwriting exceptions of which the volume exposes the bank to loss in the event of default.
Collateral requirements for RRE loans are conservative. Appraisals and evaluations are reasonable, timely, and well supported. Reviews are appropriate and reliable.	Collateral requirements for RRE loans are acceptable. Some collateral exceptions exist but are reasonably mitigated and monitored. A moderate volume of appraisals or evaluations is not well supported or is not always obtained in a timely manner. A moderate volume of reviews may not be appropriate or reliable.	Collateral requirements for RRE loans are liberal, or if policies are conservative, substantial deviations exist. Appraisals and evaluations are not always obtained, are frequently unsupported or unreliable, or reflect inadequate protection. Updated appraisals, evaluations, or valuations are not obtained in a

Low	Moderate	High
		timely manner. Reviews are not often performed or are inadequate.
RRE loan documentation or collateral exceptions are low and have a minimal impact on the bank's risk profile.	The level of RRE loan documentation or collateral exceptions is moderate; exceptions, however, are reasonably mitigated and corrected in a timely manner, if applicable. The risk of loss from these exceptions is not material.	The level of RRE loan documentation and collateral exceptions is high. Exceptions are not mitigated and not corrected in a timely manner. The risk of loss from the exceptions is heightened.
RRE loan distribution across the risk spectrum is consistent with a conservative risk appetite. Migration trends within the risk spectrum favor less risky bands. Lagging indicators, including past-dues and nonaccruals, are low and stable.	RRE loan distribution across the risk spectrum is consistent with a moderate risk appetite. Migration trends within the risk spectrum may favor riskier bands. Lagging indicators, including past-dues and nonaccruals, are moderate and may be slightly increasing.	RRE loan distribution across the risk spectrum is heavily skewed toward higher risk bands. Lagging indicators, including past-dues and nonaccruals, are moderate or high, and the trend is increasing.
The volume of RRE loans classified in accordance with interagency guidance is low and is not skewed toward more severe classifications.	The volume of RRE loans classified in accordance with interagency guidance is moderate but is not skewed toward more severe classifications.	The volume of RRE loans classified in accordance with interagency guidance is moderate or high, increasing, and skewed toward more severe loss ratings.
RRE loan and line refinancing and renewal practices raise little or no concern regarding the quality of the residential loans and the accuracy of problem loan data.	RRE loan and line refinancing and renewal practices pose some concerns regarding the quality of residential loans and the accuracy of reported problem loan data.	RRE loan and line refinancing and renewal practices raise substantial concerns regarding the quality of residential loans and the accuracy of reported problem loan data.
The volume of nonconforming, nontraditional, or subprime RRE loans is not significant. The volume of purchased RRE loans from brokers is not significant.	The volume of nonconforming, nontraditional, or subprime RRE loans is moderate and may affect the overall credit-risk profile. The volume of purchased RRE loans from brokers is moderate and may affect the overall credit-risk profile.	The volume of nonconforming, nontraditional, or subprime RRE loans is high and definitively affects the overall credit-risk profile. The volume of purchased RRE loans from brokers is high and definitively affects the overall credit-risk profile.
The number of customer complaints received for RRE loans is low when compared with the volumes of loans originated or serviced. The complaint resolution is timely, complete, and in accordance with appropriate federal and state laws.	The number of customer complaints received for RRE loans is moderate when compared with the volumes of loans originated or serviced. The complaint resolution process is untimely but complete, and in accordance with appropriate federal and state laws.	The number of customer complaints received for RRE loans is high when compared with the volumes of loans originated or serviced. The likelihood of compliance violations is high. The complaint resolution process needs substantial improvements to be timely, complete, and in full accordance with appropriate federal and state laws.

Appendix E: Quality of Credit Risk Management Indicators

Examiners should consider the following indicators when assessing the quality of credit risk management of RRE lending activities.

Strong	Satisfactory	Weak
There is a clear, sound RRE credit culture. Board and management's appetite for risk is well communicated and fully understood.	The RRE credit culture is generally sound, but the culture may not be uniform and risk appetite may not be clearly communicated throughout the bank.	The RRE credit culture is absent or is materially flawed. Risk appetite may not be well understood.
RRE lending initiatives are consistent with a conservative risk appetite and promote an appropriate balance between risk-taking and strategic objectives. New RRE loan products are well-researched, tested, and approved before implementation.	RRE lending initiatives are consistent with a moderate risk appetite. Generally, there is an appropriate balance between risk-taking and strategic objectives; anxiety for income, however, may lead to higher-risk transactions. New RRE loan products may be implemented without sufficient testing, but risks are generally understood.	RRE lending initiatives are liberal and encourage risk-taking. Anxiety for income dominates planning activities. New RRE products are implemented without conducting sufficient due diligence.
The appraisal and evaluation program is fully effective. Policies and procedures faithfully reflect relevant guidance, and controls are sufficient to ensure their consistent implementation. Staff responsible for performing or oversight of appraisals, evaluations, and reviews is competent, independent, and has the appropriate experience and training.	The appraisal and evaluation program is effective in most respects, but improvement is needed in one or more areas, such as ensuring sufficient personnel, independence, review, engagement, or collateral monitoring. Policies and procedures may require some modification, or some improvement may be needed. Staff may require additional training in some areas.	The appraisal and evaluation program is ineffective. Policies and procedures do not adequately reflect regulations or guidance or are not implemented. Staff performing appraisal-related duties does not have sufficient training or experience. Collateral values in general may be unreliable.
Management is effective. The RRE lending staff possesses sufficient expertise to effectively administer the risk assumed. Responsibilities and accountability are clear, and appropriate remedial or corrective action is taken when needed.	Management satisfactorily manages RRE lending risk, but improvement may be needed in one or more areas. RRE lending staff generally possesses the expertise to administer assumed risks; additional expertise, however, may be required in one or more areas. Responsibilities and accountability may require some clarification. In general, appropriate remedial or corrective action is taken when needed.	RRE risk management is deficient. RRE lending staff may not possess sufficient expertise or may demonstrate an unwillingness to effectively administer the risk assumed. Responsibilities and accountability may not be clear. Corrective actions are insufficient to address root causes of problems.
Diversification management is effective. RRE concentration limits are set at reasonable levels. RRE concentration risk-management practices are sound, including management's efforts to reduce or mitigate exposures. Management effectively identifies and understands correlated risk exposures and their potential	Diversification management is adequate, but certain aspects may need improvement. RRE concentrations are identified and reported, but limits and other action triggers may be absent or moderately high. Concentration management efforts may be focused at the individual product level, while portfolio level efforts may be inadequate. Correlated	Diversification management is passive or deficient. Management may not identify concentrations or may take little or no action to reduce, limit, or mitigate the associated risk. Limits may be established but represent a significant portion of regulatory capital. Management may not understand exposure correlations and their potential effect.

Strong	Satisfactory	Weak
effect.	exposures may not be identified and their risks not fully understood.	Concentration limits may be exceeded or raised frequently.
Loan management and personnel compensation structures provide strong balance among loan or revenue production, loan quality, and portfolio administration, including risk identification.	Loan management and personnel compensation structures provide reasonable balance among loan or revenue production, loan quality, and portfolio administration.	Loan management and personnel compensation structures are skewed toward loan or revenue production. There is little evidence of substantive incentives or accountability for loan quality and portfolio administration.
RRE staffing levels and expertise are appropriate for the size and complexity of RRE loan activities. Staff turnover is low, and the transfer of responsibilities is orderly. Training programs facilitate ongoing staff development.	RRE staffing levels and expertise are generally adequate for the size and complexity of RRE loan activities. Staff turnover is moderate and may result in some temporary gaps in portfolio management. Training initiatives are adequate.	RRE staffing levels and expertise are deficient. Turnover is high. Management does not provide sufficient resources for staff training.
RRE lending policies effectively establish and communicate portfolio objectives, risk appetite, loan underwriting standards, and risk-selection standards.	RRE lending policies are fundamentally adequate. Enhancement, while generally not critical, can be achieved in one or more areas. Specificity of risk appetite or underwriting standards may need improvement to fully communicate policy requirements.	RRE lending policies are deficient in one or more ways and require significant improvements. Policies may not be clear or are too general to adequately communicate portfolio objectives, risk appetite, and underwriting and risk-selection standards.
Staff effectively identifies, approves, tracks, and reports significant policy, underwriting, and risk-selection exceptions individually and in aggregate, including risk exposures associated with off-balance-sheet activities.	Staff identifies, approves, and reports significant policy, underwriting, and risk-selection exceptions on a loan-by-loan basis, including risk exposures associated with off-balance-sheet activities. Little aggregation or trend analysis is conducted, however, to determine the effect on portfolio quality.	Policy exceptions may not receive appropriate approval, significant policy exceptions may be approved but not reported individually or in aggregate, or their effect on portfolio quality is not analyzed. Risk exposures associated with off-balance-sheet activities may not be considered.
RRE loan credit analysis is thorough and timely at underwriting and periodically thereafter for servicing, account management, and collection activities.	RRE loan credit analysis appropriately identifies key risks and is conducted within reasonable time frames. Post-underwriting analysis may need some strengthening to ensure proper servicing, account management, and collection activities.	RRE loan credit analysis is deficient. Analysis is superficial, and key risks are overlooked. Credit data is not reviewed in a timely manner, and servicing, account management, and collection activities suffer as a result.
Risk grading and problem loan review and identification systems are accurate and timely. Credit risk is effectively stratified for both problem and pass credits. Systems serve as effective early warning tools and support risk-based pricing, ALLL, and capital allocations.	Risk grading and problem loan review and identification systems are adequate. Problem and emerging problem credits are adequately identified, although room for improvement exists. The number of rating grades for pass credits may need to be expanded to facilitate early warning, risk-based pricing, ALLL, or capital allocations.	Risk grading and problem loan review and identification systems are deficient. Problem credits may not be identified accurately or in a timely manner, resulting in misstated levels of portfolio risk. The number of rating grades for pass credits is insufficient to stratify risk for early warning or other purposes.

Strong	Satisfactory	Weak
MIS provides accurate, timely, and complete RRE portfolio information, including significant portfolio subsets. Management and the board receive appropriate reports to analyze and understand the effect of RRE lending activities on the bank's credit risk profile, including off-balance-sheet activities. MIS facilitates timely exception reporting.	MIS is adequate. Management and the board generally receive appropriate reports to analyze and understand the effect of RRE lending activities on the bank's credit risk profile; modest improvement, however, may be needed in one or more areas. MIS facilitates generally timely exception reporting.	MIS is deficient. The accuracy or timeliness of information may be affected in a material way. Management and the board may not be receiving sufficient information to analyze and understand the effect of RRE lending activities on the bank's credit risk profile. Exception reporting requires improvement.
The audit program for RRE lending activities is strong, comprehensive in scope, adequately staffed, and sufficiently frequent. Identified issues are clearly reported, tracked, and rapidly resolved. Audit activities are based on a comprehensive risk assessment.	The audit program for RRE lending activities is satisfactory. There are isolated and manageable weaknesses in scope, staffing, or frequency. Audit reports do not always clearly identify issues, issues are not always closely tracked, or issue resolution may be prolonged. The risk assessment process for developing the audit program has minor weaknesses.	The audit program for RRE lending activities is weak. There are significant identified weaknesses in scope, staffing, or frequency that remain unaddressed. Audit reports fail to identify issues, issues are not tracked for resolution, and remediation efforts take excessive time to complete. The risk assessment process is flawed, resulting in inadequate audit activities.
RRE lending operations are well-managed, with appropriate governance structures and oversight. Vendor management programs closely monitor critical third-party service providers for service-level performance and compliance with laws and regulations. Operational metrics and MIS are timely and comprehensive and provide for effective decision making and proactive risk management.	RRE lending critical operations are adequately managed on a reactive basis. Noncritical activities or third-party relationships receive acceptable oversight and management. Oversight processes do not ensure that internal or third-party performance levels consistently meet business standards. Risk management metrics and MIS support a reactive stance on risk management.	Oversight of RRE lending critical operations, internal and outsourced, is materially and systemically deficient. Noncritical activities and third-party relationships may also be insufficiently supervised and operating below business standards. Risk management metrics and MIS are inadequate to support timely decision making.
Compliance with applicable laws, regulations, and regulatory guidance is consistent and thorough. Identified noncompliance is isolated and quickly corrected. Customer complaints are actively monitored, analyzed, and used as a basis for improving operations, profitability, and risk mitigation.	Compliance with applicable laws, regulations, and regulatory guidance is satisfactory but could be improved. Identified noncompliance is normally corrected in a satisfactory manner. Customer complaints are captured, but analysis is not used robustly to enhance operations or mitigate compliance risk exposures.	Compliance with applicable laws, regulations, and regulatory guidance is unsatisfactory. Identified noncompliance is often systemic and not effectively corrected in a timely manner. Customer complaints are not captured, or if captured they are not used to enhance operations or mitigate compliance exposures.

Appendix F: Appraisal and Evaluation Questionnaire

1. Does the bank have a written RRE appraisal and evaluation policy?

2. Has the policy been approved by the board of directors?

3. Does the policy require that

   - appraisals and evaluations be based on the definition of market value set forth in banking regulations?
   - appraisals and evaluations be presented in a narrative format or on approved forms?
   - appraisals and evaluations be received and analyzed before making the final credit or other decision on an RRE-secured mortgage, loan, or line of credit?
   - new appraisals be undertaken when federally related transactions meet the criteria outlined in the regulation?
   - appraisals and evaluations disclose, analyze, and report in reasonable detail any previous sales of the residential property being valued that occurred within one year of the date of the appraisal or evaluation's preparation?
   - management provide appraisers or evaluators with a letter of engagement containing
     - a legal description of the property?
     - a description of the interest to be appraised?
     - a request to use all appraisal approaches to value that are both applicable and necessary to provide credible assignment results?
     - a copy of the bank's written appraisal guidelines?
     - a copy of the appraisal rules (if not contained in the institution's policy)?
     - other pertinent information such as purchase agreements, income statements of subject property, leases, and financing terms?

4. Does the policy establish criteria to determine the useful life of a previous appraisal or evaluation?

5. Does the policy establish criteria that designate when federally related transactions require a new appraisal?

6. Does the policy require that the loan approval and appraisal functions maintain adequate independence internally?

   - If not entirely independent, for instance in a small or rural bank or branch, what additional policy requirements are mandated to mitigate this risk?

7. Are appraisers' and evaluators' fees based on a set fee and not the granting of the loan or the appraised value of the residential property?

8. Does the bank require an evaluation to disclose the name and address of the preparer?

9. Are appraisal reports prepared at the request of the lender or its agent?

   - Who is responsible for ordering appraisals and evaluations?
   - What is the process for ordering appraisal and evaluations?

10. Does the bank require appraisers (and evaluators) to meet reasonable standards for education, experience, and independence? Is proof of appropriate state license or certification readily available?

11. Does the bank maintain effective internal controls, such as a list of approved appraisers (and evaluators), to help ensure that only qualified, independent individuals are selected for assignments?

    - Is the process for selecting or removing an appraiser (or evaluator) appropriate?
    - Are the criteria used for selecting or removing an appraiser (or evaluator) appropriate?

12. Does management annually review the performance of all approved RRE appraisers (or evaluators) employed or retained in the preceding 12-month period?

    - Who is responsible for generating the annual performance reviews?
    - Is the reviewer qualified to generate the annual performance reviews?
    - Do the annual performance reviews consider the appraiser's (or evaluator's) compliance with the bank's appraisal and evaluation policy and procedures?
    - Do the annual performance reviews consider the reasonableness of the market value estimates derived by the appraiser (or evaluator)?

13. If staff appraisers are used, does the bank periodically have test appraisals made by independent appraisers to check the accuracy of appraisal reports?

14. If the bank uses appraisers who are not employees of the bank, does the bank adequately investigate their report quality, reputation, and qualifications?

15. What is the process for reviewing appraisals and evaluations for integrity of content?

    - Who is responsible for reviewing appraisals and evaluations?
    - Does the reviewer have sufficient independence, expertise, and experience?

16. What specific guidelines are used to determine the adequacy of the appraisal or evaluation, and is the review process effective? Does the process evaluate

    - underlying assumptions used?
    - technical analysis used?
    - reasonableness of the market value opinion? An important part of an adequate review is that the reviewer exercises qualitative judgment in assessing the appraiser's analysis considering the availability, or lack of availability, of data. This is different

from a review performed to see, for instance, if all of the boxes are checked and the distance from subject to comparables is within GSE guidelines.

17. Do the appraisal and evaluation policies and procedures reflect the size of the bank and the nature of its RRE lending activities?

18. Do the appraisal and evaluation policies and procedures describe the process for referring problem appraisers to appropriate state licensing and certifying agencies and other authorities?

Transaction testing of appraisals, evaluations, and reviews (to be performed during file review of new underwriting):

1. Were the appraisal reports or evaluations prepared at the request of the lender?

2. Were the appraisers (or evaluators) used from the board-approved list or hired by management through board-delegated authority?

3. Were the appraisers' (or evaluators') qualifications appropriate for the types of RRE properties being appraised?

4. Were the appraisals or evaluations sufficiently current at the time the loans were funded?

5. If a reviewer provided his or her own opinion of the market value of the property that was used as a basis for making the loan, was the reviewer appropriately licensed or certified?

6. Did any appraisals or evaluations contain language that appeared discriminatory based on the age or location of the subject residential property?

7. Did the appraisals or evaluations reviewed

   - report all three approaches to value, or contain an explanation that supported the omission of one or more approaches?
   - indicate a properly supported estimate of the highest and best use consistent with the definition of market value, whether or not the proposed use of the property is in fact the highest and best use?
   - identify, by legal description or otherwise, the RRE being appraised as this information is provided to the appraiser by management?
   - identify and reflect the market value of the property rights in the residential real property being appraised?
   - include any current agreement of sale, option, or listing of the subject residential property, if available?
   - include a history of sales for comparable residential properties when such properties have been sold several times during a brief period, or if the sales prices have decreased or increased in an atypical rate for that market?

- base their conclusions on the most recent plans and specifications for proposed residential properties?
- set forth the effective date(s) of the value estimate(s) and the date of the report?
- contain summaries of actual annual operating statements for existing income-producing residential properties, made available to the appraiser or evaluator by the lender or borrower, together with a supported forecast of the most likely future financial performance?
- include current rents and occupancy levels?
- set forth all material assumptions and limiting conditions affecting the value conclusion in one separate section within the report?
- include in the appraiser's certification a statement indicating
  - the appraiser's license or certification number and state of issuance?
  - that the appraiser has no present or prospective interest either in the property being appraised or with the parties involved?
  - whether the appraiser made a personal inspection of the subject residential property?
  - that to the best of the appraiser's ability, the analyses, opinions, and conclusions were developed and the report was prepared in accordance with the bank's appraisal standards?

8. For all residential properties, do reports include "market value as-is on appraisal date"?

9. For appraisals that included the cost approach to value,

   - are values for land and improvements presented separately?
   - do cost estimates appear to be reasonable?
   - are land values supported by comparable sales?
   - do estimates for depreciation appear reasonable and consistent with estimates of effective age?

10. For appraisals that included the income approach to value,

    - do potential gross income projections appear reasonable?
    - do adjustments for vacancy and credit loss appear adequate?
    - do operating expenses appear reasonable?
    - do capitalization rates appear reasonable, and are they supported by market data?

11. For appraisals that included the sales comparison approach to value,

    - are comparable properties physically similar?
    - are comparable properties economically similar?
    - are comparable sales sufficiently recent, that is, substantial changes in the market have not occurred?
    - are adjustments to comparable properties made for sales with favorable financing?

12. Is market value estimated by reconciling the values indicated by the individual approaches to value?

13. Based on the RRE transactions, appraisals, and evaluations reviewed during the examination,

    - is there any indication of weaknesses in the bank's appraisal or evaluation policies, procedures, or internal controls?
    - is there any correlation between problem RRE loans and lines of credit (delinquent or classified) and faulty appraisals or evaluations?
    - can the faulty appraisals or evaluations be traced to certain appraisers, appraisal firms, or evaluators?
    - is an MRA and appropriate corrective action required to describe the findings regarding the bank's appraisal or evaluation program or policies?
    - are problem appraisers removed from the list of approved appraisers in a timely manner and referred to the appropriate licensing authorities?

Appendix G: Glossary

Entries marked with an asterisk (*) are as defined in the "Interagency Guidelines for Real Estate Lending Policies." Entries marked with a double asterisk (**) are as defined in the "Interagency Appraisal and Evaluation Guidelines."

Ability-to-repay (ATR): The requirement in Regulation Z that lenders make a reasonable, good-faith determination before or when consummating a covered mortgage loan that the consumer has a reasonable ability to repay the loan.

Accident and health premium: A payment by a borrower to ensure that mortgage payments continue to be paid if the borrower becomes disabled or ill.

Acquisition cost: In an FHA transaction, the price the borrower pays for the property plus any closing, repair, and financing costs (except discounts in other than a refinancing transaction). Acquisition costs do not include prepaid discounts in a purchase transaction, mortgage insurance premiums, or similar add-on costs.

Adjustable rate mortgage (ARM): A mortgage loan that allows a lender to periodically adjust the interest rate in accordance with a specified index agreed to at the inception of the loan. Also known as variable rate mortgage.

Alternative A loan (Alt-A): A term used by the industry to denote loans that do not satisfy the regular criteria for conforming or jumbo loan programs but are first-lien loans to prime quality borrowers. These loans may have an LTV ratio above 80 percent but lack PMI. These loans may be extended to a temporary resident alien, secured by non-owner-occupied property, or lack requirements that specify minimum income relative to expenses.

Amortization: The process of paying off a loan by gradually reducing the balance through a series of installment payments.

Annual escrow account statement: A report prepared by the lender or servicing agent for a mortgagor, as required by RESPA, stating the amount of taxes, insurance, and interest paid during the year, as well as the outstanding principal balance.

A- or A-minus loan: See **Alternative A loan (Alt-A).**

Appraisal:** A written statement independently and impartially prepared by a qualified appraiser (state licensed or certified) setting forth an opinion on the market value of any adequately described property as of a specific date(s), supported by the presentation and analysis of relevant market information.

"A" quality credit: The best credit rating, held by borrowers who typically receive the lowest prices that lenders offer.

"As-is" market value:** The estimate of the market value of real property in its current physical condition, use, and zoning as of the appraisal's effective date.

Automated underwriting system: A system into which a loan originator enters a borrower's application information, which is subject to verification. The system typically accesses the borrower's credit reports to determine the likelihood that the loan will be repaid as agreed. The assessment is based on the performance of similar mortgages with comparable borrower, property, and loan characteristics. The system makes preliminary recommendations regarding the loan (for example, approve, refer, or caution). Some systems also make pricing recommendations.

Automated valuation model (AVM): Online databases that match similar properties using historical sales prices to derive a range of comparable sales prices. The model considers limited factual data, such as square footage, number of rooms, property age, and lot size. Some AVMs use historical information derived from county records, while others collect information from appraisal reports, in which properties' physical characteristics have been verified.

Balloon mortgage: A mortgage for which the periodic installments of P&I do not fully amortize the loan. The balance of the mortgage is due in a lump sum (balloon payment) at the end of the term. Regulation Z (12 CFR 1026.18(s)(5)(i)) defines "balloon payment" as a "payment that is more than two times a regular periodic payment."

Balloon-payment qualified mortgage: A QM standard under Regulation Z that allows small creditors (defined by prior-year asset size and origination volumes) that operate predominantly in rural or underserved areas to make balloon mortgages. (**Note:** All small creditors, regardless of where they operate, may make temporary balloon-payment QMs during a two-year transition period after the January 10, 2014, effective date of the regulation.) Balloon-payment QMs must not have negative-amortization or IO features and must comply with the points-and-fee limits for QMs. Additionally, balloon-payment QMs must

- have a fixed interest rate and periodic payments (other than the balloon payment) that would fully amortize the loan in 30 years or less.
- have a term of five years or longer.
- not be subject to a forward commitment (an agreement made at or before consummation of a loan to sell the loan after consummation, other than to a creditor that itself is eligible to make balloon-payment QMs).
- have a determination that the consumer will be able to make the scheduled periodic payments (including mortgage-related obligations) other than the balloon payment.
- have verified and considered the consumer's income or assets and debts, alimony, and child support.
- have considered the consumer's DTI or residual income, although the rule sets no specific threshold for DTI or residual income.

Broker: A person or firm that specializes in loan originations, receiving a commission to bring together the borrower and a lender. The broker performs some or most of the loan processing functions but does not underwrite the mortgage, fund the mortgage at settlement, or service the mortgage. Typically, the loan is closed in the name of the lender that commissioned the broker's services. In some cases, the loan is closed in the broker's name through a table-funded arrangement. See **table funding.**

Broker price opinion (BPO): ** An estimate of the probable sales or listing price of the subject property provided by a real estate broker, sales agent, or sales person. A BPO provides a varying level of detail about a property's condition, market, and neighborhood, as well as comparable sales or listings. A BPO is not by itself an appraisal or evaluation, but it could be used for monitoring the collateral value of an existing loan, when deemed appropriate.

Buy-down mortgage: A mortgage in which a lender accepts a below-market interest rate in return for an interest rate subsidy paid as additional discount points by the builder, seller, or buyer.

Cap (interest rate): In an ARM, a limit on the amount the interest rate may increase per period or over the life of the loan. See **floor (interest rate).**

Capitalize: The act of converting a series of anticipated cash flows into present value by discounting them at an established rate of return.

Capitalized value: The net present value of a set of future cash flows.

Certificate of reasonable value: A document issued by the VA that establishes a maximum value and loan amount for a VA-guaranteed mortgage.

Closing: Consummation of a mortgage transaction during which the note and other legal documents are signed and the loan proceeds are disbursed. If a loan is rescindable, per Regulation Z, proceeds are not immediately disbursed.

Closing costs: Fees paid to consummate the closing of a mortgage. Common closing costs include origination fees, discount points, title insurance fees, survey fees, appraisal fees, and attorneys' fees.

Closing statement: A financial disclosure giving an account of all funds received and expected at closing, including escrow deposits for taxes, hazard insurance, and mortgage insurance. All federally insured or guaranteed loans and most conventionally financed loans use a uniform closing statement known as HUD-1, as required by RESPA, for residential mortgage transactions. As of August 1, 2015, lenders will be required to use the closing disclosure mandated in the TILA–RESPA integrated disclosure rule in connection with federally related mortgage loans (as that term is defined in RESPA).

Commitment fee (lender/borrower): A fee paid by a potential borrower to a potential lender for the lender's promise to lend money on a specified date in the future, or for a specified period of time and under specified terms. The timing of income recognition for these fees should follow GAAP using the specified contractual terms.

Commitment fee (seller/investor): A fee paid by a loan seller to an investor in return for the investor's promise to purchase a loan or a package of loans at an agreed price on a future date.

Commitment (lender/borrower): An agreement, often in writing, between a lender and a borrower to lend money at a future date or for a specified time period subject to specified conditions.

Commitment (seller/investor): A written agreement between a seller of loans and an investor to sell and buy mortgages under specified terms for a specified period.

Computerized loan origination system: An electronic system that provides subscribers with current data on available loan programs at various lending institutions. Some systems offer mortgage information services and can prequalify borrowers, process loan applications, underwrite loans, and make a commitment of funds.

Conforming mortgage: A mortgage loan that meets all requirements (loan type, amount, and age) for purchase by Fannie Mae or Freddie Mac.

Conventional mortgage: A mortgage loan that is not government-guaranteed or government-insured. There are two types of conventional loans, conforming and nonconforming. See **conforming mortgage** and **nonconforming mortgage.**

Convertible mortgage: An ARM that may be converted to a fixed-rate mortgage at one or more specified times over its term.

Correspondent: A mortgage bank that originates loans that are sold to other lenders. The correspondent performs some or all of the loan processing functions, as well as underwriting and funding the mortgage at settlement. Typically, the mortgage is closed in the correspondent's name.

Debt-to-income (DTI) ratio: The ratio calculated by using identified monthly debt obligations or payments (for example, child support or alimony) as the numerator and identified monthly income amounts or receipts as the denominator.

Direct endorsement: A HUD program that enables an eligible lender to process and close single-family applications for FHA-insured loans without HUD's prior review.

Discount rate: The rate at which future dollars are converted into present value. The time value of money can be interpreted as the rate at which individuals are willing to trade present for future consumption, or as the opportunity cost of capital.

Down-payment assistance program: A product developed to assist home buyers who can qualify for a mortgage loan except for the required down payment and closing costs.

Escrow: The portion of the borrower's monthly payments held by the lender or servicer to pay taxes, insurance, mortgage insurance (if required), and other related expenses as they become due. In some parts of the United States, escrows are also known as impounds or reserves.

Escrow analysis: The review of escrow accounts to determine whether current monthly deposits provide sufficient funds to pay taxes, insurance, and related expenses when due.

Evaluation:** A valuation permitted by the appraisal regulations for transactions that qualify for the appraisal threshold exemption, business loan exemption, or subsequent transaction exemption.

Exposure time: The estimated length of time the property interest being appraised would have been offered on the market before the hypothetical consummation of a sale at market value on the effective date of the appraisal. Exposure time is always presumed to precede the effective date of the appraisal. Exposure time is a function of price, time, and use—not an isolated opinion of time alone.[103]

Extension of credit or loan:*

- The total amount of any loan, line of credit, or other legally binding lending commitment with respect to real property.
- The total amount, based on the amount of consideration paid, of any loan, line of credit, or other legally binding lending commitment acquired by a lender by purchase, assignment, or otherwise.

Fallout: Loans in the origination pipeline that do not close, or close under terms different from initial expectations (for example, a rate-locked loan is allowed to close at a lower rate to retain the customer).

Fannie Mae (Federal National Mortgage Association): A stockholder-owned corporation created by Congress in a 1938 amendment to the National Housing Act. Fannie Mae operates mortgage purchase and securitization programs to support the secondary market in mortgages on residential property.

Federal Home Loan Bank (FHLB): A privately capitalized GSE designed to help finance the country's housing and community development needs. Certain FHLBs purchase single-family mortgages from their member financial institutions. These mortgages must meet the same requirements as mortgages that Fannie Mae and Freddie Mac are permitted to purchase (that is, one- to four-family conforming loans within the size limit established by Congress).

---

[103] *Uniform Standards of Professional Appraisal Practice*, Appraisal Standards Board, Appraisal Foundation, 2014-2015 edition.

Federal Housing Administration (FHA): A federal agency within HUD, established in 1934 under the National Housing Act. The FHA supports the secondary market in mortgages on residential property by providing mortgage insurance for certain residential mortgages.

Federally related transaction:** Any real estate-related financial transaction in which a regulated institution engages or contracts for, and that requires the services of an appraiser. See **real estate-related financial transaction.**

FHA: See **Federal Housing Administration.**

FHA loan: A loan insured by the FHA and made through an approved lender.

FHA value: The value established by the FHA as the basis for determining the maximum mortgage amount that may be insured for a particular property. The FHA value is the sum of the appraised value plus the FHA estimate of closing costs.

FICO score: FICO stands for Fair Isaac Credit Organization. A consumer has three FICO scores based on information from each national credit bureau. FICO scores are a measure of consumers' financial responsibility, based on their credit history. Most lenders look at FICO scores when evaluating a loan application.

Fixed-rate mortgage: An amortizing mortgage for which the interest rate and payments remain the same over the life of the loan.

Floor (interest rate): An investor safeguard on an ARM that limits the amount the interest rate may decline per period or over the life of the loan. See **cap (interest rate).**

Forbearance: In mortgage lending, the act of refraining from taking legal action when a mortgage is delinquent. Forbearance usually is granted only if a borrower has made satisfactory arrangements to pay the amount owed at a future date.

Foreclosure: The process by which a party, which has loaned money secured by a mortgage or deed of trust on real property (or has an unpaid judgment), requires sale of the real property to recover the money due and unpaid interest, plus the costs of foreclosure, when the debtor fails to make payment. State law governs how foreclosures are conducted. In some states, judicial foreclosures, requiring a court action, are required. In other states, nonjudicial foreclosures are permitted. After the payments on the promissory note (which is evidence of the loan) have become delinquent for several months (time varies from state to state), the lender can have a notice of default served on the debtor (borrower) stating the amount due and the amount necessary to "cure" the default. If the delinquency and costs of foreclosure are not paid within a specified period, the lender (or the trustee in states using deeds of trust) sets a foreclosure date, after which the property may be sold at public sale. Up to the time of foreclosure (or even afterward in some states), the defaulting borrower can pay all delinquencies and costs (which are then greater due to foreclosure costs) and redeem the property. Upon sale of the property, the amount due is paid to the creditor (lender or owner of the judgment), and the remainder of the money received from the sale, if any, is paid to the debtor.

Freddie Mac (Federal Home Loan Mortgage Corporation): A stockholder-owned corporation created by Congress under the Emergency Home Finance Act of 1970. Freddie Mac operates mortgage purchase and securitization programs to support the secondary market in mortgages on residential property.

General qualified mortgage: Under Regulation Z, one type of a QM loan that, among other things, may not have negative-amortization, IO, or balloon-payment features or terms that exceed 30 years. General QMs are required to have a monthly DTI ratio of no more than 43 percent calculated under the standards based on the definitions and requirements for verified obligations and income in Regulation Z's appendix Q.

Ginnie Mae (Government National Mortgage Association): A federal government corporation created as part of HUD in 1968 by an amendment to the National Housing Act. Ginnie Mae guarantees mortgage-backed securities that are insured by the FHA or guaranteed by the VA and backed by the full faith and credit of the U.S. government.

Government-sponsored enterprise (GSE): A private organization with a government charter and backing. The FHLBs, Freddie Mac, and Fannie Mae are GSEs.

Graduated-payment mortgage: A flexible-payment mortgage in which the payments increase for a specified period and then level off. These mortgages may result in negative amortization during the early years of the mortgage's life.

Growing equity mortgage: A graduated-payment mortgage in which increases in the borrower's mortgage payments are used to accelerate reduction of principal on the loan. These mortgages do not involve negative amortization.

Guarantee fee: The fee paid to a federal agency or private entity in return for its agreement to accept a portion of the loss exposure on a loan.

Guarantee fee buy-down: An arrangement in which the seller of mortgages pays a lower guarantee fee in return for less cash when the loans are sold. Guarantee fee buy-downs allow a bank to collect a higher excess servicing fee over the life of the serviced loans. See **guarantee fee.**

Guarantee fee buy-up: An up-front fee paid to a loan seller in exchange for a higher guarantee fee. Guarantee fee buy-ups increase the cash received for mortgages when they are sold and reduce the excess servicing fee to be collected over the life of the underlying serviced loans. See **guarantee fee.**

Hazard insurance: Insurance coverage that protects the insured in case of property loss or damage.

High LTV RRE loan: Any loan, line of credit, or combination of credits secured by liens on or interests in owner-occupied one- to four-family residential property that equals or exceeds 90 percent of the property's appraised value, unless the loan has appropriate credit support. Appropriate credit support may include mortgage insurance, readily marketable collateral, or other acceptable collateral that reduces the LTV ratio below 90 percent.

Interest-only (IO) loan: A loan on which the borrower is required to pay only interest for a specified number of years (for example, three or five years). IO loans can be fixed-rate, hybrid, or ARM mortgages.

Investor: A person or institution that buys mortgage loans or securities, or has a financial interest in these instruments.

Investor advances: In mortgage banking, funds advanced and costs incurred by the servicer on behalf of a delinquent mortgagor.

Jumbo loan: A mortgage in an amount larger than the statutory limit on loans that may be purchased or securitized by Fannie Mae or Freddie Mac.

Loan guaranty certificate: A VA document that certifies the dollar amount of a mortgage loan that is guaranteed.

Loan origination date:* The time of inception of the obligation to extend credit (that is, when the last event or prerequisite, controllable by the lender, occurs, causing the lender to become legally bound to fund an extension of credit).

Loan originator: A person who, in expectation of direct or indirect compensation or other monetary gain or for direct or indirect compensation or other monetary gain, performs any of the following activities: takes an application; offers, arranges, or assists a consumer in obtaining or applying to obtain, negotiates, or otherwise obtains or makes an extension of consumer credit for another person; or, through advertising or other means of communication, represents to the public that such person can or will perform any of these activities. The term "loan originator" includes an employee, agent, or contractor of the creditor or loan originator organization if the employee, agent, or contractor meets this definition. The term "loan originator" includes a creditor that engages in loan origination activities if the creditor does not finance the transaction at consummation out of the creditor's own resources, including by drawing on a bona fide warehouse line of credit or out of deposits held by the creditor.

Loan to value or loan-to-value ratio (LTV):[104] The percentage or ratio that is derived at the time of loan origination by dividing an extension of credit by the total market value of the property(ies) securing or being improved by the extension of credit, plus the amount of any readily marketable or other acceptable non-real-estate collateral. The total amount of all

---

[104] CLTV indicates that additional loans on the property have been considered in the calculation of the percentage ratio.

senior liens on or interest in such properties should be included in determining the LTV ratio. When mortgage insurance or collateral is used in the calculation of the LTV ratio, and such credit enhancement is later released or replaced, the LTV ratio should be recalculated.

Locking the loan: A borrower's exercise of his or her option to lock in an interest rate and points. A lock can be exercised at the time of application or later.

Margin: In an ARM, the spread between the index rate used and the mortgage interest rate.

Marketing period or marketing time: The time it may take to sell the property interest at the appraised market value during the period immediately after the effective date of the appraisal.

Market value:** The most probable price that a property should bring in a competitive and open market under all conditions requisite to a fair sale, the buyer and seller each acting prudently and knowledgeably, and assuming the price is not affected by undue stimulus. Implicit in this definition are the consummation of a sale as of a specified date and the passing of title from seller to buyer under conditions whereby

- buyer and seller are motivated.
- both parties are well informed or well advised and acting in what they consider their own best interests.
- a reasonable time is allowed for exposure in the open market.
- payment is made in terms of cash in U.S. dollars or in terms of financial arrangements comparable thereto.
- the price represents the normal consideration for the property sold unaffected by special or creative financing or sales concessions granted by anyone associated with the sale.

Mortgage banker: An individual or firm that originates, purchases, sells, or services loans secured by mortgages on real property.

Mortgage broker: An individual or firm that receives a commission for matching mortgage borrowers with lenders. Mortgage brokers do not fund the loans they help originate.

Mortgage insurance: Insurance coverage that protects mortgage lenders or investors in the event the borrower defaults. By absorbing some of the credit risk, mortgage insurance allows lenders to make loans with lower down payments. The federal government offers such insurance for FHA loans; private companies offer it for conventional loans. See **private mortgage insurance (PMI).**

Negative amortization: The addition of due but unpaid interest to the principal of a mortgage loan, causing the loan balance to increase rather than decrease. Negative amortization occurs when the periodic installment payments on a loan are insufficient to repay interest due.

Nonconforming mortgage: A mortgage loan that does not meet the standards of eligibility for purchase or securitization by Fannie Mae or Freddie Mac. The loan amount, the LTV ratio, the term, or some other aspect of the loan does not conform to the agencies' standards.

Nontraditional mortgage product: A type of mortgage that allows borrowers to defer payment of principal and sometimes interest. Examples include IO loans and payment option ARMs.

Normal servicing fee: The rate representative of what an investor pays to the servicer for performing servicing duties for similar loans. A bank may not use its cost to service loans as the normal servicing fee.

One- to four-family residential property:* Property containing fewer than five individual dwelling units, including manufactured homes permanently affixed to the underlying property (when deemed to be real property under state law).

Origination fee: The fee a lender charges to prepare documents, make credit checks, and inspect the property being financed. Origination fees are usually stated as a percentage of the face value of the loan.

Overage pricing: Increasing the price or cost (interest rate, fees, or points) of a mortgage loan above the bank's standard rate and fees/points schedule.

Owner-occupied: A property is owner-occupied when the primary source of repayment is not derived from third-party, nonaffiliated, rental income associated with the property (that is, any such rental income is less than 50 percent of the source of repayment).

Pipeline: In mortgage lending, loan applications in process that have not closed.

Prepayment: The payment of all or part of a loan before it is contractually due.

Primary market: For a mortgage lender, the market in which it originates mortgages and lends funds directly to homeowners.

Private mortgage insurance (PMI): Insurance coverage written by a private company that protects the mortgage lender if the borrower defaults. See **mortgage insurance.**

Production flow: The purchase of mortgage loans in combination with the rights to service those loans. The entity acquiring the mortgage loans then resells the loans but retains the accompanying servicing rights.

Prospective market value "as-completed":** According to the Uniform Standards of Professional Appraisal Practice, an appraisal with a prospective market value reflects an effective date that is subsequent to the date of the appraisal report. A prospective market value may be appropriate for the valuation of a property interest related to a credit decision for a proposed development or renovation project. Prospective value opinions are intended to reflect the current expectations and perceptions of market participants, based on available data. The prospective market value "as-completed" reflects the property's market value as of the time that development is expected to be completed.

Qualified mortgage (QM): A standard for mortgages that qualify for a conclusive or rebuttable presumption of compliance with the ATR requirements in 12 CFR 1026.43, depending on price. General and temporary QMs can be originated by all creditors. Small creditor portfolio and balloon-payment QMs can be originated only by small creditors, under certain conditions. Generally, points and fees may not exceed 3 percent of the total loan amount for all types of QMs, but higher thresholds are provided for loans less than $100,000.

Quality control (QC): In mortgage banking, policies and procedures designed to maintain optimal levels of quality, accuracy, and efficiency in producing, selling, and servicing mortgage loans.

Readily marketable collateral:* Insured deposits, financial instruments, and bullion in which the lender has a perfected interest. Financial instruments and bullion must be salable under ordinary circumstances with reasonable promptness at a fair market value determined by quotations based on actual transactions, on an auction, or on similarly available daily bid and ask price market. Readily marketable collateral should be appropriately discounted by the lender consistent with the lender's usual practices for making loans secured by such collateral. Examples of readily marketable financial instruments include stocks, bonds, debentures, commercial paper, negotiable certificates of deposit, and shares in mutual funds.

Real estate-related financial transaction:** Any transaction involving the sale, lease, purchase, investment in or exchange of real property, including interests in property, or the financing thereof; the refinancing of real property or interests in real property; or the use of real property or interests in property as security for a loan or investment, including mortgage-backed transactions.

Retail production: Mortgage loan production for which the origination and underwriting process was handled exclusively by the bank or a consolidated subsidiary of the bank.

Reverse mortgage: A mortgage loan that lets homeowners 62 years of age or older convert a portion of their home equity into cash. Reverse mortgage products are sponsored by the FHA, Fannie Mae, and a small number of private lenders, and are offered by many mortgage banks. Reverse mortgages allow borrowers to access their home equity in several ways, including a lump-sum payment, a line of credit, payments over a specified term, or payments for life. Unlike a traditional mortgage, no repayment is required until the borrower(s) no longer use the home as a principal residence.[105]

Roll rates: Roll rates measure the movement of accounts and balances from one payment status to another (for example, percentage of accounts or dollars that were current last month rolling to 30 days past due this month).

---

[105] Non-borrowing spouses may have certain rights granted by the FHA to remain in the home.

Satisfaction, also known as reconveyance: Once a mortgage or deed of trust is paid, the holder of the mortgage is required to satisfy the mortgage or deed of trust of record to show that the mortgage or deed of trust is no longer a lien on the property.

Scratch-and-dent mortgage: A mortgage that fails to meet all the underwriting requirements or standard representations and warranties in a sales transaction. These mortgages are returned by the investor or retained by the bank and sold in separate transactions, in which the deficiencies are acknowledged by the buyer.

Seasoned mortgage portfolio: A mortgage portfolio that has reached its peak delinquency level, generally after 30 to 48 months.

Secondary-mortgage market: The market in which lenders and investors buy and sell existing mortgages.

Servicing, also known as **loan administration:** A mortgage lending function that includes document custodianship, receipt of payments, cash management, escrow administration, investor accounting, customer service, loan setup and payoff, collections, and the administration of OREO.

Servicing agreement: A written agreement between an investor and a mortgage servicer stipulating the rights and obligations of each party.

Servicing fee: The contractual fee due to the mortgage servicer for performing various loan servicing duties for investors.

Servicing released: A stipulation in a mortgage sales agreement specifying that the seller is not responsible for servicing the loans.

Servicing retained: A stipulation in a mortgage sales agreement specifying that, in return for a fee, the seller is responsible for servicing the mortgages.

Settlement: The consummation of a transaction. In mortgage lending, the closing of a mortgage loan or the delivery of a loan or security to a buyer. See **closing.**

Shared appreciation mortgage: A mortgage loan in which the lender offers the borrower a below-market interest rate in exchange for a portion of the profit earned when the property is sold.

Short sale: An arrangement entered into between a loan servicer and a delinquent borrower. The servicer allows the borrower to sell the property to a third party at less than the outstanding loan balance. This saves the servicer the time and expense involved in a foreclosure action. The servicer must normally obtain the approval of the investor before entering into a short sale agreement. See **forbearance.**

Small creditor qualified mortgage: A QM standard under Regulation Z that is prohibited from having negative-amortization, IO, or balloon-payment features or terms that exceed 30 years. It is also subject to standard QM limitations for points and fees. In addition to these requirements, for a loan to be a small creditor QM, it must

- be underwritten based on a fully amortizing schedule using the maximum rate permitted during the first five years after the date of the first periodic payment.
- not be subject to a forward commitment (an agreement made at or before consummation of a loan to sell the loan after consummation, other than to a creditor that itself is eligible to make small creditor QMs).
- have verified and considered the consumer's income or assets, and debts, alimony, and child support.
- have considered the consumer's DTI or residual income, although the rule sets no specific threshold for DTI or residual income.

Subprime loan: A loan provided to a borrower who has a weakened credit history, reduced repayment capacity, or incomplete credit history. Also known as nonprime loan.

Table funding: A method of acquiring mortgage loans from third parties, such as brokers or correspondents. As defined in RESPA, table funding is a settlement at which a loan is funded by a contemporaneous advance of loan funds and an assignment of the loan to the party advancing the funds.

Temporary qualified mortgage: A QM standard under Regulation Z for loans that are eligible to be purchased, guaranteed, or insured by the USDA, the Rural Housing Service, and the GSEs. They are subject to the product feature restrictions that apply to all QMs (negative amortization, IO, balloon payments, and loan terms over 30 years, as well as the same limits on points and fees).

These QMs are permitted during a transitional period tied to the end of the conservatorship status of the GSEs, when the federal agencies issue their own QM rules, or January 10, 2021, whichever occurs first. Because HUD and the VA have adopted QM rules for this purpose, creditors may make QMs under those agencies' rules and receive the same presumptions of compliance as QMs made under Regulation Z.

U.S. Department of Veterans Affairs (VA): The VA, formerly called the Veterans Administration, is a cabinet-level agency of the U.S. government. The Servicemen's Readjustment Act of 1944 authorized the VA to offer the Home Loan Guaranty Program to veterans. The program encourages mortgage lenders to offer long-term, low-down-payment financing to eligible veterans by partially guaranteeing the lender against loss.

VA: See **U.S. Department of Veterans Affairs.**

VA loan: A loan made through an approved lender and partly guaranteed by the VA.

Value:* An opinion or estimate, set forth in an appraisal or evaluation, whichever may be appropriate, of the market value of real property, prepared in accordance with appraisal regulations and guidance. For loans to purchase an existing property, the term "value" means the lesser of the actual acquisition cost or the estimate of value.

VA no-bid: An option that allows the VA to pay only the amount of its guarantee on a defaulted mortgage loan, leaving the investor with the title to the foreclosed property. The VA must exercise this option when it is in the government's best interest. No-bid properties become OREO.

VantageScore: A credit risk score that was developed through the use of information from the three national credit reporting companies. In the past, each company had used its own proprietary formulas to create its scores.

Vintage analysis: A tool for analyzing performance trends that entails review of actual serviced portfolio behavior and its implication for future default, delinquency, and loss rates. This information can be compared with historical changes in underwriting standards, credit-scoring processes, and new product development to ensure that loan pricing is consistent with perceived product risk.

Appendix H: Abbreviations

ABA	affiliated business arrangement
ALLL	allowance for loan and lease losses
AMC	appraisal management company
APR	annual percentage rate
ARM	adjustable rate mortgage
ATR	ability-to-repay
AVM	automated valuation model
BPO	broker price opinion
CFPB	Consumer Financial Protection Bureau
CLTV	combined loan to value
CRA	Community Reinvestment Act
DU	Desktop Underwriter
ECOA	Equal Credit Opportunity Act
EIC	examiner-in-charge
EOD	end-of-draw
EVP	executive vice president
FDIC	Federal Deposit Insurance Corporation
FFIEC	Federal Financial Institutions Examination Council
FHA	Federal Housing Administration
FHLB	Federal Home Loan Bank
FRB	Board of Governors of the Federal Reserve System
FSA	federal savings association

FTC	Federal Trade Commission
GAAP	generally accepted accounting principles
GSE	government-sponsored enterprise
HECM	home equity conversion mortgage
HELOC	home equity line of credit
HLTV	high loan to value
HOA	home owners association
HOEPA	Home Ownership and Equity Protection Act
HOLA	Home Owners' Loan Act
HPML	higher-priced mortgage loan
HUD	U.S. Department of Housing and Urban Development
IO	interest-only
IORR	investor-owned residential real estate
IT	information technology
ITIN	individual taxpayer identification number
LP	Loan Prospector
LPM	loan portfolio management
LTV	loan to value
MIS	management information system
MRA	matter requiring attention
NCUA	National Credit Union Administration
OCC	Office of the Comptroller of the Currency
OREO	other real estate owned

OTS	Office of Thrift Supervision
P&I	principal and interest
PMI	private mortgage insurance
QA	quality assurance
QC	quality control
QM	qualified mortgage
RESPA	Real Estate Settlement Procedures Act
ROE	report of examination
RRE	residential real estate
SAFE Act	Secure and Fair Enforcement for Mortgage Licensing Act
TDR	troubled debt restructuring
TILA	Truth in Lending Act
USDA	U.S. Department of Agriculture
VA	U.S. Department of Veterans Affairs

References

Laws

General Powers

12 USC 24, "Corporate Powers of Associations" (national banks)
12 USC 29, "Power to Hold Real Property" (national banks)
12 USC 371, "Real Estate Loans" (national banks)
12 USC 484, "Limitation on Visitorial Powers" (national banks)
12 USC 1464, "Federal Savings Associations"

Consumer Protection

Community Reinvestment Act: 12 USC 2901, 12 CFR 25 (national banks), 12 CFR 195 (federal savings associations)
Equal Credit Opportunity Act: 15 USC 1691, 12 CFR 1002 (Regulation B)
Fair Credit Reporting Act: 15 USC 1681, 12 CFR 1022 (Regulation V)
Fair Debt Collection Practices Act: 15 USC 1692, 12 CFR 1006 (Regulation F)
Fair Housing Act: 42 USC 3601, 24 CFR 100, 24 CFR 110
Federal Trade Commission Act: 15 USC 45(a)(1)
Flood Disaster Protection Act: 42 USC 4001, 12 CFR 22 (national banks), 12 CFR 172 (federal savings associations)
Gramm–Leach–Bliley Act: 15 USC 6801, 12 CFR 1016 (Regulation P)
Home Mortgage Disclosure Act: 12 USC 2801, 12 CFR 1003 (Regulation C)
Homeowners Protection Act: 12 USC 4901
Real Estate Settlement Procedures Act (RESPA): 12 USC 2601, 12 CFR 1024 (Regulation X)
Secure and Fair Enforcement for Mortgage Licensing Act: 12 USC 5101, 12 CFR 1008 (Regulation H)
Servicemembers Civil Relief Act of 2003 (SCRA): 50 USC App. 501
Truth in Lending Act (TILA): 15 USC 1601, 12 CFR 1026 (Regulation Z)

Regulations

Appraisals

12 CFR 34, subpart C, "Appraisals" (national banks)
12 CFR 164, "Appraisals" (federal savings associations)

Authority

12 CFR 7.1006, "Bank Powers: Loan Agreement Providing for a Share in Profits, Income or Earnings or for Stock Warrants" (national banks)

12 CFR 159.5, "Subordinate Organizations: How Much May a Federal Savings Association Invest in Service Corporations or Lower-Tier Entities?" (federal savings associations)

12 CFR 160, "Lending and Investment: General Lending and Investment Powers of Federal Savings Associations" (federal savings associations)

Capital

For banks subject to the advanced approaches rule:

12 CFR 3, subpart A ("General Provisions"); subpart B ("Capital Ratio Requirements and Buffers"); subpart C ("Definition of Capital"); subpart D ("Risk-Weighted Assets—Standardized Approach"); subpart E ("Risk-Weighted Assets—Internal Ratings-Based and Advanced Measurement Approaches"); and subpart F ("Risk-Weighted Assets—Market Risk")

For non-advanced approaches banks:

12 CFR 3, subparts A, B, C, and D

Interagency Guidelines for Real Estate Lending Policies

12 CFR 34, subpart D, appendix A, "Interagency Guidelines for Real Estate Lending (national banks)

12 CFR 160.101, appendix, "Interagency Guidelines for Real Estate Lending Policies" (federal savings associations)

Real Estate Lending Standards

12 CFR 34, subpart D, "Real Estate Lending Standards" (national banks)

12 CFR 160.101, "Real Estate Lending Standards" (federal savings associations)

Record Keeping

12 CFR 27, "Fair Housing Home Loan Data System" (national banks)

12 CFR 160.170, "Lending and Investment: Records for Lending Transactions" (federal savings associations)

Safety and Soundness Standards

12 CFR 30, "Safety and Soundness Standards"

12 CFR 30, appendix C, "OCC Guidelines Establishing Standards for Residential Mortgage Lending Practices"

Comptroller's Handbook

Consumer Compliance

"Fair Credit Reporting"

"Fair Lending"
"Flood Disaster Protection"
"Home Mortgage Disclosure"
"Other Consumer Protection Laws and Regulations"
"Privacy of Consumer Financial Information"
"Real Estate Settlement Procedures Act"
"SAFE Act"
"Servicemembers Civil Relief Act"
"Truth in Lending Act"

Examination Process
"Bank Supervision Process"
"Community Bank Supervision"
"Federal Branches and Agencies Supervision"
"Large Bank Supervision"
"Sampling Methodologies"

Safety and Soundness, Asset Quality
"Concentrations of Credit"
"Other Real Estate Owned"

Safety and Soundness, Liquidity
"Liquidity"

Safety and Soundness, Management
"Internal and External Audits"
"Internal Control"

OCC Issuances

Advisory Letters

Advisory Letter 1997-7, "Affordable Mortgage Portfolios" (July 23, 1997)
Advisory Letter 1998-10, "National Registry of State Certified or Licensed Appraisers" (July 17, 1998)
Advisory Letter 2000-7, "Abusive Lending Practices" (July 25, 2000)
Advisory Letter 2002-3, "Guidance on Unfair or Deceptive Acts or Practices" (March 22, 2002)
Advisory Letter 2003-2, "Guidelines for National Banks to Guard Against Predatory and Abusive Lending Practices" (February 21, 2003)
Advisory Letter 2003-3, "Avoiding Predatory and Abusive Lending Practices in Brokered and Purchased Loans" (February 21, 2003)

Bank Accounting Advisory Series

OCC Bulletins

OCC Bulletin 1997-24, "Credit Scoring Models: Examination Guidance" (May 20, 1997) (national banks)

OCC Bulletin 1999-10, "Subprime Lending Activities" (March 5, 1999)

OCC Bulletin 1999-15, "Subprime Lending: Risk and Rewards (April 5, 1999) (national banks)

OCC Bulletin 1999-38, "Interagency Guidelines for Real Estate Lending Policies: Treatment of High LTV Residential Real Estate Loans" (October 13, 1999)

OCC Bulletin 2000-3, "Consumer Credit Reporting Practices: FFIEC Advisory Letter" (February 16, 2000)

OCC Bulletin 2000-20, "Uniform Retail Credit Classification and Account Management Policy: Policy Implementation" (June 20, 2000)

OCC Bulletin 2001-6, "Subprime Lending: Expanded Guidance for Subprime Lending Programs" (January 31, 2001)

OCC Bulletin 2004-20, "Risk Management of New, Expanded, or Modified Bank Products and Services" (May 10, 2004)

OCC Bulletin 2005-3, "OCC Guidelines Establishing Standards for National Banks' Residential Mortgage Lending Practices: Appendix C to 12 CFR Part 30" (February 2, 2005)

OCC Bulletin 2005-6, "Appraisal Regulations and the Interagency Statement on Independent Appraisal and Evaluation Functions: Frequently Asked Questions" (March 22, 2005)

OCC Bulletin 2005-18, "Interagency Advisory on Accounting and Reporting for Commitments to Originate and Sell Mortgage Loans" (May 3, 2005)

OCC Bulletin 2005-22, "Home Equity Lending: Credit Risk Management Guidance" (May 16, 2005)

OCC Bulletin 2005-27, "Real Estate Settlement Procedures Act: Sham Controlled Business Arrangements" (August 4, 2005)

OCC Bulletin 2006-41, "Guidance on Nontraditional Mortgage Product Risks" (October 4, 2006)

OCC Bulletin 2006-43, "Home Equity Lending: Addendum to OCC Bulletin 2005-22" (October 4, 2006)

OCC Bulletin 2007-14, "Working With Mortgage Borrowers: Interagency Statement" (April 18, 2007)

OCC Bulletin 2007-26, "Statement on Subprime Mortgage Lending" (July 25, 2007)

OCC Bulletin 2007-28, "Nontraditional Mortgage Products: Illustrations of Consumer Information" (August 21, 2007)

OCC Bulletin 2007-38, "Working With Borrowers: Statement on Residential Real Estate Loan Restructurings for Serviced Loans" (October 11, 2007)

OCC Bulletin 2007-40, "Limitations on Terms of Consumer Credit Extended to Military Service Members and Dependents: Department of Defense Final Rule" (October 17, 2007)

OCC Bulletin 2009-12, "Bank Secrecy Act/Anti-Money Laundering: FinCEN Guidance to Financial Institutions on Filing Suspicious Activity Reports Regarding Loan Modification/Foreclosure Rescue Scams" (April 23, 2009)

OCC Bulletin 2009-23, "Fair Credit Reporting: Accuracy and Integrity of Consumer Report Information and Direct Consumer Dispute Regulations and Guidelines: Final Rules and Guidelines Together With Advance Notice of Proposed Rulemaking" (July 20, 2009) (national banks)

OCC Bulletin 2010-25, "Property Assessed Clean Energy (PACE) Programs: Supervisory Guidance" (July 6, 2010)

OCC Bulletin 2010-30, "Reverse Mortgages: Interagency Guidance" (August 16, 2010)

OCC Bulletin 2010-33, "S.A.F.E. Act Mortgage Loan Originator Registration Requirements: Joint Final Rule" (August 25, 2010) (national banks)

OCC Bulletin 2010-42, "Interagency Appraisal and Evaluation Guidelines" (December 10, 2010)

OCC Bulletin 2011-6, "S.A.F.E. Act Mortgage Loan Originator Registration Requirements: Notice of Initial Registration Period" (February 3, 2011) (national banks)

OCC Bulletin 2011-12, "Supervisory Guidance on Model Risk Management" (April 4, 2011)

OCC Bulletin 2012-6, "Interagency Guidance on ALLL Estimation Practices for Junior Liens (January 31, 2012)

OCC Bulletin 2012-10, "Troubled Debt Restructurings: Supervisory Guidance on Accounting and Reporting Requirements" (April 5, 2012)

OCC Bulletin 2013-4, "Truth in Lending Act: Annual Dollar Trigger for Certain Home Mortgages" (February 6, 2013)

OCC Bulletin 2013-6, "Truth in Lending Act and Consumer Leasing Act: Dollar Thresholds for Exempt Consumer Credit and Lease Transactions" (February 6, 2013)

OCC Bulletin 2013-29, "Third-Party Relationships: Risk Management Guidance" (October 30, 2013)

OCC Bulletin 2013-38, "Interagency Statements on Supervisory Principles for Qualified and Non-Qualified Mortgage Loans" (December 13, 2013)

OCC Bulletin 2014-4, "Secured Consumer Debt Discharged in Chapter 7 Bankruptcy: Supervisory Expectations" (February 14, 2014)

OCC Bulletin 2014-29, "Risk Management of Home Equity Lines of Credit Approaching the End-of-Draw Periods" (July 1, 2014)

OCC Bulletin 2014-42, "Credit Practices Rules: Interagency Guidance Regarding Unfair or Deceptive Credit Practices" (August 22, 2014)

OCC Bulletin 2015-15, "Appraisals for Higher-Priced Mortgage Loans: Small-Loan Exemption Threshold Revision" (February 11, 2015)

OTS CEO Memo #276, "HELOC Account Management Guidance" (August 28, 2008)

OTS Examination Handbook, section 760, "New Activities and Services" (September 2009)

Other

FFIEC, "Instructions for Preparation of Consolidated Reports of Condition and Income (FFIEC 031 and 041)"

FFIEC, "The Detection and Deterrence of Mortgage Fraud Against Financial Institutions: A White Paper" (February 2010)